JOURNAL FÜR ENTWICKLUNGSPOLITIK

vol. XXXIV 3/4-2018

PROGRESSIVE INDUSTRIAL POLICY

Special Issue Guest Editors: Julia Eder,
Roland Kulke,
Claus-Dieter König

D1734343

Published by:
Mattersburger Kreis für Entwicklungspolitik
an den österreichischen Universitäten

Journal für Entwicklungspolitik (JEP)
Austrian Journal of Development Studies

Publisher: Mattersburger Kreis für Entwicklungspolitik an den österreichischen Universitäten

Editorial Team: Tobias Boos, Alina Brad, Eric Burton, Julia Eder, Nora Faltmann, Gerald Faschingeder, Karin Fischer, Margit Franz, Daniel Fuchs, Daniel Görgl, Inge Grau, Markus Hafner-Auinger, Karen Imhof, Johannes Jäger, Johannes Knierzinger, Bettina Köhler, Johannes Korak, Magdalena Kraus, René Kuppe, Franziska Kusche, Bernhard Leubolt, Andreas Novy, Clemens Pfeffer, Stefan Pimmer, Petra Purkarthofer, Kunibert Raffer, Jonathan Scalet, Lukas Schmidt, Gregor Seidl, Anselm Skuhra, Koen Smet, Carla Weinzierl

Publications Manager: Clemens Pfeffer
Cover: Clemens Pfeffer
Photo: Paul Kelpe
      Man and Machines (Abstraction #5), 1934
      Oil on canvas
      Board of Trustees of the University of Illinois on behalf of its
      Krannert Art Museum
      Allocated by the U.S. Government, Commissioned through
      the New Deal art projects 1943-4-209

Contents

4   JULIA EDER, ETIENNE SCHNEIDER, ROLAND KULKE, CLAUS-DIETER KÖNIG
From Mainstream to Progressive Industrial Policy

15   JAN GRUMILLER
Upgrading Potentials and Challenges in Commodity-Based Value Chains: The Ivorian and Ghanaian Cocoa Processing Sectors

46   JULIANA GOMES CAMPOS
Latin American Developmentalism in the 21st Century: An Analysis of the Governmental Industrial Policies of the Workers` Party in Brazil

73   RUDY WEISSENBACHER
A Ladder without Upper Rungs: On the Limitations of Industrial Policies in TNC Capitalism. The Case of the European Union

108   JULIA EDER, ETIENNE SCHNEIDER
Progressive Industrial Policy – A Remedy for Europe!?

143   ANITA PELLE, SAROLTA SOMOSI
Possible Challenges for EU-Level Industrial Policy: Where Do Potentials for Policy Improvement in Central and Eastern European Countries Lie?

Review-Essay

173   ARNO SONDEREGGER
Mandelas Hunderter

184   Book Review
187   Editors and Authors of the Special Issue
191   Publication Details

JOURNAL FÜR ENTWICKLUNGSPOLITIK XXXIV 3/4-2018, S. 4–14

JULIA EDER, ETIENNE SCHNEIDER, ROLAND KULKE,
CLAUS-DIETER KÖNIG
From Mainstream to Progressive Industrial Policy

Since 2000, industrial policy has celebrated a remarkable comeback in the political discourse, as well as in economic research. While industrial policy had played a crucial role in the post-WWII period in Fordist states in the Global North and developmental states in the Global South alike, this changed with the rise of neoliberalism in the 1980s. At least on the discursive level, state intervention in industrial development was banished because of its distorting effects on the 'natural' economic equilibrium (Stiglitz et al. 2013: 6; Warwick 2013: 8). In practice, however, many countries of the Global North continued to implement industrial policies in a concealed and partly modified manner. At the same time, they prevented many countries of the Global South from following suit through the enforcement of the Washington Consensus and Structural Adjustment Programs (SAPs) (Chang/Andreoni 2016).

However, as early as the 2000s, mainstream economics itself provided arguments for a partial return of industrial policy (Warwick 2013: 18ff.). Industrial policy could, according to the market failure argument, play a role closely confined to those few exceptional areas where neoclassical theory assumes that market mechanisms do not lead to optimal allocation (Rehfeld/Dankbar 2015: 491). In order to correct these 'market failures', industrial policy should, for instance, support research and development (R&D) in cases of so-called R&D and information externalities. These occur when research and development activities "generate positive spillovers that are not fully captured by the original investor" (Rodrik 2014: 470) or in the case of pioneer firms which advance into new fields where they generate information for other firms without, however, being adequately rewarded for the extraordinary costs of their 'first move'.

Another precisely defined area of activity for industrial policy, according to these mainstream approaches, is to foster efficient market allocation through horizontal competition policy, such as through anti-trust legislation (Chang/Grabel 2004: 71ff., Stiglitz et al. 2013, Nübler 2011: 4).

Beyond these areas, however, the assumption persisted that industrial policy would be ultimately futile due to 'government failure', as the state lacks both information and capacities to design and to implement effective industrial policy strategies (Warwick 2013: 23). As a result, the government failure argument assumes that state agencies supposed to carry out industrial policy are incapable of 'picking winners', i.e. of deciding which firms deserve government support and which do not. They are also, due to the selective character of industrial policy, prone to corruption and to being captured by powerful industries that use public money for their particular ends instead of creating economic and societal benefits for the majority of the population (Rodrik 2008: 7).

Nonetheless, despite the neoliberal attack, industrial policy never entirely disappeared; in the Global South, several Latin American countries, such as Argentina, Brazil and Mexico, continued to apply industrial policy strategies (Rodrik 2004: 15ff.). The so-called Newly Industrialised Countries in East Asia, particularly Taiwan and South Korea, managed to change their position in the hierarchical international division of labour, to a significant extent by relying on industrial policy strategies (Chang 2002, Wade 1990). And even capitalist core economies in the Global North, often considered as the heartland of neoliberal market orientation – particularly the USA (Mazzucato 2015) – continued to implement economic policy programmes to support and create specific industries, but did not label these explicitly as industrial policy (Lin/Monga 2013: 20).

1. The rehabilitation of industrial policy

Thus, governments around the globe continued to discuss and practise specific forms of industrial policy long before the oft-proclaimed comeback of industrial policy. Nevertheless, the revival of the term in recent years has significantly broadened the scope of the debate. In particular, Dani Rodrik, Joseph Stiglitz and Justin Lin rehabilitated industrial policy without, however, thoroughly breaking with the neoclassical framework that initially justified the disavowal of industrial policy in the majority of areas (Chang/Andreoni 2016: 3). Rodrik, in particular, challenged the 'government failure' argument, shifting the terms of the mainstream debate from the "why" to the "how" of industrial policy by arguing that 'government failure' can be avoided by a specific institutional design of industrial policy (see also Warwick 2013: 18). To this end, the 'embedded autonomy' of industrial policy bodies and 'letting losers go' instead of 'picking winners' are crucial (Rodrik 2008: 26ff.). If industrial policy bodies manage to attain "embedded autonomy", a concept originally developed by Peter Evans (1995), they dispose over the in-depth knowledge of industrial sectors and production but are not prone to being captured by specific capital fractions, thus forming so-called 'pockets of efficiency' within the state (Whitfield et al. 2015: 20). This, in turn, enables them to formulate and execute strict evaluation criteria and performance targets. By relying on these criteria and targets, they are not burdened with the onerous task of 'picking winners', but they make sure that funding is withdrawn in case of non-achievement (see also Chang/Grabel 2004: 76ff.).

Besides Rodrik's theoretical intervention, Justin Yifu Lin, the first chief economist of the World Bank from the Global South, has significantly contributed to the return of industrial policy into the mainstream debate. Against the background of his New Structural Economics, which was often perceived as a paradigm shift in relation to the World Bank economics of the Washington Consensus (critically Fine/Van Waeyenberge 2013), Lin re-introduced industrial policy as a development strategy. Simultaneously, however, he outspokenly distanced himself from the strategies of the 'old' structuralism of the 1950s and 1960s (such as import substitution or selective decoupling from the world market, cf. Beigel 2015). The industrial policy strategies of 'old' structuralism, Lin asserts against the big-push argument, were doomed to fail because these strategies aimed at emulating the industrial development of the industrialised countries in the Global North despite the "natural disadvantage [of developing economies] in heavy manufacturing industry" (Lin/Monga 2013: 30). Due to this 'natural disadvantage', large industrial plants promoted by industrial policy but without effective domestic demand and without competitiveness for exports were not viable and ultimately too costly to sustain (ibid.).

Thus, instead of trying to catch up by defying comparative advantages, Lin argues for a world market-oriented industrial policy development strategy which only deviates from a country's comparative advantage to a small degree (for a critique of this argument see below, and Chang 2013).

With this strong emphasis on world market integration, Lin's approach is therefore compatible with another crucial strand of discussion running across the debate on industrial policy, namely Global Value Chains (GVC) and industrial upgrading as a perspective of development (for an overview see Plank/Staritz 2009, Gereffi/Korzeniewicz 1994). Initially, the World Systems Theory introduced the commodity chain approach to understand the reconfiguration of centre-periphery dynamics in the increasingly globalised world economy (Hopkins/Wallerstein 1977). Gradually, however, the focus of the debate shifted to questions of business economics, such as inter-firm networks and development potentials for individual firms within GVCs. While critical perspectives, particularly coming from the Global Production Networks approach rooted in geography, analyse power relations as well as class struggles along transnational GVCs and production networks, the dominant industrial policy and development paradigm in the GVC debate remains focused on industrial upgrading, i.e. moving up the value chain into areas where more value added can be 'captured'. Accordingly, hooking into GVCs is deemed more feasible, as it does not require countries to establish entire sectors with complex intra-sector divisions of labour on their own, while at the same time accruing knowledge about complex production processes (Bair 2005, Chang/Andreoni 2016: 34).

On the political and institutional level, the "normalizing industrial policy" (2008), as famously put by Dani Rodrik in a study for the World Bank, has various manifestations. Institutions which traditionally advocated the Washington Consensus free-market strategies, such as the World Bank or the OECD, have been significantly shifting their position on industrial policy (Plank/Staritz 2013, Lin/Monga 2013: 30). Moreover, emerging economies in the Global South such as India, Brazil and China adopted far-reaching industrial policy strategies (Warwick 2013: 9-10). In the EU, the Europe2020 strategy from 2010 announced an "industrial policy for the globalisation era" (European Commission 2010), and the European Commission (2014, see also 2017) proclaimed an "Industrial Renaissance" through industrial policy, particularly considering the persistent structural imbalances revealed by the Eurozone crisis.

2. Types of industrial policy

Before we turn to the discussion on progressive industrial policy, it is important to clarify what we mean by industrial policy. Surprisingly, it is far from clear what the term 'industrial policy' stands for (for a comprehensive overview of different definitions and taxonomies, see Warwick 2013: 14ff.). Of course, definitions for all policy fields such as social policy or environmental policy vary, but industrial policy is a particularly fuzzy concept. The most common, rather broad definition refers to industrial policy as government policies which aim at affecting the structure of an economy (Stiglitz et al. 201: 2). To this end, it is possible to apply a wide variety of industrial policy instruments: direct subsidies to specific firms or sectors, tax breaks, selective credit policies and capital allocation, trade subsidies or and price controls.

Against this background, there are different taxonomies which classify various types of industrial policy (Warwick 2013: 14ff.). On the one hand, economic theory typically differentiates between horizontal industrial policy and vertical (or selective) industrial policy. While horizontal industrial policy, particularly prevalent under neoliberalism and often synonymous with competition policy, merely sets general 'framework conditions' for competition, 'vertical', i.e. interventionist or selective industrial policy goes further, in that it is based on targeted strategies which support specific activities, sectors or technologies while discriminating others. On the other hand, we can further systematise selective industrial policy based on the rationale behind it. We can distinguish strategic industrial policy, which aims at promoting specific industries to catch up or advance comparative advantages in world market competition, from reactive or defensive industrial policy, which aspires an orderly adjustment and restructuring in the light of de-industrialisation and the new international division of labour (Rehfeld/Dankbaar 2015: 493, Fröbel et al. 1981).

In reality, however, the distinction between horizontal or neutral policies and selective or interventionist policies is far less clear cut than on

Julia Eder, Etienne Schneider, Roland Kulke, Claus-Dieter König paper (Stiglitz et al. 2013: 8, Lin/Monga 2013: 21, Chang/Grabel 2004: 77). Many components of industrial policy often perceived as 'horizontal', i.e. not selectively promoting or discriminating individual sectors – such as infrastructure, innovation or exchange rate policies – actually benefit specific sectors more than others (Siglitz et al. 2013: 8-9). This has led some authors to consider any intentional, targeted attempt to support particular sectors or economic activities, i.e. selective economic policy as such, as industrial policy (Rehfeld/Dankbaar 2015: 492, Warwick 2013: 14). In this very broad definition then, industrial policy does not necessarily refer to manufacturing or industry per se (Harrison/Rodríguez-Clare 2009, Rodrik 2008: 2, Lin/Monga 2013: 21). This broad understanding of industrial policy is particularly prevalent in the Global North, as opposed to the Global South, where the term is generally more closely tied to the manufacturing sector as such (e.g. UNIDO 2011). Along the lines of this broad understanding, Stiglitz, Lin and Monga (2013: 11), for instance, extend the notion beyond manufacturing to include, in particular, R&D policies that aim at knowledge transfers. However, such a broad understanding ultimately allows grouping virtually any economic policy initiative under 'industrial policy'. It is no coincidence, therefore, that industrial policy has turned into an 'empty signifier' in the recent debate: a term charged with so many different meanings by different political forces that this overload of meanings makes it ultimately devoid of any specific or binding meaning and thus political implication. This renders it even more necessary to identify the contours of progressive industrial policy in the current debate.

3. (Progressive) Industrial policy and the Left

From the 1980s onwards, debates among the Left, particularly in Europe, barely discussed industrial policy as a tool to promote sustainable development, but for reasons partly not included in the mainstream debate. One reason was the broadly shared view that the industrialised societies were evolving towards post-industrial societies, which mainly relied on the provision of services rather than on large-scale manufacturing. Furthermore, many activists praised this development from the ecological point of view, because so-called 'brown', i.e. environmentally harmful, industries should be phased out anyway. So, the question arises: why should we promote industrial development through political intervention?

On the one hand, a country becomes more resilient to crisis with a sound industrial basis. It is easier to preserve jobs and to reduce structural dependency on other economies (Becker/Jäger 2010; Rehfeld/Dankbaar 2015: 496). Furthermore, jobs in the industrial sectors are usually better paid and more stable than in the area of services (Rehfeld/Dankbaar 2015: 497). On the other hand, the potential of industrial policy as a transition policy towards sustainability has increasingly gained strength, for example, in the German 'Energiewende' strategy promoting renewable energies (Pianta et al. 2016: 46). In our view, this last point is one of the most crucial ones for any progressive industrial policy. A well-intended mainstream industrial policy tries to develop new competitive industries (or to render the existing ones more competitive) and/or it seeks to support industries under pressure so that their decline takes place in a socially and politically responsible way. However, considering the ecological crisis, such proposals do not go far enough. Arguably, a truly progressive industrial policy would need to work at least partially against the 'rationality of the markets' by promoting social goals which transcend narrow conceptions of economic efficiency and international competitiveness

A further reason for promoting industrial policy through political intervention stems from the more recent catch-up development experiences. It is generally acknowledged that the East Asian economies (South Korea and Taiwan in particular) heavily relied on industrial industrial policy (Wade 1990). However, in his book *Kicking Away the Ladder* (2002), Ha-Joon Chang demonstrated that this was not due to industrial policy as such. Rather, any successful promotion of industrial development to some extent resorted to targeted state intervention. Therefore, it may not be accidental that one of the most important policy proposals of the Labour Party under Corbyn consists of a truly vertical industrial policy – once the UK will no longer be bound to the EU competition regulations on state aids (The Labour Party 2017).

Due to these factors, the resurgence of the debate on industrial policy has also increasingly resonated within the European Left. A vivid discussion has evolved around the question of what characterises an 'alternative' or 'progressive' industrial policy in contrast to mainstream approaches (for

JULIA EDER, ETIENNE SCHNEIDER, ROLAND KULKE, CLAUS-DIETER KÖNIG a summary of the debate see Eder/Schneider in this issue). One potential answer could be that progressive industrial policy does not limit oneself to 'picking winners' and to supporting companies until they can take off (and then privatise profits). Furthermore, it should not only promote structural change for the sake of growth and to reduce trade deficits, but also to foster a socially and environmentally sustainable industrial base. Nonetheless, this special issue does not aim at promoting or defending a pre-defined concept, but rather seeks to enrich the ongoing debate on progressive industrial policy. For this purpose, we present a variety of approaches on the topic, which do not provide an unanimous answer to the identified challenges.

The first two articles of this special issue discuss experiences with industrial policy implementation in the Global South. Jan Grumiller presents a comparison of the industrial policy strategies of Ghana and Côte d'Ivoire in the cocoa processing sector. He points to similarities and differences between the two case studies and reflects on to what extent their experiences have been progressive, but also which constraints have limited their room for manoeuvre. Juliana Gomes Campos undertakes an evaluation of the Brazilian industrial policy under the Partido dos Trabalhadores governments. She discusses the efforts of Lula da Silva's (2003 – 2011) and Dilma Rousseff's (2011 – 2016) governments in this field, but also tries to provide an explanation for the meagre outcomes. Together with the other articles of this special issue, they raise several important questions and issues concerning the design and implementation of progressive industrial policy.

The rest of the special issue consists of three articles, which discuss the current stage of uneven development in the European Union and – related to this – potentials of and challenges for progressive industrial policy from different angles. Focusing on the economic structure, Rudy Weissenbacher argues that industrial development might constitute a proxy for development in a broad sense, as the possibilities for catch-up development of peripheral countries in the European Union are rather limited in contemporary capitalism. Julia Eder and Etienne Schneider, as well as Anita Pelle and Sarolta Somosi, focus on prospects for the implementation of progressive industrial policy in the European Union. Eder and Schneider are – based on an evaluation of current power relations – not too optimistic about the establishment of progressive industrial policy on the EU level. Pelle and Somosi, on the other hand, see greater potential for EU-level policy strategies, but assert that the EU institutions should abandon the 'one size fits all' approach in order to benefit the European peripheries.

Considering that the economic crisis has not (yet?) been overcome, we believe that it is crucial to further in the Left the much-needed debate on progressive industrial policy. The articles of this special issue strive to contribute to this aim.

Acknowledgement

Editing of this introduction was financially supported by the Faculty of Social Sciences at the University of Vienna.

References

Bair, Jennifer (2005): Global Capitalism and Commodity Chains: Looking Back, Going Forward. In: Competition & Change 9 (2), 153–80. https://doi.org/10.1179/102452905X45382

Becker, Joachim/Jäger, Johannes (2010): Development Trajectories in the Crisis in Europe. In: Journal of Contemporary Central and Eastern Europe 18 (1), 5-27. https://doi.org/10.1080/09651561003732488

Beigel, Fernanda (2015): Das Erbe des lateinamerikanischen Dependentismo und die Aktualität des Begriffs der Abhängigkeit. In: Journal für Entwicklungspolitik 31 (3), 11-38. https://doi.org/10.20446/JEP-2414-3197-31-3-11

Chang, Ha-Joon (2002): Kicking Away the Ladder: Development Strategy in Historical Perspective. London: Anthem Press.

Chang, Ha-Joon (2013): Comments on "Comparative Advantage: The Silver Bullet of Industrial Policy" by Justin Lin and Célestin Monga. In: Stiglitz, Joseph E./Lin, Justin (eds.): The Industrial Policy Revolution I. The Role of Government Beyond Ideology. New York: Palgrave Macmillan, 39-42. https://doi.org/10.1057/9781137335173_3

Chang, Ha-Joon/Andreoni, Antonio (2016): Industrial Policy in a Changing World: Basic Principles, Neglected Issues and New Challenges. Cambridge Journal of Economics 40 Years Conference.

Chang, Ha-Joon/Grabel, Ilene (2004): Reclaiming Development. An Alternative Economic Policy Manual. London/New York: Zed Books.

European Commission (2010): Europe2020. A European strategy for smart, sustainable and inclusive growth. Brussels: European Commission.

European Commission (2014): For a European Industrial Renaissance. Brussels: European Commission.

European Commission (2017): Investing in a smart, innovative and sustainable Industry. A renewed EU Industrial Policy Strategy. Brussels: European Commission.

Evans, Peter (1995): Embedded Autonomy. States and Industrial Transformation. Princeton: Princeton University Press.

Fine, Ben/Van Waeyenberge, Elisa (2013): A Paradigm Shift That Never Was: Justin Lin's New Structural Economics. In: Competition & Change 17 (4), 355–371. https://doi.org/10.1179/1024529413Z.00000000043

Fröbel, Folker/Heinrichs, Jürgen/Kreye, Otto (1981): The New International Division of Labour. Cambridge: Cambridge University Press.

Gereffi, Gary/Korzeniewicz, Miguel (1994): Commodity Chains and Global Capitalism. Westport: Praeger.

Harrison, Ann/Rodríguez-Clare, Andrés (2009): Trade, Foreign Investment, and Industrial Policy for Developing Countries. In: Rodrik, Dani (ed.): Handbook of Economic Growth, vol. 4. Amsterdam: North-Holland.

Hopkins, Terence K./Wallerstein, Immanuel (1977): Patterns of development of the modern world-system. In: Review 1 (2), 111-145.

Lin, Justin/Monga, Célestin (2013): Comparative Advantage: The Silver Bullet of Industrial Policy. In: Stiglitz, Joseph E./Lin, Justin (eds.): The Industrial Policy Revolution I. The Role of Government Beyond Ideology. New York: Palgrave Macmillan, 19-38. https://doi.org/10.1057/9781137335173_2

Mazzucato, Mariana (2015): The Entrepreneurial State. Debunking Public vs. Private Sector Myths (revised edition). New York: Anthem Press.

Nübler, Irmgard (2011): Industrial Policies and Capabilities for Catching up: Frameworks and Paradigms. ILO Employment Working Paper No. 77. Geneva: ILO.

Pianta, Mario/Lucchese, Matteo/Nascia, Leopoldo (2016): What is to be produced? The making of a new industrial policy in Europe. Brussels: Rosa Luxemburg Foundation.

Plank, Leonhard/Staritz, Cornelia (2009): Introduction: global commodity chains and production networks – understanding uneven development in the global economy. In: Journal für Entwicklungspolitik 25 (2), 4-19. https://doi.org/10.20446/JEP-2414-3197-25-2-4

Plank, Leonhard/Staritz, Cornelia (2013): Renaissance der Industriepolitik – Irr- oder Königsweg? In: Kurswechsel 3/2013, 74–91.

Rehfeld, Dieter/Dankbaar, Ben (2015): Industriepolitik. Theoretische Grundlagen, Varianten und Herausforderungen. In: WSI-Mitteilungen 7/2015, 491-499.

Rodrik, Dani (2004): Industrial policy for the 21st century. https://drodrik.scholar.harvard.edu/publications/industrial-policy-twenty-first-century, 27.8.2017.

Rodrik, Dani (2008): Normalizing Industrial Policy. Commission on Growth and Development Working Paper Nr. 3. Washington: International Bank for

Reconstruction and Development/The World Bank. https://doi.org/10.1093/oxrep/gru025

Rodrik, Dani (2014): Green Industrial Policy. In: Oxford Review of Economic Policy 30 (3), 469–91.

Stiglitz, Joseph E., Justin Yifu Lin, and Celestin Monga. (2013): The Rejuvenation of Industrial Policy. Policy Research Working Paper 6628. Washington: The World Bank.

The Labour Party (2017): Richer Britain, Richer Lives. Labour's Industrial Strategy. http://labour.org.uk/wp-content/uploads/2017/10/Richer-Britain-Richer-Lives-Labours-Industrial-Strategy.pdf, 27.11.2018.

UNIDO (2011): Industrial Policy for Prosperity. Reasoning and Approach. Working Paper 02/2011. https://www.unido.org/api/opentext/documents/download/9928765/unido-file-9928765, 12.2.2017.

Wade, Robert (1990): Governing the Market Economic Theory and the Role of Government in East Asian Industrialization. Princeton, N.J.: Princeton University Press.

Warwick, Ken (2013): Beyond Industrial Policy. OECD Science, Technology and Industry Policy Papers, No. 2. Paris: OECD Publishing.

Whitfield, Lindsay/Therkildsen, Ole/Buur, Lars/Kjaer, Anne Mette (2015): The Politics of African Industrial Policy. A Comparative Perspective. Cambridge: Cambridge University Press. https://doi.org/10.1017/CBO9781316225509

Julia Eder
Department of Politics and Development Research,
Institute of Sociology, Johannes Kepler University Linz
julia_theresa.eder@jku.at

Etienne Schneider
Department of Political Science, University of Vienna
etienne.schneider@univie.ac.at

Roland Kulke
Facilitator, transform! europe, Brussels
kulke@transform-network.net

Claus-Dieter König
Senior Advisor Africa Unit, Rosa Luxemburg Foundation
claus-dieter.koenig@rosalux.org

JOURNAL FÜR ENTWICKLUNGSPOLITIK XXXIV 3/4-2018, S. 15–45

JAN GRUMILLER
Upgrading Potentials and Challenges in
Commodity-Based Value Chains:
The Ivorian and Ghanaian Cocoa Processing Sectors

ABSTRACT *This paper presents a comparative analysis of the development of forward linkages to cocoa processing in the Ivorian and Ghanaian cocoa sectors. The paper argues that Côte d'Ivoire and Ghana were able to promote the grinding sectors with varying success in the context of shifting Global Value Chain (GVC) dynamics, foreign-direct investment (FDI) oriented industrial policies and ongoing distributional conflicts. The grinding sectors in both countries should not currently be selected as high priority sectors for strategic industrial policies, due to their enclave-like character and limited opportunities for additional linkage development, with the important exception of forward linkages to chocolate manufacturing. The recent growth of local and regional chocolate and cocoa confectionery consumption, as well as protective tariffs, have furthered functional upgrading into chocolate manufacturing of locally owned and more locally embedded foreign grinders and chocolate manufacturers. The paper concludes that the opportunities for additional forward linkage development to cocoa processing in the Ivorian and Ghanaian cocoa sectors are limited, particularly in GVCs geared to traditional end markets. Hence, the paper argues that the growing opportunities in local and regional end markets, as well as related value chains, need to be leveraged through strategic industrial policies that go beyond tax or price incentives and focus on supporting locally owned and locally embedded foreign companies.*

KEYWORDS: *cocoa processing, global value chains, commodity-based industrialisation, Côte d'Ivoire, Ghana*

1. Introduction

Industrial development and export diversification into higher value-added production activities remain key development objectives for (semi-)peripheral countries. For many Sub-Saharan African (SSA) countries, however, it is difficult to emulate export-oriented industrialisation strategies of successful late-industrialisers (Morris et al. 2012: 12ff.). In the context of high commodity prices in the 2000s, discussions of the viability of commodity-based industrialisation have regained importance (e.g. Morris et al. 2012; Morris/Fessehaie 2014; Kaplinsky/Farooki 2012; Ramdoo 2012, 2015; Asche et al. 2012; ACET 2014a; AfDB et al. 2014; UNECA 2013; UNCTAD 2013). Even though commodity prices have again declined, the potential role of commodity sectors in transforming SSA economies through the creation of linkages to industrial sectors remains highly relevant.

Cocoa is one of the main soft commodities exported from peripheral countries, particularly in SSA. It has experienced significant price increases since the early 2000s, despite pronounced volatility, with nominal prices reaching levels last seen in the 1970s (ICCO 2017). Price increases were mainly driven by rising global chocolate demand – particularly in Asia – and only moderate increases in the supply of cocoa beans. More recently, prices declined, highlighting the cyclical nature of commodity prices related to fundamental and speculative factors (Terazono 2017; Ederer et al. 2016). This price volatility is one of the main reasons why a diversification away from unprocessed commodity exports is crucial for peripheral countries. The development of commodity processing sectors can furthermore support industrialisation processes if linkages to industrial sectors are developed. In this context, many cocoa producing countries (origin countries) in the (semi)periphery have established and expanded cocoa processing sectors, increasing their share of higher value-added cocoa product exports (ICCO 2017; UN Comtrade 2017). The main cocoa producers in SSA, including Côte d'Ivoire and Ghana, nonetheless continue to have a comparatively small share of higher value-added exports relative to other producers, such as Indonesia and Brazil.

This paper adds to the existing literature on cocoa processing in SSA countries (e.g. ACET 2014b; UNECA 2013; Whitfield et al. 2015; Mulangu et al. 2017) by presenting a comparative analysis of the development of forward linkages to processing in the Ivorian and Ghanaian cocoa sectors. The paper argues that Côte d'Ivoire and Ghana were able to promote the grinding sectors with varying levels of success in the context of shifting Global Value Chain (GVC) dynamics, foreign direct investment (FDI) oriented industrial policies and ongoing distributional conflicts. The grinding sectors in both countries should currently not be selected as high priority sectors for strategic industrial policies, due to their enclave-like character and limited opportunities for linkage development, with the important exception of forward linkages to chocolate manufacturing. The recent growth of local and regional chocolate and cocoa confectionery consumption, as well as protective tariffs, have furthered functional upgrading into chocolate manufacturing of locally owned and more locally embedded foreign grinders and chocolate manufacturers. The paper concludes that the opportunities for additional forward linkage development in the Ivorian and Ghanaian cocoa sectors are limited, particularly in GVCs geared to traditional end markets. Hence, the paper argues that the growing opportunities in local and regional end markets, as well as related value chains, need to be leveraged through strategic industrial policies that go beyond tax or price incentives and focus on supporting locally owned and locally embedded foreign companies.

Methodologically, this paper is based on 45 semi-structured interviews (20 of which are cited) that focus on firms in both processing segments, grinders and chocolate manufacturers, interest groups and governmental institutions, mostly conducted during field research in Côte d'Ivoire and Ghana in January, February and October 2017. 21 interviews at firm level were conducted with representatives of the management and provide a varied sample based on differences in geographic location, ownership, size, production activities, end-market orientation and degree of vertical integration. The interviews are complemented by trade as well as national and international sector data, including aggregate statistics from the International Cocoa Organization (ICCO), UN Comtrade (WITS), the Ghanaian Cocoa Marketing Board (COCOBOD) as well as the Ivorian Ministère de l'Industrie et des Mines (MIM) and Conseil Café-Cacao (CCC).

The second section of the paper presents a brief conceptualisation of the importance of structural transformation, linkage development and industrial policies in the context of the global periphery's integration in GVCs. The third section gives an overview of the cocoa GVC by specifically taking account of the changing integration of cocoa producing countries in the last decades and assessing the opportunities and constraints for forward linkage development in SSA producer countries in the context of the cocoa GVC. The fourth section discusses the development of the Ivorian and Ghanaian cocoa processing sectors and related industrial policies. The fifth section presents a comparative analysis of the sectors' developments, industrial policies and related distributional conflicts, competitiveness as well as linkage effects. The sixth section concludes by presenting industrial policy implications for the development of the cocoa processing sectors based on the analysis of the shifting GVC dynamics and local sector conditions.

2. Structural transformation, linkage development and industrial policy in the global periphery

Structural transformation and economic upgrading are key concepts in development economics. Amsden (2001: 2) defines structural transformation as "[...] a process of moving from a set of assets based on primary products, exploited by unskilled labor, to a set of assets based on knowledge, exploited by skilled labor". This transformation involves attracting labor and capital to the manufacturing sector. The concept of structural transformation is closely connected to the idea of economic upgrading, even though upgrading processes do not necessarily lead to structural transformation. In the GVC and the global production networks (GPN) literature, economic upgrading has been described as a process by which economic actors move from low-value to relatively higher value activities (Bair/Gereffi 2003; Gereffi 2005).

Economic development and structural transformation can be understood as a process of linkage development (Hirschman 1981: 75). Hirschman (1981: 65ff.) distinguished between production, consumption and fiscal linkages: production linkages include backward and forward linkages of a given product line and are defined as "[...] investment-generating forces that are set in motion, through input-output relations, when productive facilities that supply inputs to that line or utilize its outputs are inadequate or nonexistent" (ibid.65). Consumption linkages are new incomes earned with potential positive effects on domestic demand and industries. Fiscal linkages are created by taxing incomes earned in an economic sector and can be used to promote industrial development.

The debate on structural transformation, upgrading and linkage development is closely connected to the role of the state. Catch-up industrialisation has been furthered by interventionist industrial policies proactively promoting economic diversification, industrial development and upgrading processes (Chang 2011). However, the formation of a 'developmental state' (cf. Evans 1995) that has the resources, capacity, capability and policy space to promote large-scale structural transformation via a comprehensive set of industrial policies is particularly challenging in the political economy context of the global periphery. Peripheral states are impinged by their subordinated integration in the global economy and socio-structural heterogeneity (Evers 1977; Becker 2008), involving factors such as a weak industrial base and lack of an entrepreneurial class, fragmented political elites, as well as foreign capital's interests, all of which have a tendency to impede the formation of large-scale industrialisation projects (Grumiller et al. 2016; cf. Whitfield et al. 2015). Countries in the global periphery may need to rely on a more strategic and selective industrial policy approach given these political economy contexts, which entails the promotion of pockets of efficiency in the state bureaucracy in order to support transformation processes in specific economic sectors (ibid.).

This paper analyses the opportunities and constraints for forward linkage development in the cocoa sectors by discussing GVC dynamics and local sector conditions, based on an adapted conceptualisation of Morris/Fessehaie (2014: 32ff.), including: (a) the technical characteristics of the GVC (e.g. how many discrete stages of production) that determine the potential, breadth and type of backward as well as forward linkages; (b) the industry structure and governance of the GVC, in particular lead firms strategies (e.g. the concentration and integration of lead firms as well as their interest to outsource production steps); (c) the size of the local and regional market that might limit or support local processing; (d) the competitiveness of the domestic industry and firms (e.g. in terms of price, quality, lead times, etc.); (e) the location and infrastructure of a specific country (e.g. the development of roads or electricity costs); (f) the market access and trade barriers that might limit or support the integration into new GVCs or regional value chains, as well as functional upgrading opportunities; and (g) the industrial policies promoting linkage development (and thus the state's political economy and distributional conflicts). Based on this analysis, the paper discusses the feasibility of industrial policies targeting the cocoa processing sectors by taking into account the different dynamics in global, regional and local value chains (cf. Gereffi/Sturgeon 2013; Morris/Staritz forthcoming).

3. Origin countries and forward linkages in the cocoa GVC

The cocoa GVC has been described as having a bi-polar governance structure, with lead firms in the grinding of cocoa and manufacturing of chocolate segments (Fold 2002).[1] The relative absence of vertical integration along the whole chain and the high level of concentration in both processing segments put forward two sets of actors with strong control over the value chain. Chocolate manufacturers nonetheless exert greater power in the cocoa GVC, since they have control over consumer brands and often have the ability to extract rents (Fold/Neilson 2016: 202ff.; Araujo Bonjean/Brun 2016). Retailers and supermarkets also have an important role, as a significant share of chocolate products is sold through their outlets. They decide whether or not certain products are included in their offer and set the retail price. However, their control over the supply chain is rather limited compared to the dominant role of cocoa processors.

The power imbalances within the bi-polar cocoa value chain, in which multinational corporations (MNCs) source cocoa beans mainly from smallholders in the global (semi)periphery, are reflected in the declining share of value captured by cocoa producers (Barrientos/Asenso-Okyere 2009: 94; cf. World Bank 2008: 136). Cocoa producers only receive a fraction[2] of the value added along the whole chain, while chocolate manufacturing and branding, as well as retailing, contribute to over three-quarters of the value added. Grinding adds comparatively little value to cocoa beans and entry barriers are lower; however, the integration and concentration of multinational traders and grinders improves their position in the GVC.

Cocoa grinding is capital intensive and highly concentrated, but increasingly geographically dispersed. Mergers and acquisitions increased the consolidation of the cocoa trading and processing sectors, particularly since the liberalisation of the cocoa sectors in producing countries in the context of Structural Adjustment Programs (SAPs) in the 1990s (Fold 2002; Gilbert 2009; Araujo Bonjean/Brun 2016; UNCTAD 2008). The exit of chocolate manufacturers from the less profitable grinding sector has also furthered its concentration (UNCTAD 2008). Today, the grinding industry is dominated by three MNCs which account for roughly 60% of the world's cocoa processing (Terazono 2014; Gayi/Tsowou 2016: Figure 6): Barry Callebaut, Cargill and Olam.

Historically, the cocoa grinding industry was located in Europe and the US, close to the chocolate manufacturers and consumer markets. Grinding in producer countries (origin grinding) expanded in recent years due to tax and other incentives in origin countries, decreasing transportation costs for intermediate products, as well as a shift in lead firms strategies to tighten the control over the upstream segments of the chain in order to address supply constraints and insecurities (Gilbert 2009; Araujo Bonjean/Brun 2016; UNECA 2013; Blommer 2011). Origin grinding also has disadvantages, including higher operational and investment costs, an additional processing stage for exports,[3] and often limited access to beans from different origins ('single origin challenge') (ACET 2014b: 31). Nonetheless, today, grinding in origin countries makes up for nearly half of total grindings, with Côte d'Ivoire (12.6% share of global grindings in 2016/17), Indonesia (9.8%), Brazil (5.3%), Ghana (5.1%), and Malaysia (5.1%) being the largest processors of cocoa apart from the Netherlands (12.7%), Germany (9.7%) and the US (9.1%) (ICCO 2017). However, origin countries in SSA continue to have a comparatively small share of higher value-added cocoa exports (Figure 1). The growth of grinding capacity in general, and outside the traditional grinding-hubs in particular, has resulted in a global capacity overhang and a drop in cocoa grinders' margins (cf. Perkins 2015).

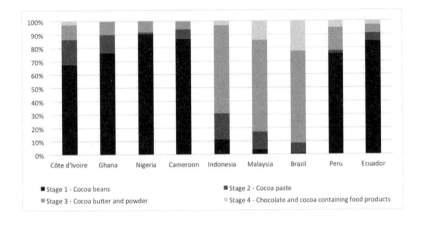

Figure 1: Value added content of key cocoa producing countries' exports (2016, per cent)

Source: UN Comtrade 2017 (WITS); cf. UNECA 2013: Figure 3.3.

Note: Stages refer to processing steps. Exports of shells, husks, etc. (HS1802) have been excluded due to their insignificance in exports. Data represents global import data by value. Malaysia has developed from a cocoa producer (esp. in the 1980s and 90s) to a processing hub for the US and Asian markets and produces a small quantity of cocoa beans today.

The manufacturing of chocolate is capital intensive and is mainly located in the largest chocolate consumer countries, the EU and the USA. Japan, Russia, Brazil, and increasingly also China and India are examples of important emerging markets for chocolate products. The chocolate manufacturing sector is also highly concentrated, with the top six chocolate manufacturers having a market share of approximately 40% (Candy Industry 2016). Some of these companies specialising in chocolate production also maintain in-house grinding capacity, or set up their own cocoa plantations to reduce the power of producers and grinders. However, most manufacturers concentrate their activities on the design of consumer chocolate products and the marketing of global brands in order to be responsive to shifting consumer demands (Fold/Neilson 2016: 202).

Production costs, as well as the size of the local and regional chocolate market, are key determinants as to whether chocolate manufacturing in origin countries (origin manufacturing) is suitable, or whether a market is mainly conquered via exports from manufacturing facilities with access to economies of scale and agglomeration (Interview 1, 18, 20; cf. ACET 2014b). The low, albeit growing, local and regional consumption in peripheral origin countries is the main reason why chocolate manufacturers are primarily situated in core and increasingly semi-peripheral countries. The production costs of chocolate can also be quite high in peripheral countries in light of often higher prices for electricity given the capital intensity of production, as well as the cost of imported inputs (e.g. milk powder and sugar). Further, high transportation costs, due to the need to cool chocolate products during transport, and a weak infrastructure also impede the manufacturing of ready-to-eat chocolate products for export in many origin countries. Production facilities of industrial chocolate also tend to be located close to manufacturers of ready-to-eat products, since the close proximity allows transportation of industrial chocolate in liquid form and simplifies just-in-time production (ACET 2014b). Origin countries with a large internal market for chocolate products (such as Brazil) have thus been more successful in functionally upgrading into chocolate manufacturing, compared to West African and smaller Latin American producer countries with limited local and/or regional demand.

However, chocolate and cocoa confectionery consumption in SSA has increased since the 2000s. In 2016, SSA countries imported 74 thousand tons of chocolate and cocoa-containing food products worth USD 278 million, an increase of 216% by volume (641 % by value) relative to 2000 (UN Comtrade 2017).[4] The growth of imports of the ECOWAS region (580% by volume and 808% by value to 20 thousand tons, worth USD 52 million), including key cocoa producers such as Nigeria, Ghana and Côte d'Ivoire, has been particularly strong. Tamru and Swinnen (2016) explain this increase in chocolate consumption in Africa in terms of rising income levels, increasing affordability (e.g. smaller packaging, low-priced products), a shift in taste (possibly related to the increasing exposure to the Western lifestyle and commercials, e.g. due to cable TV), rapid urbanisation, and the expansion of the retail sector. The growth of chocolate consumption in Africa in general, and in the ECOWAS region and origin countries' markets in particular, enhances the potential for origin manufacturing in West Africa; however, most multinational chocolate manufacturers continue to conquer African markets mainly via exports.

The increase in cocoa grinding activities has not reduced the dependency of origin countries and farmers on international markets, and particularly the international price of cocoa beans and intermediate products. The price of cocoa beans is set on futures markets through the London Cocoa Futures, the ICE Cocoa Futures, and Euro Cocoa Futures. Export prices on the national level are determined by futures prices and cocoa beans are sold at a premium or discount, depending on the quality of the beans. Intermediate products are priced in direct ratios to futures prices and thus have a similar price volatility as beans (cf. Araujo Bonjean/Brun 2016). The price volatility of ready-to-eat chocolate products, on the other hand, is much lower, since chocolate manufacturers and retailers do not necessarily pass through changes in the price of beans in the short-run (ibid.). Origin countries with an economy dependent on cocoa exports could thus reduce income volatility by increasing the export share of high value-added chocolate products, as well as by exerting greater control over the export price of cocoa beans.

4. Cocoa processing and industrial policy in Côte d'Ivoire and Ghana

The cocoa sectors of Côte d'Ivoire and Ghana share many similarities, but also have differences (see Grumiller et al. 2018; Hütz-Adams et al. 2016). Côte d'Ivoire (43%) and Ghana (20%) are by far the largest producers of cocoa beans, with around 63% of the global cocoa beans production in 2016/17, producing mainly Forastero cocoa beans ('bulk cocoa') (ICCO 2017). Both economies are highly dependent on the exportation of cocoa, as exemplified in the export share of cocoa products in total merchandise exports of 43% in Côte d'Ivoire (2015) and 18% in Ghana (2016) (UN Comtrade 2017). The sectors in Côte d'Ivoire and Ghana are regulated by the Conseil du Café-Cacao (CCC) and COCOBOD, respectively. The Ivorian cocoa sector was deregulated during the SAPs of the 1990s; however, the sector has been re-regulated since 2011 in the context of an IMF-backed debt relief deal (Agritrade 2012), whereas Ghana withstood the deregulation and the abolishment of COCOBOD. The expansion of grinding capacities and output since the 1990s and the mid-2000s respectively (Figure 2) shifted their integration into the cocoa GVC from supplying cocoa beans to supplying cocoa beans and intermediate products (esp. cocoa liquor, butter and powder), particularly for processors located in key consumption markets (Figure 1).

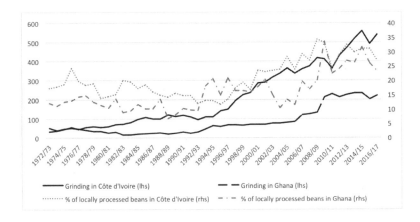

Figure 2: Growth of grinding output in Côte d'Ivoire and Ghana (thousand tons, 1972/73 – 2016/17)

Source: ICCO 2017, author's calculation.

4.1 Côte d'Ivoire

The Ivorian grinding sector dates back to the establishment of SACO by Cacao Barry (FR) in 1962 (Losch 2001), and particularly gained dynamism in the mid-1990s with the increasing investments of MNCs (Barry Callebaut, Cargill, ADM and Cémoi). The capacity expansions of MNCs, and the investments of smaller foreign and Ivorian companies, resulted in a significant increase in the total grinding capacity, from 350,000 tons in 2003/04 to 741,000 tons, with 2,161 direct employees in 2016/17 (MIM 2016; CCC 2017a). The Ivorian grinding sector operates at a capacity utilisation rate of around three-quarter in recent years, and is dominated by four large multinational grinders which total 72% of the overall grinding capacity (ibid.). Côte d'Ivoire is, together with the Netherlands, the largest grinder in the world, with 540,000 tons of processed beans and a 12.6% share of global grindings in 2016/17 (ICCO 2017; Figure 2). The *Rassemblement des Républicains* government officially aims to process 50% of its bean output in Côte d'Ivoire by 2020 (CCC 2017b); however, only 27% of produced beans were processed locally in 2016/17 (Figure 2).

Following the general trend towards origin grinding, investments in the grinding sector have increased, as a result of export tax incentives, investment zone benefits and deregulation in the 1990s. The substantial growth in grinding capacity was nonetheless hampered due to the political instability in the 2000s, to the benefit of investments in the Ghanaian grinding sector. Deregulation resulted in intensified operations of multinational grinders and an increased concentration of cocoa trading, at the cost of independent and locally owned exporters. Multinational grinders intensified their upstream activities (sourcing and exporting), since the abolishment of the Ivorian cocoa marketing board (CAISTAB) in 1999 increased their counterparty risk and opened a window of opportunity to increase control over the value chain (cf. Gilbert 2009: 300; Araujo Bonjean/Brun 2016: 344f.).

The key incentive for cocoa processors to grind in Côte d'Ivoire is the single export tax (*droit unique de sortie* - DUS) on cocoa and coffee products. The DUS was calculated based on the weight of the cocoa products produced – and not on the weight of the beans processed – which effectively reduced the export tax for grinders, depending on the product to be exported, by around 25% (Ecobank 2014). The tax was introduced after independence and suspended in 1989 due to pressure from the Bretton Woods institutions, but it was reintroduced during the 1991/92 season due to fiscal deficits after a sharp devaluation of the CFA franc (IMF 1998: 42ff.; IMF 2000: 30ff.). Initially, the incentive was to be abolished after five years; however, the DUS was not reformed until the 2012/13 cocoa season (Agritrade 2012). The reform of the DUS was particularly challenging for small-scale grinders due to their higher cost of finance and smaller margins. In addition, various small-scale grinders were only established a few years before the DUS reform and thus were not able to pay off their full investment costs under the pre-reform DUS (Ecobank 2014).[5]

At the end of 2016, after continuous pressure from local processors, a new conditional DUS incentive for processers was introduced in order to achieve the goal of processing 50% of total bean output locally (Interview 7, 12). Processers who agree to increase their capacities within five years – by between 7.5% and 15%, depending on their size – are eligible to export processed cocoa products at a reduced DUS rate (a reduction of between 1.4 and 5 percentage points of the 14.6% DUS for cocoa paste, butter and powder, and duty free exports for finished chocolate products). CCC reported that Barry Callebaut, Cargill, ICP, FORAGRI and Tafi have agreed to increase their capacities until 2022 (ibid.). In addition to the DUS, investment incentives (a share of the investment might be deductible from the taxable income in the following years) and other temporal restricted tax benefits (including exemptions from corporate tax) provided in investment zones incentivise processers to invest in Côte d'Ivoire.

Chocolate manufacturing in Côte d'Ivoire continues to be limited; however, the dynamics of the sector have recently evolved due to rising local and regional demand in the context of a 35% common external tariff (WTO 2017) on chocolate products in the ECOWAS region. Most importantly, two local grinding companies, the French chocolatier Cémoi and the Ivorian grinder Tafi, functionally upgraded to chocolate manufacturing to supply the local and regional markets (see Grumiller et al. 2018 for more details). In recent years, the growth of artisanal chocolate manufacturers has expanded as well (e.g. Instant Choco, Mon Choco). Exports of chocolate products (in particular industrial chocolate) have increased significantly since the mid-1990s, from negligible volumes to USD 148 million in 2016 (representing 35,000 tons) (UN Comtrade 2017).[6]

4.2 Ghana

Ghana has a long history in cocoa processing; however, until the 1990s, processing was largely limited to the state-owned and now partially privatised Cocoa Processing Company (CPC)[7] and to the joint venture West African Mills Company (WAMCO). Particularly since the mid-2000s, MNCs and local private investors have expanded grinding capacities to around 489,000 tons, with around 2,100 employees[8] in 2016/17

(COCOBOD 2017; ICCO 2017). Ghana is the seventh largest grinder in the world, with 220,000 tons of processed beans (representing five per cent of global grinding) (ibid.). MNCs with processing capacities include Barry Callebaut, Cargill, Olam and Touton, holding between them nearly 60% of the operational grinding capacities (COCOBOD 2017). The largest operational Ghanaian companies are CPC and Niche Cocoa Industry. The grinding sector has faced a severe setback after various grinding companies stopped operations due to the limited availability of discounted beans and the abolishment of COCOBOD's working capital credit facility, which occurred because various grinders did not pay back their debt in 2014/15 (Interview 4, 5, 13, 16, 17).[9] The New Democratic Congress (NDC) government in the past, and the current New Patriotic Party (NPP) government aim to increase the share of locally processed beans in total output to 50%; however, only 23% of total output was processed locally in 2016/17 (Figure 2).

Investments in grinding were incentivised by a discount on light crop beans, export-processing zone (EPZ) benefits and indirectly by the political instability in Côte d'Ivoire since the 2000s. Grinders benefit from a 20% discount on light beans; however, since light crop beans trade at a lower price on the international market, the real discount of light crop is equivalent to around 7.5% (COCOBOD 2017). The discount on light beans results in a lower average FOB price; grinders are thus indirectly subsidised by smallholders, which explains why farmers and to some extent COCOBOD are opposed to incentives which support the grinding sector (cf. Whitfield et al. 2015: 244ff.). Processors have argued that the discount on light crop is crucial in order to process profitably in Ghana, in particular since high electricity costs and unreliable power supply impede cocoa processing (Interview 4, 5, 13, 14, 15, 16, 17; cf. ACET 2014b: 38f.).[10] The incentives of the EPZs most importantly include tax-free importation for production in EPZs and the suspension of corporate income tax for 10 years, with a reduction by 17 percentage points thereafter (from 25% to 8%) (GFZB 2017). Cocoa processors situated in an EPZ are authorised to sell up to 30% of their annual production on the local market (ibid.), which particularly benefits local grinders such as Niche Cocoa and CPC that have already or want to upgrade to chocolate manufacturing and produce for the local market.

The goal of the government to increase the share of locally processed beans to 50% by 2020 could already be achieved at the current total grinding capacity and given the cocoa bean production levels in recent years; however, capacity utilisation (around 64% of operational capacity in 2016/17) remains well below the installed capacity, due to the limited availability of light crop beans, which are sold at a discount (cf. COCOBOD 2017; ICCO 2017). Various grinding companies ceased operations in 2014/15, but the total grinding volume did not drop significantly due to existing overcapacities. Ghana would need to expand incentives for grinding companies in order to achieve the government's goal (cf. Mulangu et al. 2017), since the share of light crop beans in total output is expected to decrease due to quality improvements in the production of cocoa and the increasing use of hybrid seeds (Interview 5, 17).

The chocolate manufacturing sector in Ghana is small; however, there have been some important new developments, similar to the situation in Côte d'Ivoire (see Grumiller et al. 2018 for more details). CPC is the largest manufacturer and produces bars of chocolate and other products, mainly for the local market under the Golden Tree label. Niche Cocoa Industry, a Ghanaian processor which mainly sells intermediate products to MNCs such as Touton and Olam, recently functionally upgraded to chocolate manufacturing and aims at the local, regional and Asian markets in particular (Interview 14). Some small-scale and artisanal chocolate manufacturers exist as well (e.g. 57chocolate, fairafric). Exports of chocolate products nonetheless remain insignificant.

The Ghanaian government and COCOBOD are currently developing a new strategy for the cocoa sector, based on the Cocoa Sector Development Strategy approved in 1999, which seeks to intensify the promotion of the chocolate manufacturing sector (Interview 16, 17). The new strategy could include a two per cent discount on main crop beans for local chocolate manufacturers as well as the promotion of local chocolate and cocoa confectionery consumption, e.g. via school feeding programs (Interview 17). A discount on main crop beans for local grinding has been repeatedly demanded by the industry as well, but so far lacks political support, in particular due to the continuing opposition of smallholders (Interview 1, 5).

5. Distributional conflicts, competitiveness and linkages in the Ivorian and Ghanaian cocoa processing sectors

The Ivorian and Ghanaian cocoa sectors are examples of the successful development of forward linkages and functional upgrading into more capital intensive, albeit still low value- added, activities in the context of a cash-crop based GVC. The growth of the grinding sectors has been furthered by tax and price incentives, changing sector regulations and GVC dynamics, in particular the shifting strategies of lead firms that seek to strengthen their control over the upstream segments of the chain and secure access to cocoa beans in light of potential scarcity in bean supply, as well as technological advances, especially in transportation (cf. Fold 2002; Gilbert 2009; Araujo Bonjean/Brun 2016). The industrialisation process has been FDI-led, and multinational grinders exploiting tax and price incentives dominate the sectors. The head start of the Ivorian grinding sector is explained by the deregulation of the cocoa sector in the mid-1990s and the earlier application of incentives, in particular the large DUS 'discount' for processed cocoa products. Ghana was able to expand its grinding sector from the mid-2000s in the context of the political insta-bility in Côte d'Ivoire and the introduction of the discount on light beans for local processing. The grinding sectors of both countries also benefit from their global importance in cocoa bean production and the interest of lead firms in maintaining strategic relationships with COCOBOD and CCC. Incentives, and to a lesser extent spillovers and a working capital facility, also furthered the creation of locally owned grinding companies. The growth of the grinding sector was – in addition to the substantial growth in local and regional chocolate consumption and high regional tariffs on chocolate imports – key for the creation of additional forward linkages to chocolate manufacturing in Côte d'Ivoire and Ghana. In both countries, locally embedded companies[11] with existing grinding capaci-ties – the French chocolatier Cémoi and the Ivorian grinder Tafi in Côte d'Ivoire, as well as the Ghanaian grinder Niche Cocoa – function-ally upgraded into chocolate manufacturing in order to start producing, particularly for the local and regional markets.

5.1 Distributional conflicts related to industrial policies

The industrial policy design focusing on tax and price incentives created distributional conflicts. In both countries, the 'subsidisation' of the MNC-dominated grinding sectors has reduced the income of smallholders and/or the government. This has created distributional conflicts, particularly between smallholders and grinders, to some extent restricting the support for cocoa processing via incentives financed from cocoa income. The smallholders' political weight has been more pronounced in Ghana, and the parties' dependencies on votes from cocoa farmers in democratic elections has counteracted MNCs lobbying for an enlargement of incentives (cf. Whitfield et al. 2015: 244ff.). In Côte d'Ivoire, the Bretton Woods institutions played a more important role in the reforms of the DUS. Today, neither the Ivorian nor the Ghanaian government support the development of cocoa processing via a comprehensive set of strategic industrial policies beyond the FDI-oriented incentive structure. Only Ghana continues to support the CPC more directly. However, some advances are visible, for example in the new conditionality of the DUS in Côte d'Ivoire, as well as the recent discussions on the reform of the Cocoa Sector Development Strategy in Ghana. The policy focus on cocoa production and the lack of strategic industrial policies to promote cocoa processing show the difficulty to create and sustain support for industrialisation projects in light of distributional conflicts, and the diverging interests and needs of MNCs, locally owned firms, smallholders and the political elite, as well as foreign institutions, such as the World Bank.

5.2 Competitiveness

In general, the grinding sectors in both countries struggle to be competitive (Interview 1, 2, 3, 4, 5, 8, 10, 12, 13, 14, 15, 16, 17, 18). In addition to the global capacity overhang and low margins, higher investment costs, the export of intermediate products in solid form, as well as the 'single origin challenge', the key constraint remains operational costs. In Côte d'Ivoire, the grinding sector can operate without DUS incentives (Interview 7, 8, 12), which is indicated by the stagnation of grinding levels after the DUS-reform in 2012 (Figure 2). Grinders nonetheless retained new investments after the 2012 DUS-reform (Interview 7, 12). In Ghana, the high costs of electricity and unreliable power supply make the discount on light beans – and thus the subsidisation of grinders at the cost of small-holders – a 'necessity' in order for grinding to be profitable (Interview 1, 2, 15, 16, 17, 18). Lower operational costs enhance the policy makers' ability to adjust FDI-oriented incentive structures: Ivorian policy makers initially abolished the DUS-incentives and later implemented conditional DUS-incentives. Policy makers in Ghana, in contrast, are severely constrained, since the discount on light beans is a 'necessity' in order to sustain the sector until the long-term electricity problem is resolved, but room for conditionality nonetheless exists. Smaller grinders in both countries have, in addition, difficulties in accessing finance and some companies have older and less efficient machinery (Interview 4, 7, 8, 10, 13, 14; cf. UNECA 2013: 144ff.). Smaller firms also often struggle to find buyers and rely on selling to intermediaries, in particular to multinational grinders (Interview 4, 8, 13, 14).

The comparatively small chocolate manufacturing sectors in both countries are oriented towards the local and regional markets and, with the exception of a few small manufacturers that focus on niche export markets, are not competitive on the global market, due to high investment, operational, input and transportation costs, and despite duty-free, quota-free market access to key consumption markets such as the EU and the US (Interview 1, 5, 6, 10). In addition, the sector suffers from market and product development strategies. The larger locally owned and multinational manufacturers focus on the relatively protected local and regional markets; however, they struggle to penetrate the regional ECOWAS market due to non-tariff measures (e.g. infrastructural and bureaucratic obstacles) and regional as well as international competition (Interview 1, 4, 6, 10, 14). Artisanal and smaller manufacturers struggle with access to, and the high cost of, finance, and generally have niche market strategies. Some of the firms struggle to comply with the high regulatory standards in export markets (Interview 6, 11).

5.3 Linkage effects

Whether or not strategic industrial policies in support of a specific sector can be justified heavily depends on the sector's potential for linkage effects. The export-oriented and MNC-dominated grinding sectors in both countries had for many years an enclave-like character with limited employment and linkage creation, but the recent functional upgrading processes of locally owned and locally embedded foreign grinders has furthered the growth of the chocolate manufacturing sectors. The grinding sectors have some backward (e.g. to the transporting and cardboard packaging industry) and forward linkages (esp. to chocolate manufacturing) to the local economy (Interview 1, 2, 4, 5, 7, 8, 12, 14, 15, 16, 17, 18, 19). Machines and spare parts are, however, imported. Multinational grinders often run sustainability programmes targeting cocoa production and smallholders in the context of the industry's fear of supply shortages, as well as of quality and traceability issues (ibid.; cf. Barrientos 2016). The limited employment creation in the capital-intensive grinding sector, as well as the FDI-dominance and profit repatriation, constrain the creation of consumption linkages. Fiscal linkages are difficult to assess; however, they are likely to be small in the context of extensive tax and price incentives. The situation is particularly problematic in Ghana due to the 'necessity' to subsidise the sector in the light of high operational costs.[12] The potential to create fiscal linkages is more pronounced in Côte d'Ivoire, and the situation has improved since the DUS reform in 2012. Evidence for meaningful linkages between MNCs and locally owned grinders, in particular in terms of technological transfers, is limited as well. (Interview 1, 4, 8, 10, 13, 14, 15, 17; cf. ACET 2014b: 38f.). The activities of MNC grinders had nonetheless some positive impact on investments by local actors (e.g. in the case of a former manager of Cémoi who co-founded the Ivorian grinder and manufacturer Tafi) (Interview 10).

Chocolate manufacturing (including marketing and branding) has broader linkage potentials in relation to grinding, but the linkage effects of the manufacturing sectors in Côte d'Ivoire and Ghana have been almost negligible due to the small scale of the sectors. Potentials for backward linkages exist to the milk (milk powder is generally imported), sugar (Côte d'Ivoire has sugar production) and more sophisticated packaging (which is generally imported from China) industries – also in order to reduce input prices – as well as for forward linkages to design, branding, marketing and distribution. The potential to develop backward linkages to chocolate manufacturing, such as the creation of a milk industry, might be undercut by the recently ratified Economic Partnership Agreements between the EU and Côte d'Ivoire, as well as with Ghana, which further deregulate the importation of bulk milk powder from the EU, albeit from low levels, and only include restrictive infant industry clauses (cf. Grumiller et al. 2018).

6. Conclusion – industrial policy implications

The analysis of the GVC dynamics and local sector conditions has highlighted the opportunities and challenges for the development of cocoa processing in Côte d'Ivoire and Ghana. The paper concludes that the opportunities for additional forward linkage development in the Ivorian and Ghanaian cocoa sectors are limited, particularly in GVCs geared to traditional end markets. Hence, the paper argues that the growing opportunities in local and regional end markets, as well as related value chains, need to be leveraged through strategic industrial policies that go beyond tax or price incentives and focus on supporting locally owned and locally embedded foreign companies.

The development of grinding sectors has been relatively successful, but the future growth of the grinding sectors is constrained by global overcapacities, generally high operational and/or investment costs, and the dominance of MNCs, which mainly seek to exploit tax and price incentives in the context of distributional conflicts. In addition, the grinding sectors should currently not be selected as a high priority sector for strategic industrial policies due to their enclave-like character and limited opportunities for linkage development, with the important exception of forward linkage development to chocolate manufacturing of locally owned and embedded foreign grinders and chocolate manufacturers.

The development of the chocolate manufacturing sectors continues to be constrained by limited export opportunities. Simultaneously, the substantial increase of local and regional chocolate consumption, albeit from a low level, has opened a window of opportunity for the growth and promotion of origin manufacturing. Rising consumption levels, and high tariffs protecting the domestic and regional ECOWAS markets, has furthered functional upgrading into chocolate manufacturing of locally owned and embedded foreign grinders and manufacturers; however, they lack the support of strategic industrial policies. It is unlikely that functional upgrading into chocolate manufacturing will be emulated by MNCs with grinding facilities in Côte d'Ivoire or Ghana in the near future, since most companies' main business is grinding (and to some extent the production of industrial chocolate) and not the manufacturing of branded ready-to-eat products. Hence, Ivorian and Ghanaian grinders are more likely to upgrade into chocolate manufacturing (like Niche Cocoa in Ghana or Tafi in Côte d'Ivoire). Multinational chocolate manufacturers might invest in Ghana or Côte d'Ivoire in order to be better able to tackle the local and regional markets (e.g. Nestlé in Nigeria and Cémoi in Côte d'Ivoire); however, as of now the size of the markets do not seem to be sufficiently attractive for most companies. Another opportunity could be exports to markets with similar climate conditions and demand for more heat-resistant chocolate products, but many of these markets are already contested by MNCs or are protected by tariffs (cf. van Huellen 2014). The growth of origin manufacturing will thus mainly be determined by the future development of local and regional demand for chocolate products – luxury products – in low and lower middle-income countries in (West) Africa and the ability to capture market shares in niche export markets.

This paper argues that the constrained opportunities for additional forward linkage development in the Ivorian and Ghanaian cocoa sectors need to be leveraged by strategic industrial policies, in addition to tax and price incentives. The industrial policy design should thus extend its focus beyond global exports and specifically seek to leverage the opportunities in local and regional value chains by mitigating the challenges of locally owned and more locally embedded foreign grinders and chocolate manufacturers. The resources invested for the promotion of both processing sectors must be carefully aligned with the global, regional and local market opportunities, as well as with the growth and potential to develop the local, regional and niche export markets in order to avoid extensive and long-term overcapacities. The development of regional market opportunities will not only depend on the growth of chocolate consumption, the local firms' competitiveness and the protective tariff structure for chocolate imports, but also on the reduction of non-tariff measures.

Carefully administered price and tax-discounts for origin grinding and manufacturing play an important role in the development of the processing sectors, but the incentives should be conditional, as in the case of Côte d'Ivoire. The conditionality of incentives could be linked to additional investments, capacity utilisation rates, employment creation, and the creation of other linkages. Multinational grinders should furthermore be incentivised to foster linkages with locally owned grinders, in particular with respect to technology transfer. Further infrastructural improvements, particularly in the Ghanaian electricity sector, are of crucial importance in order to reduce operational costs and ensure the growth and sustainability of the sectors, as well as increasing the policy space. The further development of a grinding hub (see ACET 2014b) in Côte d'Ivoire or Ghana to achieve economies of scale and agglomeration, and thus to some extent overcome the 'single origin challenge', would benefit from cooperation between the two countries, but the current global and national overcapacities in the grinding sector call for careful expansion planning.

In both countries, in particular locally owned and locally embedded foreign grinders and chocolate manufacturers need to be supported by strategic industrial policies, since most MNCs are not likely to invest in manufacturing in the near future in light of limited local and regional market opportunities. Locally owned companies would benefit from subsidised access to finance, and (smaller) chocolate manufacturers in particular need support in R&D for product development as well as market diversification strategies. Smaller and artisanal chocolate manufacturers also need assistance to comply with regulatory standards in export markets. The promotion of backward linkages to chocolate manufacturing should be a long-term goal and is crucial in order to reduce input costs and increase linkage effects.

In addition to the development of forward linkages, it is also important to have a policy focus on commodity production and trade per se to ensure higher and sustained income for commodity producers, as well as to create consumption and fiscal linkages via process and product upgrading. Ideally, the cooperation between the two major producers, Côte d'Ivoire and Ghana, could be fostered in order to exert market power and reduce their dependency on international markets and prices, for example via the regulation of cocoa production or buffer-stocks. A 'cocoa cartel' that tries to go beyond increased cooperation and coordination is likely to face various difficulties (see Oomes et al. 2016: 95), in particular since cocoa is easier to substitute and produce relative to oil. There have been recent signs that the cooperation between Côte d'Ivoire and Ghana, as well as industrial policy measures in the respective cocoa sectors, are expanding in the context of the 'Abidjan Declaration' and a USD 1.2 billion loan request from the African Development Bank in 2017; nevertheless, the implementation and results remain to be seen (Interview 1, 7, 12, 16, 17). The loan could finance the building of storage and warehousing facilities necessary for buffer-stocks, the promotion of local and regional processing and consumption, as well as a stabilisation fund and a cocoa exchange commission for the management of production (AfDB 2017).

Acknowledgement

I would like to thank Cornelia Staritz, Bernhard Tröster, Werner Raza and Hannes Grohs, and two anonymous referees, for comments that greatly improved the quality of the paper.

1 The cocoa GVC has two major processing steps following the production of cocoa beans: grinding (producing intermediate products such as cocoa liquor, butter and powder), and the manufacturing of chocolate and cocoa confectionery.

2 The share of cocoa beans in the value of a bar of milk chocolate in the UK is estimated to have dropped from an average of 27% between 1976 and 1985 to nine per cent between 1996 and 2005 (Gilbert 2006). A cost breakdown for UK milk chocolate in 2004 estimated the producer price of the final retail price to be only four per cent, while grinders and manufacturers receive around 51% and retailers 28% (the rest includes other ingredients, advertising, transport) (ibid.). A similar cost analysis by Cocoa Barometer (2015) estimates the value added of cocoa producing (seven per cent), transporting and trading (six per cent) as well as processing (eight per cent) to be relatively low compared to the value added of chocolate manufacturing (35%) and retailing (44%).

3 Close proximity to chocolate manufacturers enables grinders to transport cocoa liquor and butter in liquid form on a just-in-time basis. This reduces costs since the products do not need to be re-melted (Gilbert 1997 in Fold 2002). The same applies to industrial chocolate (ACET 2014b).

4 Data represents global exports. Updated data from Grumiller et al. (2018).

5 Grinders with highly efficient machines, particularly employed by MNCs, complain that the multiplier used to calculate the equivalent tonnage of beans used to make cocoa products increases their tax burden (they produce more cocoa products

from cocoa beans compared to what would be allowed to export under the current calculation method) (Ecobank 2014: 4). CCC is currently addressing this problem by developing multipliers adjusted to the efficiency of the machines used by different grinders (Interview 7, 12).

6   Data represents global imports.

7   CPC is listed on the Ghanaian Stock Exchange since 2003. Today, COCOBOD, the Finance Ministry and the state-run SSNIT own around 94% of CPC (Reuters 2017). CPC had financial difficulties in 2017.

8   Data provided by CCC respectively COCOBOD regarding employees in the grinding sector should be regarded as rough estimates, since grinding capacity and total grindings in Côte d'Ivoire are much larger relative to Ghana, but employment in the sectors is at the same level.

9   The credit-facility enabled grinders to buy beans on credit as well as process and sell their products in order to pay back the credit. The facility thus reduced cash-flow requirements, which particularly benefited Ghanaian and smaller grinders. The abolishment of the credit-facility also put profitable companies under pressure due to changing cash-flow requirements (Interview 5, 17).

10 Ghana has a comparatively unstable power supply, which often makes investments in expensive electric generators necessary. Electricity prices in Ghana are higher compared for example to Côte d'Ivoire or EU countries. The World Bank estimates electricity prices for standardised warehouses in business hubs to be at 24.5 ¢/kWh in Ghana, 12 ¢/kWh in Côte d'Ivoire and 10.8 ¢/kWh in the Netherlands (World Bank 2017).

11 The key issue is not so much nationality of ownership but rather the embeddedness and the strength of ties (economic, cultural, societal) that link a firm to a specific location and its economic fabric (Morris et al. 2016).

12 Based on an assessment of PricewaterhouseCoopers, processors argue that the benefits in terms of investment and employment creation outweigh the costs of incentives (Kolavalli/Vigneri 2017: 125f.); however, this is contested by different stakeholders (Interview 1, 5) and there is no clear evidence on the net effects, due to a lack of transparency.

References

ACET (2014a): African Transformation Report. Growth with Depth. In: African Center for Economic Transformation, http://africantransformation.org/wp-content/uploads/2014/02/2014-african-transformation-report.pdf, 05.01.2018.

ACET (2014b): The Cocoa Agri-Processing Opportunity in Africa. In: A Dalberg study for the African Center for Economic Transformation, http://acet-forafrica.org/publication/the-cocoa-agroprocessing-opportunity-in-africa/, 07.01.2018.

AfDB/OECD/UNDP/UNECA (2013): African Economic Outlook. Structural Transformation and Natural Resources. In: OECD publishing, Paris, http://dx.doi.org/10.1787/aeo-2013-en, 05.01.2018. https://doi.org/10.1787/aeo-2013-en

AfDB (2017): High hopes for cocoa farmers in Africa, as AfDB plans big for producing countries. In: African Development Bank, https://www.afdb.org/en/news-and-events/high-hopes-for-cocoa-farmers-in-africa-as-afdb-plans-big-for-producing-countries-17247/, 31.10.2017.

Agritrade (2012): Special report: Côte d'Ivoire's cocoa sector reforms 2011-2012. In: Agritrade, http://agritrade.cta.int/en/layout/set/print/Agriculture/Commodities/Cocoa/Special-report-Cote-d-Ivoire-s-cocoa-sector-reforms-2011-2012, 31.11.2017.

Amsden, Alice (2001): The Rise of "The Rest": Challenges to the West from Late-Industrializing Economies. Oxford, New York: Oxford University Press. https://doi.org/10.1093/0195139690.001.0001

Araujo Bonjean, Catherine/Brun, Jean-François (2016): Concentration and Price Transmission in the Cocoa-Chocolate Chain. In: Squicciarini, Mara/Swinnen, Johan (eds.): The Economics of Chocolate. Oxford: Oxford University Press, 339-362. https://doi.org/10.1093/acprof:oso/9780198726449.003.0017

Asche, Helmut/Neuerburg, Philipp/Menegatti, Matteo (2012): Economic diversification strategies: A key driver in Africa's new industrial revolution. In: UNIDO, development Policy, statistics and research branch, working paper 2/2012.

Bair, Jennifer/Gereffi, Gary (2003): Upgrading, Uneven Development, and Jobs in the North American Apparel Industry. In: Global Networks 3(2), 143-169. https://doi.org/10.1111/1471-0374.00054

Barrientos, Stephanie (2016): Beyond Fair Trade: Why are Mainstream Chocolate Companies Pursuing Social and Economic Sustainability in Cocoa Souring? In: Squicciarini, Mara/Swinnen, Johan (eds.): The Economics of Chocolate. Oxford: Oxford University Press, 213-227. https://doi.org/10.1093/acprof:oso/9780198726449.003.0012

Barrientos, Stephanie/Asenso-Okyere, Kwadwo (2009): Cocoa value chain: challenges facing Ghana in changing global confectionary market. In: Journal für Entwicklungspolitik 25(2), 88-107. https://doi.org/10.20446/JEP-2414-3197-25-2-88

Becker, Joachim (2008): Der kapitalistische Staat in der Peripherie: polit-ökonomische Perspektiven. In: Journal für Entwicklungspolitik 24(2), 10-32. https://doi.org/10.20446/JEP-2414-3197-24-2-10

Bessi, Benjamin (2017): Interview avec Benjamin Bessi, Directeur Général de Cemoi Côte d'Ivoire. In: Interview conducted by Marcopolis, http://www.marcopolis.net/cemoi-un-des-premiers-transformateurs-de-cacao-en-cote-d-ivoire.htm, 17.10.2017.

Blommer, Peter (2011): A Collaborative Approach to Cocoa Sustainability. The supply threat is real. Aggregation of farmers remains the single biggest challenge to overcome. In: The Manufacturing Confectioner, May 2011, 19-26.

Candy Industry (2016): 2016 Global Top 100 Candy Companies, http://www.candyindustry.com/2016-Global-Top-100-Part-4, 31.04.2017.

CCC (2017a): Data. In: Provided by the Conseil Café-Cacao in October/December 2017.

CCC (2017b): Évolution de la Filière Café-Cacao de 2012 à 2017. 4ème Édition des Journées Nationales du Cacao & du Chocolat. In: CCC report presented in Abidjan between the 29th of Septembre and the 1st of October at the CAISTAB-Plateau, http://www.conseilcafecacao.ci/docs/2016/CATA-LOGUE_JNCC_2017.pdf, 07.01.2018.

Chang, Ha-Joon (2011): Industrial Policy: Can We Go Beyond an Unproductive Confrontation? In: Lin, Justin/Pleskovic, Boris (eds.): Annual World Bank Conference on Development Economics – Global 2010: Lessons from East Asia and the Global Financial Crisis. Washington D.C.: World Bank, 83-109.

Cocoa Barometer (2015): Resources and Data. In: http://www.cocoabarometer.org/Resources_and_Data.html, 05.01.2017.

COCOBOD (2017): Data. In: Provided by the Cocoa Marketing Board and the Cocoa Marketing Company in October 2017.

Divine Chocolate (2017): Divine Chocolate – About Us. In: http://www.divinechocolate.com/us/about-us/, 07.01.2018.

Ecobank (2014): Côte d'Ivoire's cocoa grinders: at the crossroads. In: Middle Africa Insight Series, Soft Commodities, Cocoa, 29th January 2014, http://ecobank1.aznresearch.com/upload/201406040521177811163jBenJTFhcc.pdf, 31.10.2017.

Ederer, Stephan/Heumesser, Christine/Staritz, Cornelia (2016): Financialization and commodity prices – an empirical analysis for coffee, cotton, wheat and oil. In: International Review of Applied Economics 30(4): 462-87. https://doi.org/10.1080/02692171.2015.1122745

Evans, Peter (1995): Embedded Autonomy. States and Industrial Transformation. Princeton, N.J.: Princeton University Press.

Evers, Tilman (1977): Bürgerliche Herrschaft in der Dritten Welt. Zur Theorie des Staates in ökonomisch unterentwickelten Gesellschaftsformationen. Köln: Europäische Verlagsanstalt.

Fold, Niels (2002): Lead Firms and Competition in 'Bi-polar' Commodity Chains: Grinders and Branders in the Global Cocoa-chocolate Industry. In: Journal of Agrarian Change 2(2), 228-247. https://doi.org/10.1111/1471-0366.00032

Fold, Niels/Neilson, Jeff (2016): Sustaining Supplies in Smallholder-Dominated Value Chains: Corporate Governance of the Global Cocoa Sector. In: Squicciarini, Mara/Swinnen, Johan (eds.): The Economics of Chocolate. Oxford: Oxford University Press, 195-212. https://doi.org/10.1093/acprof:oso/9780198726449.003.0011

Frank, Andre Gunder (1966): The Development of Underdevelopment. In: Monthly Review 18(4), 17-31. https://doi.org/10.14452/MR-018-04-1966-08_3

Gayi, Samuel/Tsowou, Komi (2016): Cocoa industry: Integrating small farmers into the global value chain. In: UNCTAD report UNCTAD/SUC/2015/4.

Gereffi, Gary (2005): The global economy: Organization, governance and development. In: Smelser, Neil/Swedberg, Richard (eds.): Handbook of Economic Sociology. Second Edition. Princeton, NJ: Princeton University Press and Russell Sage Foundation, 160-182.

Gereffi, Gary/Sturgeon, Timothy (2013): Global Value Chains and Industrial Policy: the role of emerging economies. In: Elms, Deborah/Low, Patrick (eds.): Global Value Chains in a changing world. Geneva: WTO publications, in cooperation with the Fung Global Institute and the Temasek Centre for Trade and Negotiations.

GFZB (2017): Ghana Free Zones Board – Incentives. In: GFZB, http://www.gfzb. gov.gh/investment%20opportunity/incentives.php, 05.12.2017.

Ghana-IEPA (2016): Stepping Stone Economic Partnership Agreement between Ghana, of the one part, and the European Community and its Member States, of the other part. In: Official Journal of the EU, L 287/3.

Gilbert, Christopher (2006): Value Chain Analysis and Market Power in Commodity Processing with Application to the Cocoa and Coffee Sectors. In: Universita Degli Studi Di Trento, Dipartimento Di Economia, Discussion paper No. 5.

Gilbert, Christopher (2009): Cocoa Market Liberalization in Retrospect. In: Review of Business and Economics, 54(3), 294-312.

Grumiller, Jan/Raza, Werner/Staritz, Cornelia (2016): Framework to Assess Institutional Setups for Industrial Policies. In: Background paper financed by the Deutsche Gesellschaft für Internationale Zusammenarbeit (GIZ), a summary of the report has been published online: http://www.equip-project.org/ wp-content/uploads/2017/09/D-Institutional-Setup-July-2017.pdf, 31.10.2017.

Grumiller, Jan/Raza, Werner/Staritz, Cornelia/Grohs, Hannes/Arndt, Christoph (2018): Perspectives for export-oriented industrial policy strategies for selected African countries: case studies Côte d'Ivoire, Ghana and Tunisia. In: ÖFSE Report, https://www.oefse.at/publikationen/research-reports/, 10.07.2018.

Hirschman, Albert (1981): Essays in Trespassing: Economics to Politics and Beyond. Cambridge/New York: Cambridge University Press.

Hütz-Adams, Friedel/Huber, Claudia/Knoke, Irene/Morazán, Pedro/Mürlebach, Mara (2016): Strengthening the competitiveness of cocoa production and improving the income of cocoa producers in West and Central Africa. Bonn: Südwind e.V.

ICCO (2017): Database provided by the International Cocoa Organization (ICCO) in December 2017.

IMF (2000): Côte d'Ivoire: Selected Issues and Statistical Appendix, IMF Staff Country Report no. 00/107, Washington, D.C.: IMF Publication Services.

IMF (1998): Côte d'Ivoire: Selected Issues and Statistical Appendix, IMF Staff Country Report no. 98/46, Washington, D.C.: IMF Publication Services.

Kaplinsky, Raphael/Farooki, Masuma (2012): Promoting Industrial Diversification in Resource Intensive Economies. In: UNIDO report, Vienna.

Kolavalli, Shashi/Vigneri, Marcella (2017): The Cocoa Coast: The Board-Managed Cocoa Sector in Ghana. Wahsington DC: International Food Policy Research Institute.

Losch, Bruno (2001): La libéralisation de la filière cacaoyère ivoirienne et les recompositions du marché mondial du cacao: vers la fin des «pays producteurs» et du marché international? In: Oléagineux Corps gras Lipides 8(6), 566-576. https://doi.org/10.1051/ocl.2001.0566

MIM (2016): Secteur de la Transformation du Cacao. In: http://www.industrie.gouv.ci/index.php/article/Resultats-projet-pacir-onudi-coteivoire?page=secteur_cacao, 10.11.2017.

Morris, Mike/Kaplinsky, Raphael/Kaplan, David (2012): "One Thing Leads to Another" – Promoting Industrialisation by Making the Most of the Commodity Boom in Sub-Saharan Africa. Cape Town: Centre for Social Science Research.

Morris, Mike/Fessehaie, Judith (2014): The industrialization challenge for Africa: Towards a commodities based industrialization path. In: Journal of African Trade 1, 25-36. https://doi.org/10.1016/j.joat.2014.10.001

Morris, Mike/Plank, Leonhard/Staritz, Cornelia (2016): Regionalism, end markets and ownership matter: Shifting dynamics in the apparel export industry in Sub Saharan Africa. In: Environment and Planning A, 48(7), 1244-65. https://doi.org/10.1177/0308518X15614745

Morris, Mike/Staritz, Cornelia (forthcoming): How global value chains change industrialization paths and industrial policies for developing countries. In: Gereffi, Gary/Ponte, Stefano/Raj-Reichert, Gale (forthcoming): Handbook on Global Value Chains. Cheltenham: Edward Elgar Publishing, forthcoming 2018.

Mulangu, Francis/Miranda, Mario/Maïga, Eugenie (2017): Cocoa pricing options and their implications for poverty and industrialization in Ghana. In: Agricultural Economics, 48(4), 481-490. https://doi.org/10.1111/agec.12349

Oomes, Nienke/Tieben, Bert/Laven, Anna/Ammerlaan, Ties/Appelman, Romy/Biesenbeek, Cindy/Buunk, Eelco (2016): Market Concentration and Price Formation in the Global Value Chain. In: SEO Amsterdam Economics Study.

Perkins, Isaac (2015): Global Cocoa processing: Ground to a Halt. In: Brown Brothers Harriman & Co., Commodity Markets Update Oct. 2015, 14-15.

Prebisch, Raúl (1981): The Latin American periphery in the global system of capitalism. In: Cepal Review 13, 143-150.

Ramdoo, Isabelle (2013): From Curse to Purse. Making Extractive Resources work for Development. In: ECDPM Discussion paper 136.

JAN GRUMILLER

Ramdoo, Isabelle (2015): Resource-based industrialization in Africa: Optimising linkages and value chains in the extractive sector. In: ECDPM Discussion Paper 179.

Reuters (2017): Ghana Stock Exchange says trading of CPC's shares suspended. In: Reuters, 29th August, https://af.reuters.com/article/commoditiesNews/ idAFL8N1LF69D, 05.10.2017.

Squicciarini, Mara/Swinnen, Johan (2016): From Cocoa to Chocolate: Process, Products, and Agents. In: Squicciarini, Mara/Swinnen, Johan (eds.): The Economics of Chocolate. Oxford: Oxford University Press, xxv-xxvi. https://doi.org/10.1093/acprof:oso/9780198726449.001.0001

Tamru, Seneshaw/Swinnen, Johan (2016): Back to the Roots: Growth in Cocoa and Chocolate Consumption in Africa. In: Squicciarini, Mara/Swinnen, Johan (eds.): The Economics of Chocolate. Oxford: Oxford University Press, 439-456.

Terazono, Emiko (2014): Welcome to the world of Big Chocolate. Three companies will dominate processing sector. In: Financial Times, December 18, 2014.

Terazono, Emiko (2017): Signs of pick-up in global demand boost cocoa industry. In: Financial Times, July 14, 2017.

UN Comtrade (2017): UN Comtrade Database. In: https://comtrade.un.org/ or https://wits.worldbank.org/, 01.05.2018.

UNCTAD (2008): Cocoa Study: Industry Structures and Competition. In: Study prepared by the UNCTAD secretariat, UNCTAD/DITC/COM/2008/1, http://unctad.org/en/Docs/ditccom20081_en.pdf, 05.01.2017.

UNCTAD (2013): Commodities and development report. Perennial problems, new challenges and evolving perspectives. In: UNCTAD report, UNCTAD/SUC/2011/9, http://unctad.org/en/PublicationsLibrary/suc2011d9_en.pdf, 05.01.2018.

UNECA (2013): Economic Report on Africa 2013: Making the Most of Africa's Commodities. Industrializing for Growth, Jobs and Economic Transformation. In: Economic Commission for Africa, Addis Ababa/Ethiopia.

van Huellen, Sophie (2014): West Africa's Cocoa Sector. The Need for Regional Integration and Value Addition at Origin. In: Background paper for the African Development Bank.

Whitfield, Lindsay/Therkildsen, Ole/Buur, Lars/Klær, Anne Mette (2015): The Politics of African Industrial Policy. A Comparative Perspective. New York: Cambridge University Press. https://doi.org/10.1017/CBO9781316225509

World Bank (2008): World Development Report. Washington DC: World Bank.

World Bank (2017): Doing Business database – explore economy – getting electricity. In: World Bank, http://www.doingbusiness.org/, 31.12.2017.

WTO (2017): Tariff Download Facility. In: World Trade Organization, http://tariffdata.wto.org, 31.12.2017.

List of Interviews

In total, 45 interviews with representatives of companies, interest groups and governmental institutions were conducted. The list presented below only includes interviews cited in this paper.

Interview 1: (Senior) Researchers of the African Center for Economic Transformation (ACET), 24.01.2017, 27.01.2017 and 22.10.2017.

Interview 2: Senior researcher of the International Food Policy Research Institute (IFPRI), 30.01.2017 and 24.10.2017.

Interview 3: Employee of a multinational grinding company in Ghana, 31.01.2017.

Interview 4: Senior manager of a Ghanaian grinder and manufacturer, 02.02.2017.

Interview 5: Former senior manager of COCOBOD, 03.02.2017.

Interview 6: Owner of an artisanal chocolate manufacturing company in Côte d'Ivoire, 16.10.2017.

Interview 7: Representative of CCC (unofficial interview), 16.10.2017.

Interview 8: Various managers of an Ivorian grinding company, 17.10.2017.

Interview 9: Employee of an Ivorian grinding company, 17.10.2017.

Interview 10: Manager of an Ivorian grinding and manufacturing company, 18.10.2017.

Interview 11: Owner of an artisanal chocolate manufacturing company in Côte d'Ivoire, 19.10.2017.

Interview 12: Representative of the Groupement des exportateurs (GEPEX), 19.10.2017.

Interview 13: Former manager of a Ghanaian grinding company, 24.10.2017.

Interview 14: Various interviews with managers of a Ghanaian grinder and manufacturer, 25.10.2017.

Interview 15: Former manager of a multinational grinding company in Ghana, 27.10.2017.

Interview 16: Senior managers of CMC, 27.10.2017.

Interview 17: (Senior) Researchers of COCOBOD, 27.10.2017.

Interview 18: Representative of a multinational grinding company with grinding facilities in Côte d'Ivoire and Ghana, 08.01.2018.

Interview 19: Manager of packaging company in Ghana, 24.10.2018.

Interview 20: Manager of a chocolate branding company in London, 12.01.2018.

ABSTRACT *Dieser Artikel präsentiert eine komparative Analyse über die Entwicklung von Vorwärtsverknüpfungen (forward linkages) in den ivorischen und ghanaischen Kakaosektoren. Der Artikel zeigt auf, dass sich die Vermahlungs- und Verarbeitungssektoren (grinding sectors) in Côte d'Ivoire und Ghana im Kontext von sich veränderten globalen Wertschöpfungskettendynamiken, auf ausländische Direktinvestitionen ausgerichteten Industriepolitiken sowie andauernden Verteilungskonflikten mit unterschiedlichem Erfolg entwickelten. Die grinding sectors in beiden Ländern sollten derzeit nicht als prioritäre Sektoren für strategische Industriepolitik ausgewählt werden, da sie von einem Enklavencharakter sowie nur begrenzten Möglichkeiten für die Entwicklung von zusätzlichen Vorwärtsverknüpfungen charakterisiert sind. Das rezente Wachstum der lokalen Schokoladenindustrien stellt eine wichtige Ausnahme dar, da diese von der Entwicklung der grinding sectors sowie dem gestiegenen lokalen und regionalen Schokoladenkonsum, in Kombination mit Schutzzöllen, profitierten. Der Artikel argumentiert, dass die lokalen kakaoverarbeitenden Industrien durch strategische, über Preis- und Steueranreize hinausgehende, industriepolitische Maßnahmen unterstützt werden sollten, um auch die Möglichkeiten in lokalen und regionalen Wertschöpfungsketten besser nutzen zu können.*

Jan Grumiller
Austrian Foundation for Development Research
j.grumiller@oefse.at

JOURNAL FÜR ENTWICKLUNGSPOLITIK XXXIV 3/4-2018, S. 46–71

JULIANA GOMES CAMPOS
Latin American Developmentalism in the 21st Century: An Analysis of the Governmental Industrial Policies of the Workers' Party in Brazil

ABSTRACT *This paper aims to analyse the feasibility of the return of industrial policies to foster development as a post-neoliberal alternative in the era of globalisation. With Partido dos Trabalhadores government, Brazil was considered one of the main countries in the Pink Tide. The government plan promised to foster industry modernisation and reduce poverty by bringing the state back into the picture to coordinate a project between public institutions, private sector and civil society in order to improve the country's position in the global economy. This paper thus analyses PT industrial policies to investigate the characteristics of a post-neoliberal development model in Latin America as an alternative to neoliberalism.*

KEYWORDS *PT, Brazil, industrialisation, developmentalism, post-neoliberalism*

1. Introduction

Since the end of the 1990s, Latin America has seen a wave of governments with a leftist stance – known as the Pink Tide group – and a rejection of neoliberal ideas of minimal state intervention and intense international competitiveness. These ideas had pushed the countries back to a position of dependence on natural resources and cheap labor export through the depletion of the national industrial base (Heidrich/Tussie 2009: 37).

Industrial policies have regained popularity as the main tool to help countries to catch up with the Global North in the post-neoliberal context.

However, the dimensions to formulate and implement these policies must encompass far broader and more complex policies than in the Import Substitution Industrialisation (ISI) era. Significantly, post-neoliberalism is not a unified theoretical alternative, but encompasses approaches that range from the most radical to the most progressive ones[1]. A detailed discussion of the whole scope of post-neoliberal approaches is, however, beyond the scope of this article. As a matter of purpose, this research specifically concentrates on neostructuralism, the post-neoliberalism approach developed by the Economic Commission for Latin America and the Caribbean (ECLAC). The neostructuralist approach advocates for growth with equity, through technical progress based on knowledge accumulation, and is commonly connected with the Chilean and Brazilian former new-leftist governments during the 2000s (Bielschowsky 2009: 177).

The *Partido dos Trabalhadores* (PT - Workers' Party) government in Brazil positioned the country as an important actor in the post-neoliberal discussion, due to its outstanding role in Latin America, the size of its internal market, and its already diverse industrial base, which does not solely rely on the extraction of natural resources. The PT has actively promoted industrial policies aimed at updating the Brazilian industrial base and fostering innovation. However, when quantitative results are analysed, the pattern of decreased industrial participation and increased share of export of natural resources in the GDP has slightly changed, when compared to the Washington Consensus era in the 1990s (Doctor 2012: 806; Milanez/Santos 2015: 13).

These quantitative results, combined with the recent economic and political crisis that culminated in the impeachment of Dilma Rousseff and the return of a conservative government with neoliberal ideals in 2016, are part of a broad discussion on the effectiveness and expected long-term results claimed by ECLAC's neostructuralist strategy (Leiva 2008a; Boito/Saad-Filho 2016). Critics of the approach doubt the capacity of neostructuralism to go beyond the neoliberal model and to present a feasible alternative to it. Others, in contrast, recognise that all post-neoliberal alternatives remain at the mercy of global capitalism, albeit with a more positive perspective. It is argued that even cases that adopted more reformist policies and that try to operate within the contradictions of neoliberalism

– commonly considered more as *status-quo* defending and likely to be temporary solutions – have opened up space to several counter-hegemonic possibilities from below (Chodor 2015: 180).

This study, thus, aims to investigate the Brazilian case in an attempt to contribute to the diverse discussion of the effectiveness of industrial policies in a post-neoliberal alternative. It is divided into four parts. After this brief introduction, the next section presents the theoretical formulation of industrial policies in a neostructuralist approach, as well as its critique. The third section discusses the methodology employed – the analysis of the industrial policies in Lula's and Dilma's mandates in the literature, combined with expert semi-structured interviews carried out by the author in Brazil in 2016-17. Expert selection was based on the interviewees' connection to government, and with knowledge of industrialisation, of PT, and of neostructuralism. Finally, the paper concludes by presenting the main findings of the case study.

2. Latin America & industrial policies: theoretical perspectives

Historical evidence has shown that today's developed countries had been actively promoting interventionist policies in trade and industry during their catching-up process (Di Maio, 2009: 107; Chang, 2003: 43). Following the example of countries in the Global-North already in an advanced level of industrialization, Latin American countries have been promoting industrial policies that can be traced back to the 1940s through the promotion of the Import Substitution Industrialisation (ISI) model. This is commonly associated with the structuralist's thinkers of ECLAC. Adopting a historical-structural method, structuralism argues that the economic relations between the 'centre' and the 'periphery' tended to increase the underdevelopment conditions and deepen the gap between developed and developing countries (Bielschowsky 2009: 173). Structuralism sees the periphery – as commodity exporter – in an unfavourable position in international trade, contradicting the general benefits deriving from free trade in David Ricardo's comparative advantage theory (Bracarense 2015: 125).

JULIANA GOMES CAMPOS

Singer (1975: 46) argued that the significant difference between the more productive export sectors – commonly foreign-owned – and the almost subsistence production for the domestic sector in underdeveloped countries, showed that the export sectors were not becoming an integral part of the underdeveloped country's economy. Indeed, the foreign investment in the periphery with the purpose of maintaining them as providers of food and raw materials for the centre reduces the spread of technical progress and the periphery's capacity for capital accumulation. Thus, ISI focused on fostering an industrial base to replace foreign produced goods as a way to break away from the circle of dependency and underdevelopment (Bielschowsky 2009: 182).

Under ISI, the state played a central role in protecting national industries, by implementing multiple exchange rates, high tariffs and restrictive quotas on imports. It also promoted industrial growth via substantial subsidies that targeted those sectors with the highest potential for industrial upgrading and productivity growth. This extensive government intervention also pushed for institutional transformation: ministries and public agencies were expanded to include a variety of regulatory and subsidy activities, and national and development banks, new utilities, and holding companies to administer public investment were created to support industrial development (Melo/Rodríguez-Clare 2006: 6).

ISI presented ambiguous results – by the late 1960s Brazil, Argentina and Mexico could be characterised as semi-industrialised countries with Colombia and Chile not far behind, while countries such as Bolivia and Honduras remained dependent on commodities exports (Munck, 2008: 53). However, the extensive size and functions of the state led to a great concentration of power that was not matched by accountability. Large-scale industrial development and infrastructure programmes were funded via the excessive borrowing of foreign capital, resulting in the accumulation of a massive amount of debt in the late 1970s. This situation, combined with external factors in the world economy, drove the region to a widespread debt crisis in the 1980s, labeled as the "lost decade" (Melo/Rodríguez-Clare 2006: 6; Kerstenetzky 2014: 173).

During the debt crisis, ISI in Latin America reached its saturation point and industrial policies lost their leading role as development agents. With the introduction of neoliberalism through the Washington Consensus

(WC) in the region, the reasons for underdevelopment were understood as rooted in excessive state intervention in regulating economic relations, and thus, deregulation and privatisation were seen as essential to let market forces alone provide the 'right' signals for the allocation of investment and efficient production. In this sense, industrial policy was seen as harmful, since it was prone to rent-seeking, production inefficiency and adversely affecting the effectiveness of the market ability to efficiently implement resource allocation, thus impeding the industrial base of a country to fully pursue its comparative advantage (Taylor 2009: 27; Lall 2004: 1-2).

The period was also marked by the promotion of a new form of regional integration known as 'open regionalism' and the establishment of the *Mercado Común del Sur* (MERCOSUR - South American trade bloc) by Brazil, Argentina, Paraguay and Uruguay. Although Latin America had already experienced attempts of regional integration during its ISI period, its focus remained on implementing ISI strategies in industrial development at a national level (Sanahuja 2012: 2). The new attempt at regional integration in the neoliberal context tried to align with the policies of the WC through regional agreements to lower trade barriers and tariffs; this was done in order to move away from protectionism, to promote international competitiveness, and to intensify the integration in the global economy (Dabéne 2009: 21-22; Sanahuja 2012: 2-3).

However, the opening of the economies and the change to an export-led model forced uncompetitive local industries into international competition without minimal protection, bankrupting many small and medium-sized enterprises (SMEs), while the ones with international potential were privatised and incorporated to multinational corporations. This situation led to early deindustrialisation and massive job losses in most countries in the region (Scholz 2014: 13). By the end of the 1990s, unable to deliver on its promises, the leading thinkers of the WC recognised the necessity of moving away from the excessive focus on competition and perfect market forces, in a recognition that institutions play an essential role in efficient markets (Marangos 2009: 207; Saad-Filho 2010: 7).

This new focus led to the introduction of the so-called Post-Washington Consensus (PWC). PWC promoted the idea of policies directed to create a suitable institutional environment for economic growth. Institutions were intended to provide a supporting structure that promotes the diffusion of technological information, funding precompetitive research, and providing tax incentives for Research and Development (R&D) to stimulate the growth of industrial clusters and venture capital. These incentives are supervised by a network of decentralised agencies specialising in activities such as export promotion and Foreign Direct Investment (FDI) attraction (Marangos 2008: 207).

At the same time, following a wave of elected leftist governments, industrial policies re-entered mainstream political discourse with a broader definition. The new industrial policy formulation takes into consideration the necessity to acquire technological and organisational capabilities with a comprehensive structure that promotes learning-based production through rent-seeking incentives but that is also able to curb rent seeking *tout court*. These structures, it is argued, should be combined with industrial friendly macroeconomic management (Stiglitz et al. 2009: 543). This extended view, characterised as a post-neoliberal perspective, aims to break with neoliberal practices and moves beyond the proposals of the PWC (Yates/Bakker 2012: 64; Peres/Primi 2009: 14).

2.1 Neostructuralism and the renewed role of Industrial Policies (IP)

Post-neoliberalism can be categorised as a combination of an ideological project and a set of policies and practices that focus on redirecting a market economy to social concerns and the revival of citizenship through politics of participation and cross-sector alliances. Thus, as a government project, post-neoliberalism aims to preserve elements of the export-led growth model by committing to a certain level of fiscal restraint for economic stability, and to remain responsive to the global economy, while promoting social equity through conscious government spending and different stakeholder alliances (Grugel/Riggirozzi 2012: 1; Yates/Bakker 2014: 64).

Neostructuralism – a post-neoliberal approach developed by the ECLAC – argues that economic globalisation is not a phenomenon that will automatically lead to catching-up in terms of technological capabilities and increased well-being. Interdependent economies, particularly the ones in the Global-South, need even more refined measures of policy intervention that will lead them to the so-called 'high road' of globalisation, namely measures of policy intervention to profit from world market integration. This goal can only be attained when combined with social development, strong institutions and improved macroeconomic policies, in order to brace the economy against international financial volatility (Bielschowsky 2009: 185-188; ECLAC, 2012: 270).

In this sense, compared to PWC, neostructuralism has substantially broadened the market economy model scope in developing countries by incorporating the issue of coordination among governmental and nongovernmental economic agents. Other themes, such as the formal exploration of increasing returns to scale and the availability of new technology, as well as knowledge production, information externalities and other forms of industrial organisation, also assume importance in the new approach (Todaro/Smith, 2012: 156).

Also, neostructuralism aims to tackle the flaws of its structuralist ISI past. ECLAC claims that, analytically, neostructuralism has remained close to structuralism by keeping its historical-structural orientation, while adding Schumpeterian approaches (the focus on knowledge formation and accumulation, the effects of path-dependency and changes in techno-economic paradigms) to countercyclical macroeconomic policies, citizenship and social cohesion, and an agenda coherent with the globalised environment in which developing countries function (Bielschowsky 2009: 179). Focusing on a more systemic and proactive form of public intervention would enable support to the private sector as a means to overthrow structural constraints in innovation, productive transformation and upgrade. It would allow for the expansion of development to generate growth and equity. In this context, industrial policies return to play an important role in fostering production growth and development in the context of rapid technical transformation (Devlin/Moguillansky 2011: 2).

Institutions must be strengthened, and accountability mechanisms settled, to avoid government corruption, and efficiently coordinate public agencies and the private sector, execute industrial policies and monitor their progress. The coordination and execution of horizontal and vertical industrial policies must have a clear-cut strategic view towards changing existing production patterns towards more knowledge intensive ones. Thus, the government partnership with the private sector should focus on selecting a small set of industrial sectors, not companies, which will change

JULIANA GOMES CAMPOS

the direction of production to value-added goods and thus create spillovers (vertical industrial policy). Regarding horizontal policies, public-private partnerships and civil society should team up to complement vertical policies in order to change production patterns. This would focus not only on horizontal issues directly related to production, such as sound macroeconomic policies, technological innovation and investment, but also on more general areas that indirectly affect production, such as infrastructure, health, education, and working conditions (Melo/Rodríguez-Clare 2006: 5, 16).

Regarding regional integration, there is a shift from open regionalism to a post-hegemonic form (Riggirozzi/Tussie 2012). Neostructuralism does not reject globalisation, but embraces it in its various forms. It keeps the goal of strengthening regional institutions and institutional structures and seeks international competitiveness, while also focusing on signing preferential, reciprocal trade agreements at bilateral and sub-regional levels – particularly South-South agreements – guided by government supported export-oriented companies to know which markets should be prioritised to improve production development. This can be evidenced by the importance given to South-South relations and industrial policies, such as the 2008 Common Industrial Policy Programme (*Programa de Integración Productiva* - PIP) of MERCOSUR (Riggirozzi 2010: 9; MERCOSUR 2015: 20).

Industrial policy in neostructuralism has, thus, the intention of creating the necessary systemic competitiveness for the world market, a situation where macroeconomic equilibrium and productive modernisation go along with social and environmental equilibrium. This synergy would create a self-expanding virtuous circle that forges an efficient development project in the era of globalisation (Leiva 2008a: 13).

Although neostructuralist strategies have been praised as feasible alternatives to neoliberalism, with positive results in many countries, critics argue that their active support for manufactured export-led growth has deep contradictions and flaws that jeopardise their expected long-term results. The systematic exclusion of power relations in the neostructuralist mode of theorisation directly affects the possible positive results (Leiva 2008a: 97).

Neostructuralism promises a virtuous cycle, dependent on adequate technical, social-scientific capacity (i.e. human capabilities), and strong government institutions where those capabilities can influence and be exercised, to move beyond the corporatist standpoint and actively interact with government agencies and other stakeholders for long-term goals in production development. By ignoring power relations in the state-private sector-civil society nexus, neostructuralism becomes unable to explain the weak technical and social capacities, weak mechanisms for good governance, and lack of support of the private sector for common long-term goals. In this sense, issues such as new modes of unequal exchange, denationalisation and highly limited technology, and know-how transfers that remain concentrated within transnational companies (TNCs), are not adequately addressed by the approach (Melo/Rodríguez-Clare 2006: 18; Leiva 2008a: 97).

Authors also argue that neostructuralist macroeconomic priorities are not industry-friendly. Macroeconomic discipline to control inflation and high exchange rates does not generate an increase in savings and investments in the internal market. Thus, SMEs, infrastructure and technological capacity are directly affected. The neoliberal macroeconomic tripod – overvalued currency, high real interest rates and primary surplus (when the level of income is higher than the current spending) – makes industrial policies hardly achievable without harming SMEs (Ban 2012: 7; Saad-Filho 2015).

Thus, for critics, neostructuralism is a status-quo defending approach, since it ignores the main characteristics of its own structuralist roots in order to understand how the accumulation logic of capitalism undermines it. By believing that the high road for globalisation is an inevitable process if only the right policies were adopted, the proposal remains attached to the idea that development is a natural process, and ignores the historical North-South relations as much as it does PWC with its exclusive focus on institutional reform (Leiva 2008a: 225; Missio et al. 2015: 248).

3. The PT and the return of industrial policies

The debt crisis of the 1980s triggered the end of ISI and signaled the adoption of neoliberalism under the WC in Brazil. Industrial policy lost its importance as the mean to achieve growth and development, and a process of industry and infrastructure privatisation took place. This situation put the industrial base – which was already weakened and technologically backward because of the stagnation of the 1980s debt crisis – under pressure to compete with foreign companies and capital. The industry share in GDP fell drastically, and a new power structure took shape, through a few strategic industries and the re-structuring of a few private national groups (Suzigan/Furtado 2006a: 173). This new power structure – combined with external factors – increased unemployment as well as unequal income distribution, and intensified dissatisfaction among the national industrial elite (Boito 2007: 71).

This situation opened up an interesting and divided debate on industrialisation in Brazil, namely the question of whether the country had suffered deindustrialisation and 'regressive specialisation' since the WC programmes, or whether the country was just moving to the next step of advanced economies in a post-industrialisation context, where industry loses its share of GDP due to technological sophistication and the disintegration of certain productive processes (Urraca-Ruiz et al. 2013: 2-3).

A third view claims that the Brazilian process of deindustrialisation is relative and sector-specific, and thus possible to reverse through industrial policies that aim at reorienting the country towards the advanced economies and improving its participation in global value chains (Milani 2011: 7; Urraca-Ruiz et al. 2013: 7). This view was able to bring together a heterogeneous – and contradictory – alliance between the national industrial bourgeoisie, the social movements, and the working class to elect PT and Luís Inácio Lula da Silva in 2002, initiating a post-neoliberal and a leftist phase in the country (Boito/Saad-Filho, 2016: 194).

3.1 Lula's industrial policies

Historically, industrial policies have been constantly influenced by different powers within the country, with different levels of success. During the ISI period, as several governments (both democratically elected and dictatorship) added new agencies, institutions, policies and instruments to a ISI strategy with a highly influential developmentalist state, different political actors were created and/or strengthened around the industrial policy agenda: old and new elites, business associations and trade unions, and regional and sectoral bodies (Suzigan 2006b: 74).

Trade unions and nationalist groups influenced the nationalisation of oil production (Petrobrás). Industrial associations focused on a more pro-developmentalist agenda. Business elites backed the dictatorship and focus on high technology sectors, such as aircraft (EMBRAER), computers, the promotion of the automotive industry, and nuclear energy (Angra I & II). Notwithstanding these developments, the groups that influenced the government under ISI never acted as a unified coalition for a single, coherent development strategy (Schneider 2015: 116).

Therefore, the historical context in which the PT brought industrial policies back to the development agenda was marked by a complex institutional environment, where several actors and stakeholders at the national and international level were exerting their influence on policymaking and decision-taking (Almeida et al. 2014: 9).

This was also one of the main points mentioned by the expert interviewees when the context for the formulation of industrial policies in the era of globalisation was discussed; they pointed out that the huge power disputes within the government, and the commitment to the Right and international organisations such as the IMF for governability jeopardised a full/consequent implementation of industrial policies (Interviews 1/2, December 2016; Interview 4, January 2017).

A second challenge was related to the return of industrial policy *per se* as a goal for economic and social development in a globalised and open economy context. The stagnation of the 1980s and market-governed policies from the 1990s in Brazil created several obstacles to the implementation of an industrial development agenda. The main ones were the disadvantageous heritage left by neoliberalism, with unfavourable macroeconomic policies, privatisations, disarticulated institutions and instruments for industrialisation, and lack of investment in an already outdated infrastructure. Combined with an equality gap and lack of human capability (i.e. skilled work force fostered through a strong and inclusive education system), PT was left with a difficult environment for its objective of catching up with the Global North in terms of knowledge production and new technologies (Suzigan and Furtado 2006a: 173-174).

Those challenges created a government with a hybrid policy regime: it remained committed to economically liberal goals and instruments rooted in the WC, while adopting more interventionist instruments and policies commonly associated with neostructuralism. The government discourse emphasised the necessity of a gradual structural change through a national development project supported by a "new social pact" directed towards the forgotten population (Erber 2006: 19; Ban 2012: 1)

Efforts should have been directed towards macroeconomic stabilisation in order to generate an increase in savings and investments, focusing on the internal market – SMEs, infrastructure and technological capacity. The stabilisation would come with several institutional reforms from the fiscal to the social security sectors, uniting labour and productive capital on a solidarity synergy (Erber 2006: 20).

In this scenario, the *Política Industrial, Tecnológica e de Comércio Exterior* (PITCE - Industrial, Technology, and International Trade Policy) – was implemented. It was based on the, albeit affected and weakened by neoliberal deindustrialisation, diverse industrial base of the country, and was aimed at reducing external vulnerability. It was supported by the necessity for technological modernisation by targeting different sectors and productive chains, with a particular focus on the oil production chain, construction, pharmaceutical and agribusiness sectors, sectors that would be essential to generate and expand innovation, competitiveness and international dynamism (Cano/Gonçalves da Silva 2010: 7).

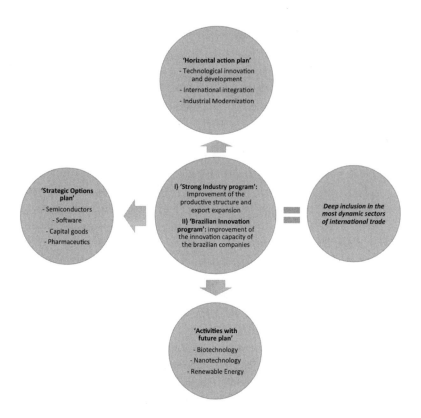

Figure 1: PITCE General Strategy
Source: dos Reis, 2006, own figure and translation

However, when the results of the PITCE were assessed, it turned out that its proposals were not all successfully implemented, due to the scenario left by neoliberal reforms. The results generated by the PITCE encompassed a broad package of measures with heterogeneous stages of planning and implementation, due to the incompatibility with the macroeconomic policies and the necessity to re-organise and strengthen the institutions for the promotion of industrial development. Nevertheless, it was able to open up a path of industrial reforms (Laplane/Sarti 2006: 285).

JULIANA GOMES CAMPOS

The sharp currency devaluation by the end of Lula's first mandate contributed to a decrease to zero of the trade deficit for manufactured products. This measure, along with the constraints for growth of the domestic sector caused by the monetary policy, payment of the IMF debt, and the positive international scenario for trade pushed by the Chinese economy, which opened a space to deepen South-South relations and insert Brazil as an important player in the world economy with BRICS and the G20, stimulated the expansion of the industrial production for export, as international restrictions were considerably reduced (Cano/Gonçalves da Silva 2010: 6).

There was a clear movement to create a resilient internal market to support the national industry. There was consequently a strong promotion of credit expansion, growth of household demand, unemployment reduction, increase of minimum wage, and the introduction of affirmative action policies and transfer cash programmes to reduce inequality as the means to boost national production (Cano/Gonçalves da Silva 2010: 15). There was also a move to upgrade and strengthen the national value chain of oil, with Petrobrás taking the lead. As argued by Expert 3, Petrobrás prioritised national goods – such as ships and other resources – to initiate a recovery process of the naval industry in Rio de Janeiro and develop the Northeast region of the country (Interview 3: December 2016).

With more freedom from external agents, after paying its debt to the IMF, and a more stable economy, PT was able to deepen its industrial policy strategy (Laplane/Sarti 2006: 285; Kupfer 2013). The Productive Development Policy (PDP) was launched to overcome PITCE limitations – such as the lack of coordination and proper instruments to foster innovation – and expand its action to a greater number of sectors by improving accountability mechanisms and creating institutions to promote industrialisation, such as the creation of the Brazilian Agency for Industrial Development (ABDI) (Guerriero 2012: 156).

Figure 2: PDP General Strategy
Source: ABDI, PDP presentation, 2008, own figure and translation

The PDP proposal was to converge with macroeconomic policy and give sustainability to the favourable growth moment the country was experiencing. The stable macroeconomic moment opened a space for horizontal policy measures to close structural gaps that would upgrade production and promote development, such as promoting investment on the infrastructure and supporting education through financial and quotas programmes to foster a specialised workforce. The PDP formulation tried to expand instruments to stimulate the innovation capacity and combine them with

JULIANA GOMES CAMPOS

investments to increase the supply capacity and avoid inflation and trade imbalances (ABDI 2008: 9; Guerriero 2012: 157-158).

Experts 1 and 3 – although they defended the position that the government could and should have done more regarding institutional change – praised the government's intention to move away from the rigidity of the first mandate by taking advantage of the favourable international scenario and acting quickly when the Global Financial Crisis hit the country (Interviews 1/3: December 2016). Existing programmes from the ISI era to support SMEs were adapted and relaunched. There was an effort to ease the obstacles for investment, production and export. Fiscal exemption was conceded to national products as an attempt to promote national producers. Tax exemption to buy machines and equipment was given to companies that exported at least 80% of their production (Cano/Gonçalves da Silva, 2010: 8).

Among the interviewees, the action of the Brazilian development bank (BNDES) was considered as one of the main supporters of the PT industrial strategy. They particularly emphasised its role in the second mandate in line with PDP, that explicitly focused on fostering international competitiveness by investing in the main sectors and companies of the Brazilian production system (Interviews 1/2, December 2016; Interview 4, January 2017).

Indeed, the plan was in line with their approach to South-South relations and the strengthening of MERCOSUR members' national companies through the region's productive integration in the framework of MERCOSUR's PIP. Under programmes within PIP guidelines, such as those to intensify and complement the automotive chain (FOCEM Auto) and the (Producers Qualification of Oil and Gas) chain in MERCOSUR (FOCEM P&G), the MERCOSUR was able to go beyond the idea of open regionalism from the neoliberal era by investing in regional infrastructure, such as the 550 million USD in the construction of the transmission line between La Paz (Paraguay) and the Itaipú hydroelectric power plant (ABDI n.d.; JIE September 2017).

Moreover, the country remained committed to the already established industrial cooperation partnership with Argentina. Since Lula's first mandate, they deepened and consolidated their bilateral economic, political and institutional relations and acted as active leaders in MERCOSUR to promote their national industries (KAS 2015). However, when compared to *Alternativa Bolivariana para las Américas* (ALBA) and Venezuela's leading role in it during the 2000s, Brazil's efforts were moderate. Economically weaker states complained that Brazil's foreign policy aspirations to broaden South-South relations left questions of asymmetries and inequalities within the bloc unaddressed (Vázquez/Ruiz Briceño 2009: 44)

Another central issue for industrial policies in the post-neoliberal context is the task of innovation. As pointed out by neostructuralists, competitiveness could not rely on cheap labour. It must, rather, change the export pattern to increase technological innovation and to raise labour productivity, creating a more 'genuine' form of competitiveness (Leiva 2008a: 13).

Interviewees pointed out that this was one of the main issues where Lula's government had many coordination flaws. Expert 1 pointed out that:

> "(...) the share of imported components in the industry rose considerably, thus, it weakened the industry [since there was no R&D knowledge transfer for upgrade]. When you analyze it as whole, in the second part of the 2000s, the industrial production rose, there was more regulation, which is something very positive. But at the same time, with these problems I mentioned" (Interview 1, December 2016).

There was also a lack of infra-structure policies to boost innovation: "[t]here was a rise in the consumption capacity [of the internal market]. (...) But to develop a technological industry, it is also necessary a [comprehensive development] policy that will develop urbanization, infrastructure" (Interview 3, December 2016). Indeed, the widespread protests of 2013, which started because of a high increase in the public transport tariff, were a reaction of the population against the lack of infrastructure investment of the government in roads and public transport alternatives (Saad-Filho 2013: 3-4).

Moreover, as discussed by Gudynas (2010: 2) and interviewees 1 and 5, despite the high importance of sustainable development and a more 'green consciousness' that neostructuralism should bring to industrial polices, PT – as many of its peers in Latin America – did not reverse the importance of their extractivist sector, e.g. Petrobrás and agri-business, particularly the food processor JBS. The government remained committed to build an infrastructure to answer the needs of those groups and not of the population as a whole. This contradictory combination shows the struggle for cohesion and more effective results in such a heterogenous power alliance for a long-term productive development plan (Interview 1, December 2016; Interviewee 5, March 2017).

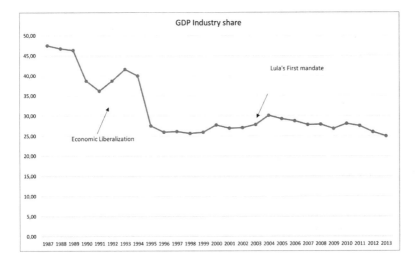

Figure 3: Industry share in the Brazilian GDP since the economic liberalisation
Source: IPEA 2016: GDP Industry data – November 2016, own chart

Thus, the PDP's main goal was to invest and innovate to sustain the growth momentum. However, the Global Financial Crisis in 2008, and difficulties in coordinating an alliance of heterogenous power groups directly affected the policy implementation. The PDP was redirected – along with other measures – to work as an anti-cyclical policy to reduce the crisis's immediate harmful shocks. Its redirection proved to be useful as a way to limit the negative effects of the crisis and to return to high rates of growth by 2010. Due to this reason, the share of industry of GDP did not rise further (Kupfer 2013).

3.2 Dilma's industrial policies

Dilma's government was marred by an already unfavourable international scenario, left by the 2008 Global Financial Crisis (ABDI 2013: 10). In this context, the PT launched its third industrial policy phase, known as *Plano Brasil Maior* (PBM – Great Brazil Plan). The main goal was to sustain growth by tackling the flaws of PITCE and PDP. Noteworthily, the PBM recognised that the state should coordinate and regulate the development process better, and guide the country to improve its position in the world economy (Guerriero 2012: 229; Curado 2017: 139).

The plan covered the promotion of innovation and technological development, the expansion of the internal and external market for the Brazilian companies, and the guarantee of social, inclusive growth. Also, there was a focus on investment via cosolidated enterprises, such as Petrobras, on innovation to lead the country to a change in production pattern and modernisation. Internal market dynamism remained an essential tool to shield the national companies against the unfavourable international scenario (Guerriero 2012: 229-230).

Official documentation shows that Dilma's government tried to intensify the action of state institutions to coordinate industrial policy implementation (Curado 2017: 139). Indeed, Expert 1 (December 2016) pointed out that Dilma had a more 'industrial' approach compared to Lula as "(...) she favored the industry a lot. She made a series of concessions, incentives and subsidies." The external scenario forced the PBM to focus on recovering the industrial base through investment in innovation and technological development, based on the dynamism of the internal market. However, the same unfavourable international scenario, and Dilma's lack of political power curbed the PBM results, as pointed out by Expert 2 (Interview 2, December 2016): "(...) something more structural took form but there were clearly no conditions of implementation. (…) Dilma's government had no political condition to implement [a project] (...)".

The more industrialist approach, with a stronger state presence of Dilma's government, was not seen favourably by private institutions, such as private banks, and it was impossible to build alliances with the private sector and elites that are still in power, such as traditional and conservative parties, especially the Brazilian Democratic Movement MDB (former

PMDB) – the current party in power under the presidency of Michel Temer, and which actively supported the impeachment of Dilma Rousseff. Private institutions directly attacked the government when it expanded the role of public banks, and felt there was strict regulation over their actions (Interview 2, December 2016).

The industrial project was also hit by several cases of corruption involving Petrobrás and other companies supported by, and with high investment from, the government. The accusations led to a perceived lack of legitimacy and support of the PT. Petrobrás, the main actor of the industrial projects involving the oil and gas chains, has had all its on-going contracts stalled because of the called 'Car Wash' federal police corruption investigation (Expert 5, March 2017).

This scenario was combined with the still contradictory role of the neoliberal macroeconomic policies. Since the first year of Dilma's first mandate, the government pushed for a huge primary surplus, increasing the already high interest rates (Interview 3, December 2016). This affects, once more, the task of innovation for the Brazilian industrial base. There were, indeed, measures from PBM implemented to foster innovation [i.e. sector specific financial programmes and tax wave on petrochemical products to foster competitiveness and innovation]; however, those results can only be evaluated in the long-run, and most of them were halted because of the economic and political crisis (Interview 5, March 2017).

Finally, in the context of growth retraction, the government maintained the already exhausted strategy of anti-cyclical policies of aggregate demand, which had been implemented to resolve the crisis of 2008. This situation led to a deeper economic crisis – transformed into a political crisis by opposing powers – that led to the end of Dilma's short-lived second mandate, with her controversial impeachment in August 2016 (Barcia 2016; Curado 2017: 145).

4. Conclusion

As the Brazilian case has shown, the industrial policies formulated during the PT government were not translated into a significantly increased share of industrial participation in GDP, as compared to the neoliberal era. The government was, indeed, successful in promoting an internal market based on mass consumption as an anti-cyclical measure after the 2008 financial crisis. It was able to maintain industry dynamism by giving exceptions to some sectors, as well as other measures. However, it was not able to deeply change essential aspects, namely, to boost innovation and technology, to create infrastructure and to improve the satisfaction of basic needs.

Nevertheless, neoliberalism is clearly not the undisputed way for developing countries to improve their position in the world economy while trying to create a more inclusive society in the era of globalisation. The administrative mistakes of PT, and the lack of enforcement and political reform, led to capacity inability to curb the country's historical corruption and to fully reverse the deindustrialisation trend. Notwithstanding these factors, it was able to bring industrial policies back to the development agenda, showing that there is still space for policy manoeuver in the context of WTO rules and open market economies.

However, neostructuralism's belief in the high road to globalisation as an inevitable process if only the right policies were adopted, marginalises power relations in the analysis of economy and society. This claim proved to be particularly strong because of the contradictory character of the Brazilian government's neoliberal macroeconomic policies when combined with industrial policies, creating a scenario that consistently turned down better results from the policies adopted. The government's inability to push for structural reforms, the resistance of some sectors of the elite to the government, the PT's pact with the right to keep the project moving, and the commitment to international financial institutions, cannot all be understood as a 'simple' lack of management ability to implement the 'right' policies, as neostructuralism would claim.

In this sense – for a development project that wants to foster innovation through the return of the state and industrial policies in order to be able to effectively stop deindustrialisation – it is, indeed, essential to reshape existing power structures, and not only to accommodate them. If not, opportunities for a profound change of the current global economic structure that reproduces the center-periphery-nexus will be continuously lost.

1   Leiva, claims that, while neostructuralism can be characterised as "status-quo defending", with its progressive focus on politics, institutions and culture that helps to legitimise and regulate the export-oriented regime of accumulation introduced by neoliberalism, the so-called 21st century socialism advocated by countries such as Venezuela can be understood as "status-quo transforming". This transforming characteristic is marked by its attempt to redirect society's economic surplus and reshape existing power structures by a gradual process that promotes a mixed economy and strengthens the state's role to guide economic surplus to development purposes that includes less powerful groups of the society (Leiva 2008a: 225).

References

Ban, Cornel (2012): Brazil's liberal neo-developmentalism. New paradigm or edited orthodoxy? In: Review of International Political Economy 20 (2), 298-331. https://doi.org/10.1080/09692290.2012.660183

Barcia, Manuel (2016): Dilma Rousseff's impeachment was led by the white, wealthy men who now make up the Brazilian cabinet. In: Independent, 15.05.2016. http://www.independent.co.uk/voices/dilma-rousseffs-impeachment-was-led-by-the-white-wealthy-men-who-now-make-up-the-brazilian-cabinet-a7030761.html, 25.03.2017.

Bielschowsky, Ricardo (2009): Sixty years of ECLAC: Structuralism and Neo-structuralism. In: Cepal Review 97, 171-192.

Boito, Armando (2007): Estado e Burguesia no Capitalismo Neoliberal. In: Revista de Sociologia e Política. Curitiba 28, 57-73.

Boito, Armando/Saad-Filho, Alfredo (2016): State, State Institutions, and Political Power in Brazil. In: Latin American Perspectives 43(2), 190-206. https://doi.org/10.1177/0094582X15616120

Bracarense, Natalia (2013): Economic Development in Latin America: Lessons from History of Economic Thought. In: Journal of Economic Issues XLVII(1), 113-134. https://doi.org/10.2753/JEI0021-3624470105

Cano, Wilson./Gonçalves da Silva, Ana Lucia (2010): Política Industrial do Governo Lula. In: Texto para Discussão IE/UNICAMP 181, 1-27.

Chang, Ha-Joon (2003): The Market, the State and Institutions in Economic Development Ch. 2. In: Chang, Ha-Joon (ed.).: Rethinking Development Economics. London: Anthem Press, 41-60.

Chodor, Tom (2015): Neoliberal Hegemony and the Pink Tide in Latin America: Breaking Up with TINA? London: Palgrave Macmillan. https://doi.org/10.1057/9781137444684

Curado, Marcelo (2017): Por que o governo Dilma não pode ser classificado como novo-desenvolvimentista? In: Revista de Economia Política 37 (146), 130-146. https://doi.org/10.1590/0101-31572016v37n01a07

Dang, G./Sui Pheng, L. (2015): Infrastructure Investments in Developing Economies. Singapore: Springer Science and Business.

Devlin, Robert./Moguillansky, Graciela (2011): Breeding Latin America Tigers: Operational Principles for Rehabilitating Industrial Policies. Chile: ECLAC.

Di Maio, Michele (2009): Industrial Policies in Developing Countries: History and perspectives. In: Cimoli, Mario/Dosi, Giovanni/Stiglitz, Joseph E. (eds.). Industrial Policy and Development: The Political Economy of Capabilities Accumulation. Oxford: Oxford University Press. https://doi.org/10.1093/acprof:oso/9780199235261.003.0005

Doctor, Mahrukh (2012): Brazil's New Government and Trade: An Evaluation of Policy and Performance. In: Critical Sociology 38(6), 799-807. https://doi.org/10.1177/0896920512440573

Dos Reis Alvarez, Roberto (2006): A Política Industrial, Tecnológica e de ComércioExterior (PITCE) e a atuação da ABDI. In: Workshop PCI (Rede TSQC – ABRACI –FINEP).

ECLAC (2012): Structural Change for Equality: An Integrated Approach to Development. In: Thirty-fourth Session of ECLAC, San Salvador, 27-31. August, 2012.

Erber, F.S. (2006). "Inovação tecnológica". In: Facto, Jun./Jul. 2006.

Grugel, Jean/Riggirozzi, Pía (2012): Post-neoliberalism in Latin America: Rebuilding and Reclaiming the State after Crisis. In: Development and Change 43(1), 1–21. https://doi.org/10.1111/j.1467-7660.2011.01746.x

Gudynas, Eduardo (2010): The New Extractivism of the 21st Century: Ten Urgent Theses about Extractivism in Relation to Current South American Progressivism. In: Americas Program Report. Washington, DC: Center for International Policy.

Guerriero, Ian Ramalho (2012): Formulaçao e Avaliação de Política Industrial e o Caso da PDP. In: Tese (doutorado) – Universidade Federal do Rio de Janeiro. Instituto de Economia.

Heidrich, Pablo/Tussie, Diana (2009): Post-Neoliberalism and the New-Left in the Americas: The Pathways of Economic and Trade Policies. In: Macdonald, Laura/Ruckert, Arne (eds.): Post-Neoliberalism in the Americas. UK: Palgrave Macmillan, 37-53. https://doi.org/10.1057/9780230232822_3

IPEA (2016): Produto interno bruto (PIB) - indústria - referência 2000. http://www.ipeadata.gov.br/Default.aspx, 04.11.2016.

KAS (2015): Relatórios dos países: Brasil e Argentina. In: http://www.kas.de/brasilien/pt/publications/42326/,12.01.2018.

Kerstenetzky, Celia Lessa (2014): The Brazilian Social Developmental State: A Progressive Agenda in a (Still) Conservative Political Society. In: Williams, Michelle (ed.): The End of the Developmental State?, London: Routledge, 172-196.

Khan, Shahrukh Rafi (2011): Towards New Developmentalism: Context, Program, and Constraints. In: Khan, Shahrukh Rafi and Christiansen, Jens (eds.): Towards New Developmentalism: Market as Means rather than Master. New York: Routledge, 252-278.

Kupfer, David (2013): Dez Anos de Política Industrial. In: Revista Valor Econômico,. Available in: http://www.ie.ufrj.br/clipping/download/dezanos.pdf, 08.07.2013.

Lall, Sanjaya (2004): Reinventing Industrial Strategy: The Role of Government Policy in Building Industrial Competitiveness. In: G-24 Discussion Paper Series 28, 3-34.

Laplane, Mariano Francisco (2014): A indústria ainda é o motor do crescimento? Teoria e evidências. In: Jackson de Toni, Jackson (ed.): Dez anos de política industrial. Balanço e Perspectivas (2004-2014), 23-39.

Laplane, Mariano./Sarti, F. (2006): Prometeu acorrentado: o Brasil na indústria mundial no início do século XXI. In: Carneiro, R. (Org.): A Supremacia dos Mercados e a Política Econômica do Governo Lula. São Paulo: Editora Unesp, 271-291.

Leiva, Fernando Ignacio (2008a): Latin American Neostructuralism: The contradictions of post-neoliberal development. Minnesota/USA: University of Minnesota Press.

Marangos, John (2009): What happened to the Washington Consensus? The evolution of international development policy. In: The Journal of Socio-Economics 38, 197-208. https://doi.org/10.1016/j.socec.2008.07.007

Melo, Alberto/Clare-Rodríguez-Clare, Andrés (2006): Productive Development Policies and Supporting Institutions in Latin America. In: Inter-American Development Bank (BID) – Competitive Studies Series Working Paper C-I 06.

MERCOSUL (n.d.): Saiba mais sobre o MERCOSUL. In: http://www.mercosul.gov.br/saiba-mais-sobre-o-mercosul, 12.01.2018.

MERCOSUR (2015): MERCOSUR: Structuras y Agendas. In: http://www.mercosur.int/innovaportal/file/7338/1/mercosur_academico_final_es_web.pdf, 29.12.2017.

Meyer-Stammer, Jörg (1997): New patterns of governance for industrial change: Perspectives for Brazil. In: Journal of Development Studies 33 (3), 364-391. https://doi.org/10.1080/00220389708422470

Milanez, Bruno/Santos, Rodrigo S.P. (2015): Topsy-Turvy Neo-developmentalism: Naan Analysis of the Current Brazilian Model of Development. In: Revista de Estudios Sociales (53), 12-28. https://doi.org/10.7440/res53.2015.01

Milani, Ana Maria Rita (2011): Questões para se pensar o desenvolvimento no Brasil. especialização regressiva e pauta exportadora no período 2003-2010. In: IPEA - CODE 2011: Anais do I Circuito de Debates Acadêmicos, 1-19.

Munck, Ronaldo (2008²): Contemporary Latin America. London: Palgrave Macmillan. https://doi.org/10.1007/978-1-137-09082-9

Peres, Wilson/Primi, Annalisa (2009): Theory and Practice of Industrial Policy. Evidence from the Latin American Experience. In: CEPAL: Serie desarollo productiveo 187.

Portal ABDI (2016): Política Industrial. http://www.abdi.com.br/Paginas/politica_industrial.aspx, 17.11.2016.

Portal ABDI (n.d.): Ações ABDI FOCEM. http://www.abdi.com.br/Paginas/acao_resumo.aspx?i=105, 12.01.2018.

Riggirozzi, Pía/Tussie, Diana (2012): Chapter 1. The Rise of Post-Hegemonic Regionalism in Latin America. In: Riggirozzi, Pía/Tussie, Diana (eds.): The Rise of Post-Hegemonic Regionalism in Latin America. Dordrecht et al.: Springer, 1-16.

Saad-Filho, Alfredo (2010): Growth, Poverty and Inequality: From Washington Consensus to Inclusive Growth. In: DESA Working Paper 100.

Saad-Filho, Alfredo (2013): Brazil: Development Strategies and Social Change from Import-Substitution to the "Events of June". In: Studies in Political Economy 94, 3-29. https://doi.org/10.1080/19187033.2014.11674952

Saad-Filho, Alfredo (2015): A Critical Review of Brazil's Recent Economic Policies. In: Centre for Development Policy and Research - Development Viewpoint (84).

Sanahuja, José Antonio (2012): Post-liberal Regionalism in South America: The Case of UNASUR. In: EUI Working Papers, RSCAS 2012/05.

Schneider, Ben Ross (2015): The Developmental state in Brazil: comparative and historical perspective). In: Brazilian Journal of Political Economy 35 (138), 114-132. https://doi.org/10.1590/0101-31572015v35n01a07

Scholz, Richard (2014): Paradigms in Development Economics. In: Politik und Wirtschaft – Volkswirtschaftliches Forschungsseminar. Universität Leipzig.

Singer, Hans Wolfgang (1975): The Strategy of International Development: Essays in the Economics of Backwardness. London: The Macmillan Press. https://doi.org/10.1007/978-1-349-04228-9

Stiglitz, Joseph E. et al. (2009): The Future of Industrial Policies in the New Millennium: Toward a Knowledge-Centered Development Agenda Ch. 20. In Cimoli, Mario/Dosi, Giovanni/Stiglitz, Joseph E. (eds.): Industrial Policy and Development: The Political Economy of Capabilities Accumulation. New York: Oxford Press, 541-560.

Suzigan, Wilson./Furtado, João (2006): Política Industrial e Desenvolvimento". In: Revista de Economia Política 26 (102), 163-185.. https://doi.org/10.1590/S0101-31572006000200001

Taylor, Marcus (2009): The Contradictions and Transformations of Neoliberalism in Latin America: from Structuring Adjustment to 'Empowering the Poor'. In: Macdonald, Laura and Ruckert, Arne (eds.): Post-Neoliberalism in the Americas. UK: Palgrave Macmillan, 21-36. https://doi.org/10.1057/9780230232822_2

Todaro, Michael P./Smith, Stephen C. (2012¹¹): Economic development. Boston: Pearson.

Urraca-Ruiz, Ana et al (2013): Qualificando o caráter 'regressivo' da especialização industrial do Brasil. In: Conferência Internacional LALICS 2013. http://www.redesist.ie.ufrj.br/lalics/papers/50_Qualificando_o_carater_regressivo_da_especializacao_industrial_do_Brasil.pdf, 20.09.2016.

Vázquez, Mariana/Ruiz Briceño, José (2009): O Mercosul na época de Lula e Kirchner: um balanço, seis anos depois. In: Revista Nueva Sociedad especial em Português 98, 33-48.

Vogeler, Colette Sophie (2016): Conventional Paths for New Challenges: Change and Continuity in Economic Policy in Brazil. Baden-Baden: Nomos. https://doi.org/10.5771/9783845265506

Yates, Julian S. /Bakker, Karen (2014): Debating the 'post-neoliberal turn' in Latin America. In: Progress in Human Geography 2014, 38(1), 62-90. https://doi.org/10.1177/0309132513500372

List of Interviews

Interview 1: Academic in the field of political economy and development and specialist in developmentalism, 15.12.2016.

Interview 2: Academic in the field of economics and specialist in development banks, 19.12.2016.

Interview 3: Former member of PT and academic in the field of economics, 20.12.2016.

Interview 4: Academic in the field of political economy and specialist in leftist theories, 31.01.2017.

Interview 5: Former member of the Ministry of Sciences and Technology of Dilma's government and academic in the field of economics, 11.03.2017.

ABSTRACT *Dieser Beitrag diskutiert die Frage, ob im Zeitalter der Globalisierung die Wiederbelebung industrieller Politiken zur Förderung von Entwicklung eine post-neoliberale Alternative sein kann. Die Regierungsverantwortung der Partido dos Trabalhadores (PT) in Brasilien machte das Land zu einem zentralen Repräsentanten der „Pink Tide", der politischen Transformation Lateinamerikas unter linken Regierungen Anfang des 21. Jahrhunderts. Der Regierungsplan versprach die industrielle Modernisierung zu fördern und die Armut zu reduzieren, indem der Staat wieder die Rolle des zentralen Vermittlers zwischen öffentlichen Institutionen, privaten Sektoren und der Zivilgesellschaft einnehmen und in weiterer Folge auch die Stellung des Landes in der globalen Ökonomie verbessern sollte. Im Beitrag wird die Industrialisierungspolitik der PT folglich als Fallbeispiel genutzt, um mögliche Charakteristika eines post-neoliberalen Entwicklungsmodells in Lateinamerika als Alternative zum Neoliberalismus zu untersuchen.*

Juliana Gomes Campos
juliana.gcampos@live.com

Journal für Entwicklungspolitik XXXIV 3/4-2018, S. 45–70

Rudy Weissenbacher
A Ladder without Upper Rungs:
On the Limitations of Industrial Policies in TNC Capitalism.
The Case of the European Union[1]

Abstract *Global production and trade is significantly organised by Transnational Companies (TNC). In this article, I will argue that even if one considers industrial development as a proxy for development or leading to development in a broad sense, the prospects for 'progress' in contemporary capitalism are very limited. I will revisit theory, method, and proxies for 'development' and 'industrial development', as used by Arrighi and Drangel (1986) and Arrighi et al. (2003). I will adapt their approach for a core-periphery typology in the EU, and use it in order to estimate industrial convergence compared with convergence in 'development' (in EU language: convergence and cohesion). Furthermore, I will suggest additional proxies to estimate (spatial) politico-economic power in the hierarchy of TNC capitalism. I will close with concluding remarks on policies, from a dependency perspective.*

Keywords *EU, core-periphery, uneven development, commodity chains, manufacturing*

1. The Three-Tier World-System according to Giovanni Arrighi and Jessica Drangel

I follow in my inquiry the three-tier system of core – semiperiphery – periphery, as suggested by Giovanni Arrighi and Jessica Drangel (1986). The authors clarified, adapted and qualified the World-System Analysis, as introduced by Immanuel Wallerstein (1979, 1984, 1985). They use the term semiperiphery "exclusively to refer to a position in relation to the world division of labor and never to refer to a position in the interstate system" (ibid:15). Although both spheres, (the economic) world division of labour and the geopolitical "hierarchy of the interstate system" (ibid), are important and interrelated, it is "the separation of the two types of command [that] is a peculiarity of the capitalist world-economy" (ibid:16). The economic activities of this world-economy are pursued in commodity chains[2]; therefore, it is not a sectoral distribution that decides upon the allocation of states as belonging to the core, semi-periphery, or periphery.

It is rather "the unequal distribution of rewards among the various activities that constitute the single overarching division of labor defining and bounding the world-economy" (ibid:16). These economic activities are called "nodes of the commodity chain" (ibid:16). Arrighi and Drangel "take only the level of aggregate rewards as indicative of the core and peripheral status of an activity" (ibid:18). What is the nature of these economic activities? Are there economic activities that can be considered core or peripheral? These questions seem to have utmost importance for development studies, a) in the light of the historical experience of core-periphery categorisation, and b) for possible future development scenarios. Other than modernisation theoretical accounts which more or less regard progress as a movement from agricultural production to industrial production (as claimed in the British experience), Arrighi and Drangel reject the idea of invariant characteristics:

> "We further assume that no particular activity (whether defined in terms of its output or of the technique used) is inherently core-like or periphery-like. Any activity can become at a particular point in time core-like or periphery-like, but each has that characteristic for a limited period. Nonetheless, there are always some products and techniques that are core-like and others that are periphery-like at any given time." (Arrighi/Drangel 1986:18)

We will return to this question shortly. Since Arrighi and Drangel's model is a three-tier system, we first need to explain the logic behind it (the relations between enterprises and the states), and the identification of the three tiers. The authors outline their interpretation of the capitalist enterprise, which they perceive as engaging in a mix of activities and

RUDY WEISSENBACHER

creating competitive pressure by introducing profit-oriented innovations. The success of an enterprise lies in its ability to upgrade its mix of activities at the expense of other enterprises:

> "[A]s the capitalist enterprise is a locus of "accumulation" (of assets, expertise, specialized knowledge, and organization), the present capability of an enterprise to upgrade its mix of activities will to some extend depend upon its past success in doing so." (ibid:21)

The core enterprises that successfully upgrade their activities are, Arrighi and Drangel (1986:21) claim, quoting Schumpeter, "aggressor by nature and wield the really effective weapon of competition". Arrighi and Drangel (1986:19ff.) draw on Schumpeter's conception of "creative destruction", but they interpret it spatially instead of chronologically. With Schumpeter, profit-oriented innovations create windfall profits for a few, and losses for the majority of enterprises. In the phase of economic prosperity, a productive revolution occurs which then leads – during a depression phase – to the elimination of old and outdated elements of the industrial structure. Competition is dampened in the prosperity phase, but in the depression phase, the majority of enterprises overrate their chances of being equally successful, and so engage in cut-throat competition. While this was a "cluster in time", Arrighi and Drangel (1986:20) use this concept for a "cluster in space": zones of predominant prosperity and zones of predominant depression (cf. also Arrighi et al. 2003:17). Core enterprises compete by outsourcing the consequences of competition to peripheral enterprises (or peripheral capital). A relatively small group of core enterprises cluster in a "core zone" and produce a spatial polarisation. Such an arrangement would be volatile (if core and periphery arrangements changed easily), but core enterprises and core states have developed together, producing a rather stable form of spatial polarisation. Arrighi and Drangel (1986:22) observe that the "competitive struggle among capitalist enterprises has not taken place in a political void, but has been closely interrelated with the formation of states – that is, of formally sovereign territorial jurisdictions".

States have been integral to the formation of the global economy, and commodity chains have operated across state boundaries. However, states differ in their ability to influence the commodity chains, and "the modalities by which the social division of labor operates" (ibid:22). The position of states in their relation to enterprises (or commodity chains) contains weaknesses. States are seen as having the priority of securing their monopoly of power in their territories, and not the creation of wealth. They compete against other states, attempting to upgrade their position in the division of labour.

> "The main difficulty is that economic command is largely dependent upon an innovative participation in the world division of labor [...], and that capitalist enterprises have progressively become specialized agencies of such participation [...]. The problem of upgrading a state's mix of core-peripheral activities is thus largely a problem of being able to attract and develop organic links with "core capital" [...]. This capacity is only in part reflection of state's political power [...] it depends equally if not more on the extent to which a state has already developed organic links with core capital and, therefore, already encloses within its jurisdiction a predominantly core mix of activities." (ibid:24)

However, core states do have, and peripheral states lack, the capability

> "(1) to control access to the most remunerative outlets of all major commodity chains, (2) to provide the infrastructure and services required by core-like activities, and (3) to create a political climate favorable to capitalist entrepreneurship. This means that core states control advantages of core locations and can use that control to develop a symbiotic relation with the core capital that is already located within their jurisdiction, and to attract more core capital from peripheral locations." (ibid:25)

This symbiotic relationship between core states and core capital enhances, for both, the ability "to consolidate and reproduce their association with predominantly core-like activities" (ibid:26), while the opposite is true for peripheral states which face an "endemic inability [...] to escape their association with predominantly peripheral activities" (ibid:26). Semi-peripheral states are those that have an about even mix of core-like and peripheral activities. They may try and strengthen linkages between the two types of activities within their boundaries and by doing so escape some world market pressure. Also, they can compete with core-activities outside their territory, but with peripheral activities as well. The actions of semi-peripheral states make a difference, as they are not passive recipients of mixes of core-peripheral activities (upgrading or preventing from down-grading, ibid:27f.). Actual upgrading from semi-periphery to core status, however, seems possible in exceptional cases only:

"[T]he inability of the bulk of semiperipheral states to move into the core (and of peripheral states to move into the core) is the obverse of the success of some states to upgrade their mix of core-peripheral activities and move to a higher position." (ibid:28)

Candidates for upgrades to core or semi-periphery are found at the borders between the three tiers. Arrighi and Drangel (1986:29) adapt the concept of "perimeter", introduced by Peter Lange (1985) They call these upper areas the perimeter of the core and the perimeter of the periphery. Arrighi (1985:247) 'redefines' these perimeters as a

"no man's land that separates the unambiguously semiperipheral from the unambiguously core states, the perimeter of the core is not a line demarcating two zones but is itself a zone – a relatively empty but quite wide zone. Indeed, the two perimeter zones may even be subject to a progressive widening consequent upon core-periphery polarization."

In their empirical analysis, Arrighi and Drangel (1986:30) emphasise "that there is no operational way of empirically distinguishing between peripheral and core-like activities and therefore of classifying states according to the mix of core-peripheral activities that falls under their jurisdiction". There is no complete map of commodity chains, and conse-quently no assessment of the competitive pressure at their nodes. Further-more, the relationships of competition and cooperation are constantly changing. Arrighi′and Drangel (1986:31) point out, however, that such problems were not unique to their concept:

"Mixes of core-peripheral activities play in world-systems theory a role analo-gous to that played by "marginal utility" in neo-classical price theory or "labor embodies" in Ricardian and Marxian theories of value. All such "quantities" play a key role in their respective conceptualizations but cannot be subjected to direct measurement. What matters is to be able to derive from the conceptualization a set of empirically verifiable hypotheses that can provide us with indirect measurements of key variables."

Rather conventionally, Arrighi and Drangel (1986:31ff.) use GNP per capita in a common currency (US dollar) as an indicator for the aggregate rewards in order to test their hypothesis of a three tier system. I emphasise a few of their findings. The state composition of the three-tier system has not changed substantially from 1938 to 1983: "In sum, 95% of the states for which we could find data (and 94% of total population) were in 1975/83 still on or within the boundaries of the zone in which they were in 1938/50" (ibid:44). There were (temporary) downward movements, however, from 1938/1950 to 1960/1970 (Germany and UK from core to perimeter of the core, and France and Belgium from perimeter of the core to the semi-periphery). 74 out of 93 states remained in one of the three zones (10 in the core zone, 20 in the semi-periphery, and 44 in the periphery) and are described as "organic members" (ibid:49). The organic members are then used to estimate the "economic activities" prevailing in different zones.

We have already seen that Arrighi and Drangel reject the idea of invariant characteristics for core-like or peripheral activities. Especially as far as industrialisation and industrial production are concerned, this aspect seems important for development studies. The findings of Arrighi and Drangel (1986:53ff.) suggest that views of progress based on modernisation theory (from agricultural to industrial production) are of limited explanatory value. Furthermore, they question the claim that the capability to industrialise qualifies as a means or sign of an *overall* development or dependency characteristic. Using data on the average labour force employed in "industry" and on the share of "manufacturing" in GDP for the countries in the three tiers, they found that "the gap between the degree of industrialization" of the core *vis-à-vis* the semi-periphery and the periphery narrowed significantly after 1960. In the late 1970s, "the semiperiphery not only caught up with but overtook the core in terms of industrialization" (ibid:55). Arrighi and Drangel (1986:55f.) argue that semiperipheral countries lost "economic command" in terms of industrialisation in the period of 1938-1948, and

RUDY WEISSENBACHER

"so there are good reasons for supposing that in this period core-like activities were largely industrial activities. Interestingly enough, it was at the end of this period that Prebisch and his associates first introduced the concept of core-periphery relations and formulated it in terms of a primary activities-industrial activities dichotomy." (ibid:55)

From the 1950s to the 1960s, "a positive correlation between industrial activities and core-like activities is still in evidence" (ibid) but gaps in industrialisation and GDP between core, semiperiphery and periphery are narrowing. The authors call 1960 to 1965 transitional years: the gaps in industrialisation are decreasing "but there is no corresponding relative decline in core states' economic command". The authors explain this by "the fact that the positive correlation between industrial and core-like activities was losing strength". In the following two decades, "a weakened positive correlation turned into an increasingly strong *negative* correlation". In the period from 1965 to 1980, "the periphery and the semiperiphery continued to industrialize" and "the core began to de-industrialize". While the industrialisation gap narrowed (between core and periphery) or almost disappeared (between core and semiperiphery), the economic command of the semiperiphery (compared to the core) remained constant, and that of the periphery (compared to the core) worsened (ibid:55f.): "In sum, the industrialization of the semiperiphery and periphery has ultimately been a channel, not of subversion, but of reproduction of the hierarchy of the world-economy" (ibid:56).

But what replaces industrial production as core activity? Arrighi and Drangel (1986) draw on Arrighi (1985:275), who argues that

"the growing importance of vertically integrated TNC's in all branches of economic activity (from agriculture and mining to manufacturing, distribution, and banking) dissolves and blurs any previously existing correlation between the core-periphery dichotomy [...] and distinctions based on the kind of commodity produced (e.g., industry versus agriculture) or even on the techniques of production used (e.g., high productivity versus low productivity)".

The distinguishing feature between core, semiperipheral, and peripheral states seems to have become the ability to control commodity chains:

> "The relevant distinction is between activities that involve strategic decision making, control and administration, R&D, and other "brain" activities, on the one hand, and activities of pure execution, on the other. […] [C]ore states are those where TNC's concentrate their brain activities, and peripheral states are those where they concentrate their muscle-and-nerve activities. Under these circumstances, semiperipheral states would be of two types: states that have attained the core position of the previous stage of development of the world economy but that have not yet moved on to the core position of the new stage; and countries where TNC's locate a fairly balanced mix of brain and muscle/nerve activities." (Arrighi 1985:275)

These inquires suggest that there is a persistent path dependence in the spatial division of labour that makes an upgrading of a state's position difficult. Core states and core enterprises grow and develop together in a symbiotic relationship, but the nature of the commodity chains is changing. The control over the commodity chain gained importance in relation to industrial production and its geographical distribution. Semiperipheral or peripheral countries could close the gap to core countries as far as industrialisation is concerned without closing the gap in terms of distribution of GNP per capita. Based on this research, Arrighi (1990) talked of a "developmentalist illusion", arguing against the assumption that 'industrialization' was the equivalent of 'development' and 'core' the same as 'industrial'. Following Arrighi and Drangel (1986), Arrighi et al. (2003) demonstrate [that] industrial convergence has not been accompanied by a convergence in the levels of income and wealth enjoyed on average by the residents of the former First and Third Worlds (ibid:4).

They base their empirical analysis on studies that found evidence of a core or OECD "convergence club" at the upper end of the world income distribution (ibid: 6 and 8). The convergence among these countries was not accompanied by an overall (global) convergence of income. In order to show the convergence of industrial production against the non-convergence of income, they relate a country's income (measured by the Gross National Product per capita – GNPPC – in relation to the weighted average of core countries' income of a given year) to its industrial development (measured by the share of manufacturing in the GDP of a country in relation to the share of manufacturing in the GDP of core countries in any given year). Measured by "the proportions of GDP in manufacturing" in core and periphery and semiperiphery, "industrial convergence in this period was due exclusively to First World de-industrialization", argue Arrighi et al. (2003:15), while the unevenness in economic performance between peripheral and semi-peripheral countries increased significantly.

2. Industrial convergence without development?
An inquiry into a Three-Tier System of the European Union

2.1 Core, semiperiphery, and periphery in the European Union

In 2015, the European Central Bank (ECB 2015) expressed its disappointment at the degree of convergence within the EU/EMU between 1999 and 2014, and acknowledged the limitations of mainstream neoclassical economics. The arguments put forward by authors from the European Dependency School (EDS), research networks that applied elements from the Latin American dependency school on the European situation in the 1970s and 1980s (cf. Weissenbacher 2015&2018), still hold: neither of the two ways of challenging polarisation in an "integration of unequal partners" have materialised, these being either: a) a balanced industrialisation between core and periphery, or b) more re-distributive funds from the core to the periphery. Since b) is seen as being out of the question in the EU setting, for the ECB (2015:31) "achieving sustainable real convergence by means of sound national economic policies is important to support the economic and social cohesion of EMU".

The key elements of economic growth and convergence in neoclassical economics are (still) 'technology', 'innovation', and 'research and development'. The ECB's (2015:38ff.) presentation, however, reflects the difficulty of neoclassical theory in explaining technological progress that "appeared like manna from heaven" (Maier et al. 2006: 57). Drawing on the externalities or endogenous growth model (cf. ibid:96ff.), the ECB (2015:40) suggests that an "alternative way" is necessary "to endogenously create growth, and for convergence to be explained in a theoretical model, innovation must be 'produced' in a separate sector of the economy". If it is the public sector that is responsible for financing and producing technology and innovation, it may be no surprise that "[c]ountries that spend more on R&D tend to exhibit higher income levels" (ECB 2015:42). The data the ECB presents seem to support the thesis that those regions that can afford more technological investments have an advantage. This opens different development paths in addition to neoclassical convergence, from persisting development gaps to divergence (cf. Weissenbacher 2008:94). Consequently, as Maier et al. (2006:101) put it, the "question of convergence cannot be answered by [neoclassical] theory but must be passed on to empiricism". This obsession with productive forces and technological progress seems to be the fetish of the ideology of the capitalism of transnational companies (TNC), a mode of production that has created productive forces capable of providing "a good life for all".[3]

Economic convergence is conventionally measured by beta and sigma convergence. The former tries to capture whether there is a 'catching-up' process between low and high income countries by means of higher economic growth, while the latter "refers to a reduction in the dispersion of income levels across economies" (ECB 2015:31). The ECB (2015:31) argues that "real convergence mainly pertains to the [beta]-dimension of convergence, with [sigma]-convergence being a by-product; sustainable convergence is the key precondition for economies that are catching up to be resilient to shocks". Other authors stress the importance of Sigma-convergence "because it speaks directly as to whether the distribution of income across economies is becoming more equitable" (Young et al. 2008:1084) and "that the concept of Sigma-convergence is more revealing of the reality as it directly describes the distribution of income across economies without relying on the estimation of a particular model" (Monfort 2008:5). I will follow Arrighi and Drangel (1986) and Arrighi et al. (2003) in the attempt to estimate core-periphery relations in the EU at the country level. Consequently, I am not interested in estimating the actual living situation of people in the core and periphery of the EU, but the (relative) relations between core and periphery and their change over time.

Calculations that use Sigma-convergence usually observe statistical variations among the EU28 or EU15 groups; EuroStat presents data that refer to EU28=100 or EU15=100. I will relate, however, EU countries to the EU core. While Arrighi et al. (2003) used the OECD "convergence club" as the core proxy, they relate the periphery and the semiperiphery to, I will use the undisputed core country of Europe, Germany, as the sole EU core reference (Germany=100). Germany certainly has core characteristics different from the US, and therefore the interpretation in terms of industrialisation will differ somewhat. The main argument of de-industrialisation, however, seems to hold for both Germany and the USA, according to the data I used. If one takes 1960=100 as base line, then the share of manufacturing industry in all branches (gross value added) as proxy for industrialisation will start to show declining values no later than the 1970s (table 1). It will not be a surprise that these data suggest a lead by TNC from the USA – as compared to those from Germany – in the outsourcing process towards the (semi)periphery. The widening of the gap between the US and Germany slowed down in the 1990s, when the German economy was faced with the integration of Eastern Germany. However, the German "wage-dumping policy" (Flassbeck/Spiecker 2011), which brought the German economy a significant competitive edge, seems to have stopped de-industrialisation. One could read the confrontational protectionist policies by the Trump administration as a reaction to a weakening of US control of global TNC capitalism, with its commodity chains.

The obvious difference between the US and Germany (in the data presented) is the higher share of industrialisation of the smaller and more export-oriented German economy in all available data.

The main objective in this article is, however, the core-periphery system in the European Union, and the question regarding industrial policies for convergence and cohesion if the logic of TNC capitalism remains unaltered.

I will suggest a contemporary core-periphery system of the European Union at the national level. (Data for the resident/citizen concept of Gross National Income (GNI) per capita at purchasing power standards (PPS) do not seem to be easily available at the regional level.) The GNI per capita (PPS) considers income from residents of one country that is earned in other countries, and subtracts domestic income by nationals from other countries. PPS is an artificial common currency that respects countries' different price levels (cf. Eurostat n/y1&2).

The purpose of this sketch is to find a working classification of a core-periphery system in the EU that could be used for further research. I used the data on GNI per capita (PPS) provided by the AMECO database (EU Commission n/y). Data for EU15 are available from 1960 and data for EU28 from 1990. I related the data to Germany = 100 and used an average over each available decade (cf. Table 2).

Arrighi and Drangel (1986) worked within the world system and commodity chains. Their assessment aimed at a working scheme for the global level. Following the dependency paradigm, and staying geographically in Europe, particularly the EU, I was interested as to whether a three-tier system could be observed in the EU as well. There would be candidates for Arrighi and Drangel's (1986) perimeters (of the periphery and of the core) in the EU also (Slovakia and the Czech Republic in the 1990s/2000s, and Ireland and Finland (1990s) or Spain and Italy (2000s), respectively). With a much more limited data set than Arrighi and Drangel (1986) and Arrighi et al. (2003), I, however, intend to stick to a three-tier system between EU core and EU periphery and try to explain some of the special cases. The data, indeed, suggest a three-tier system in the EU. I use the upper three quintiles of GNI per capita (100=Germany) to approximate core = 81-100, semiperiphery = 61-80, and periphery = 41-60. Due to the restricted space, I need to limit my presentation and interpretation. Historical data can be found, however, in tables 2 and 4 (more detailed interpretation in Weissenbacher, forthcoming).

In the current decade, the consistent hard core countries (except Belgium) plus Ireland still score higher than Germany (cf. tables 2 and 3). Belgium has lost ground, and so did Finland, France, and the UK. Italy has even dropped to the semiperiphery, which it leads, followed by Spain down to the Czech Republic. Portugal lost and Slovakia gained, both appearing as a crossover (perimeter?) between semiperiphery and periphery, which is led by Greece and Estonia (which have declined from their previous positions), down to Romania, and far behind to Bulgaria. Tables 2 and 3 offer a synopsis. Most of the countries are "organic members", as Arrighi and Drangel (1986) put it, of their group during the observation period, and therefore their overall classification fits their historical record. According to the AMECO data, Greece started as a periphery and wound up as a peripheral country. The GNI per capita increase that suggested a rise to semiperiphery (of EU15/EU28) seems somewhat a surprise, especially if we look at the share of manufacturing in total gross value added over the entire observation period (table 4). I ranked Greece therefore as periphery. Slovakia has risen to the threshold between periphery and semiperiphery, yet whether it really advances to the semiperiphery remains to be seen. The historical data suggest an overall peripheral classification. Similarly I ranked Portugal, which reached the threshold due to a recent decline, as a peripheral country. Spain had loomed into the core before it declined. A treatment as semiperiphery seems justified. Italy remains the commuter between core and semiperiphery, the perimeter of the core. Recent tendencies in the Italian political economy suggest a characterisation as belonging to the semiperiphery for the time being (cf. Weissenbacher forthcoming). The UK seems to have had recovered from semiperipheral status, but recent developments also suggest a decline. I will keep the UK in the core group, although there is reason to believe that this might change in the not too distant future. We will return to the Irish case in the following chapter.

2.2 A ladder without upper rungs: commodity chains and the confusion of industrial development with development

Following Arrighi and Drangel (1986), industrial production, as we have seen, lost its core characteristics in the 1960s. This is pretty much in line with the ever more pronounced 'new international division of labour' that brought an outsourcing and re-organisation of production from the core to the (semi)periphery, especially with the global economic crisis of the 1970s. Consequently, TNC strategy has changed the focus from organising production (industrialisation) in the territories/jurisdictions of the countries of their home bases to controlling (production in) the commodity chains (CC). It is important to remember that it is not territories and their governments or jurisdictions that control CC but core transnational companies (TNC). If I use the spatial expression of control by core countries, it will be used as proxy for the symbiosis the core TNC developed with core territories/jurisdictions they use as home bases. Historical experience saw a rather persistent divide between core and periphery, which is also reflected in the dataset for the EU. Furthermore, recent research by UNCTAD (2013:122) suggests that 80% of world trade is organised by TNC in CC, and about 60% of global trade consists of intermediate goods and services. As far as the core-periphery distribution of such CC activity is concerned, the predominant share of investments still stems from what UNCTAD considers the 'developed world'.

In my inquiry I use the undisputed European core country, Germany, as a reference for changes in industrial production and income levels per capita. With the latter, we have already seen that there were fluctuations, yet during the observation period the three-tier system showed remarkable persistence against the pretence of the overall core integration model of the EU28, which is convergence and cohesion. The matter of industrialisation directly concerns the political economy of the EU and immediate economic policy. Can re-industrialisation or more industrialisation (more industrial production) in the EU (semi)periphery bring development or convergence? The findings of the Arrighi research groups suggest that even if one termed climbing the ladder in this hierarchy 'development', such 'development' was unlikely.

In order to numerically estimate the EU situation in terms of industrialisation, I used the share of manufacturing industry in all branches (gross value added) at current prices (expressed in ECU/Euro) as proxy for industrial development or level of industrialisation, and related each country to Germany (=100, cf. table 4). I averaged the yearly data (where available from the AMECO database) over decades. The interpretation of the findings necessarily varies from Arrighi et al. (2003). They used the OECD convergence club and marked the de-industrialisation of these core countries as an important reduction in the industrialisation gap: the core de-industrialised and the (semi)periphery industrialised. I do not treat groups of countries but rather single countries, and the reference country is Germany, the industrial export champion. But the de-industrialisation process of core countries can still be reproduced with this data. If we take the core countries of table 3 plus Italy (and without Ireland, which will be explained later) than we will get the following picture (in table 4): Luxembourg de-industrialises from the 1980s to the 2010s (no earlier data). Belgium, Denmark, France, Italy, the Netherlands, and UK de-industrialise *vis-à-vis* Germany from the 1960s to the 2010s (UK data: from 1970s), with one important exception: the 1990s. I interpret the 1990s as the decade which statistically reflects the integration of the former German Democratic Republic into the Federal Republic (first eastern enlargement of the EC/EU), a process which weakened the German economy. For Austria, Finland, and Sweden this comparative recovery of industrial production *vis-à-vis* Germany lasted into the 2000s.

In the Southern EU (semi)periphery, Greece and Portugal did participate in the industrialisation process of the overall (semi)periphery, according to these data, until the 1980s, but the accession to the EC/EU as 'unequal partners' stopped the process, unsurprisingly so if one follows the analysis of authors from the European dependency school (Weissenbacher forthcoming). Data for Spain start in the accession decade, and if one takes the 1990s as the German decade of 'weakness', then we can see immediate de-industrialisation.

The data for the EU28 start with the 1990s. If one compares tables 2 and 4, the difference is striking. While in table 2, which represents a proxy for hierarchies of wealth, the grey rows (enlargement countries after EU15) are grouped at the 'peripheral' side, the tendency in table 4, with a proxy for industrialisation, shows a different story. These countries are grouped with the core country, Germany. Furthermore, if we assume, for the sake of the argument, a strict three-tier system following these industrialisation data (a three-tier system of the three upper quintiles of Germany=100, sorted from bottom to top, cf. table 4), then the current decade would find this typology: *Industrialised countries* (higher than 80) are Austria, Poland, Lithuania, Slovakia, Slovenia, Germany, Hungary, Romania, Czech Republic, Ireland; *Semi-industrialised countries* (61-80): Denmark, Belgium, Croatia, Italy, Estonia, Sweden, Finland; *low industrialised countries*: (60 and lower): Cyprus, Luxembourg, Greece, UK, Malta, France, the Netherlands, Latvia, Portugal, Spain.

It cannot be a surprise that the countries Stöllinger (2016) calls the "Central European (CE) manufacturing core" (Germany, Austria and the Viségrad countries Czech Republic, Hungary, Poland, and Slovakia) are among the 'industrialised countries' in this typology. It also indicates the Austrian dependence on Germany. Austria's FDI stocks balance had only turned positive recently, due to its engagement in the production networks with the regional EU enlargement countries which joined in 2004 (table 6, cf. Becker/Disslbacher/Weissenbacher 2015). Stöllinger

(2016:803) starts with general assumptions that the Arrighi research groups (discussed above) had rejected for core countries (and accepted for semiperipheral and peripheral countries only): "[We] will consider a decline in the value added share of the manufacturing sector as an adverse structural shift for an economy". Stöllinger (2016:804) is here drawing, however, on literature which was written in a time when industrial production was still considered a 'core activity' by the Arrighi research group:

> "Closely related to our work is Chenery (1960) who links manufacturing value added per capita, i.e. manufacturing intensity in several manufacturing industries to domestic supply and demand conditions which are proxied by income per capita. He finds a positive relationship between manufacturing intensity and income per capita for all industries." (Stöllinger 2016:804)

For Arrighi's research groups, industrial production had ceased to be the distinctive core activity (in core territories) in the 1960s, and upward shifts by industrialisation processes were seen as being possible, afterwards, above all within the group of peripheral and semiperipheral countries. Stöllinger (2016:806f.) presents literature that considers consequences of CC participation as possible in either direction, catching-up or increasing uneven development. 'Offshoring' of production from the core is on Stöllinger's (2016:805) radar, but he does not focus on explaining why it is possible for countries to maintain their core status despite the fact that the

> "flip side of this agglomeration of manufacturing activities in the CE manufacturing core is a significant decline in the share of EU manufacturing value added exports in other EU Member States, in particular in high-income countries including the Nordic and the Benelux countries and above all France and the United Kingdom" (Stöllinger 2016:814).

The evidence presented in this article suggests that the observations of the Arrighi research groups for the capitalist world system are also true for the European Union, namely that it is the ability to control TNC commodity chains that enables a core status to prevail, or, in other words, that 'core activity' goes well beyond organising manufactured production on one's own territory. Again, I need to refer to Weissenbacher (forth-coming) for detailed (historical) interpretation, but the current EU situation tends to be in line with the arguments of Arrighi's research groups as well. For all (semi)peripheral countries except Greece, the convergence in industrial production is much more pronounced than the income situation (for Portugal, the situation seems more balanced). The situation of the semiperipheral countries Cyprus, Malta, Italy, and Spain will be explained below. For all core countries except the special case of Ireland, the situation is the other way round, as convergence in industrial production is well below the income situation. Ireland is an example of the phenomenon of extreme financialisation, part of which was a domestic loan expansion due to cheap credit, made possible by Ireland's entry to the Eurozone. Mortgage debt more than trebled from 2002 (47.2 billion euro) to the onset of the crisis of 2008 (139.8 billion euro) (Wickham 2012:66ff.). As far as manufacturing production is concerned, the dependence of the Irish economy on TNC is seen as a weakness, part of which "is the practice of transfer pricing whereby the foreign-owned companies tend to inflate the value of their output in the Irish economy in order to avail of the state's low tax on manufacturing profits" (Kirby 2010:22). Irish data for manufacturing in the AMECO database start with the 1990s, with an already high percentage that would overtake the German level in the following decade. The 2010s seem to surpass the industrial success story of Finland, but not as pronounced regarding the income situation. Italy's progress in manufacturing industry (according to these data) does not show such massive jumps and also loses out in the 2000s. Italy has never reached the per capita income levels of Finland and Ireland (compared to Germany=100) and loses massively in the 2010s. For our purpose, the success stories and the upward shift to the core are particularly interesting. Following the model of Arrighi's research groups, industrialisation ceased to be a characteristic of core countries in the second half of the 1960s. If this is true also for the EU (the overall core integration model), we would therefore expect that additional efforts in industrialisation would – in optimal cases – lead to upward movement among peripheral and semiperipheral countries, but not to the shift of a semiperipheral country to the core. If we take the core countries of the 1970s, namely Austria, Belgium, Denmark, France, Germany, Luxembourg, The Netherlands and Sweden, and compare them to the core countries of the 2010s, then there are three countries that have entered the core zone: Finland from the semiperiphery, UK re-entering from the semiperiphery, and, surprisingly, Ireland marching through from the periphery. Additionally, we will keep Italy on the radar, because it seems to have reached the perimeter of the core, and then the core, by 'traditional' core means, namely industrialisation. It is important to remember that Finland was already considered a core country in Arrighi and Drangel's (1986) global scheme in the years 1975-1983, and Ireland belonged to the perimeter of the core.

The striking issue (but not a surprise following Arrighi's working groups) is that, with a few exceptions, the 'convergence' to the German level (Germany=100) on part of the (semi)peripheral countries is higher, in many cases very much higher, in terms of industrial production (table 3), than the 'convergence' in the income level (table 1). The exceptions are Greece and Cyprus, Malta in the 2000s, and Spain, beginning with the 2000s. I interpret the Spanish situation with the 'pseudo boom' that poured foreign capital into the economy's non-tradable sector (cf. Becker/Weissenbacher 2014). All in all, there is a trend that supports the Arrighian notions: a) industrial production ceased to be a core characteristic; b) the core countries keep the core status by controlling the global (European) commodity chains; c) core TNC are able to control and exploit manufacturing production in the periphery and semiperiphery. We will discuss these aspects in a moment.

2.3 Further evidence of the control of TNC

In order to further establish this argument, I suggest using additional proxies for quantification. I use – taking from the OECD database on outward activities of TNC (OECD n.y.) – a) the figures of *TNC in the manufacturing sector* (of all available country data) in the EU28 area, and b) the turnover of these TNC in the EU28 area in 2014. I use these data as a proxy for the extent of control of European commodity chains. I took into account the size of countries and therefore calculated a TNC per capita amount and a TNC turnover per capita amount (Euro millions at current prices). In order to make these data comparable with the data of GNI per capita and share of manufacturing industry, I, again, related them to Germany (=100). They confirm the Arrighian thesis of control of European commodity chains versus productive activity in the manufacturing sector (for details and graphics: Weissenbacher, forthcoming). For most *core countries*, the number of TNC with outward activities in the EU28, as well as their turnover (both per capita), are above or at least around the level of GNI income per capita (compared to Germany=100), while the share of manufacturing production lies below the comparative income level. Some countries are extreme (top: Luxembourg with 1012 TNC per capita and a turnover of 1966, both compared to Germany = 100). Only Ireland, Italy (which has lost its core position), and the UK (which might again lose its core position) are exceptions to this overall core trend. The opposite is true for *(semi-)peripheral EU countries*. The GNI income per capita is below the share of manufacturing production (with the exceptions mentioned above), but above the number of TNC per capita, as well as their turnover per capita levels. These data paint an intense picture of the core – (semi)periphery situation in the European Union. The status of the core means the control of TNC and European commodity chains. This is very clear in the cases of the hard core (Austria, Belgium, Denmark, Germany, Sweden) and also Finland. It seems to explain the persistent role of France, despite its weaker GNI per capita positions. But what about Ireland? And the seemingly weakened Italy and UK? Also, the Netherlands are not included (no data). And we need to explain more the – at first glance – somewhat surprising positions of Cyprus and Malta (which may be historically explained by their British legacy).

Let us have a look at TNC home countries as yet another proxy for the amount of power in the global political economy. Among the 100 largest global non-financial TNCs in 2016 (as presented by UNCTAD 2017b), exactly one half was considered to have an EU country as its home base. (To be sure, there are also other European TNCs among the top 100, i.e. from Switzerland.) 15 TNCs are considered to have the UK as their 'home economy', 11 from France and also 11 from Germany, three from Spain, two each from Ireland and Italy, and one each from Belgium, Denmark, Finland, Luxembourg, the Netherlands, and Sweden (table 5). From this perspective, it seems clear why the UK can preserve its position as a core country. The level of France's TNC control in the top 100 seems also in line with its persistent role as core country, despite weakening GNI per capita levels. Semiperipheral Italy (in GNI per capita terms) controls three percent of foreign assets in this top 100 list, and also semiperipheral Spain. With the exception of Austria, all the smaller countries of the hard core control one TNC in the top 100 list. Ireland is listed as homebase for two TNCs, but with a low share of foreign sales and employment.

Another proxy I suggest for regional/country 'control' of TNC is Foreign Direct Investments (FDI). There is an entire data set available for FDI outward stock in Millions of (current) US dollar (UNCTAD 2016, 2017a). These data indicate the extent to which TNC control investments abroad, but not specifically in the EU28 area and not for the manufacturing sector in particular (as with the OECD data above). Table 6 shows the differences in political-economic power in numbers. I calculated averages over decades for the FDI net (outward and inward) stock and averages of country populations over the respective decades (population data from Eurostat or national sources) to receive FDI stocks per capita for each decade. In order to make the data comparable to the data we used so far, I again calculated a relation to Germany (=100). Table 6 (first three columns) shows absolute figures and the net FDI stocks averaged for each decade, and the relation to Germany (=100), respectively. The core – (semi)periphery divide is again apparent. The demarcation line of net FDI stocks runs between Spain and Italy, which might indicate the better position of Italy in the hierarchy. Very generally, the (semi) peripheral countries do have negative values in net FDI stocks, which means they import more FDI than they export. The situation is reversed in the core countries.

The most striking exception in the sphere of semiperipheral countries are Cyprus and Malta. The explosion of their inward and outward FDI stock in the decade of EU accession seems to indicate that these two countries are being used as bridgeheads into the EU, but also as nodes of tax avoidance (Garcia-Bernardo et al. 2017 , cf. Weissenbacher forthcoming). However, there are also cases in core countries that merit our attention. There is, above all, Luxembourg boasting exorbitant FDI inward and outwards stock data, which indicates a special TNC network country (with special tax regulations). Among the core countries, Luxembourg is followed by Ireland, also with striking data for inward and outward

FDI stocks. Among the hard core countries, Belgium and the Netherlands also display extreme data. Their data reflect the ability of TNC to transfer prices to, and evade taxes in, the most preferred jurisdictions (Weissenbacher forthcoming). Among the core countries, Ireland might surely be considered as having shaky foundations, because it seems to depend on the integration into two core structures, the US and the EU core, for upholding its position in the commodity chains (Wickham 2012:75).

3. Room to manoeuver? A few concluding remarks

Neither for the Latin American nor the European Dependency School is industrial development synonymous with development in a broad (societal) sense. What I have tried to show in this article, following the (world systems) approach of Arrighi and Drangel (1986), and Arrighi et al. (2003), is that even if – due to the current lack of feasible alternatives – industrial development (under current circumstances, without changing the mode of production) is the only policy proxy for development, one should not raise one's hopes too high. There is some room to manoeuver within the sphere of the (semi-)periphery, but climbing to a core level is unlikely, and reserved to special cases such as Ireland, which experienced a hard landing with the crisis of 2008ff. And the Irish case can hardly count as one of successfully climbing the ladder by means of industrialisation, but can rather be explained by circumstances that seemed favourable for transnational companies (TNC). Industrialisation or industrial policy for (semi-)peripheral countries will usually mean accepting a lower place in the commodity chains (or, metaphorically speaking, hoping to climb a ladder without the upper rungs). The place at the top of the international hierarchy depends on the (usually historically grown and therefore 'path-dependent') ability to control or influence TNC and their commodity chains.

It is my understanding of the dependency schools (Latin American and European) that they regarded a change of the mode of production as necessary. Speculating on the elasticity of international demand may be a tactic, but does not seem to be a sound (long-term) strategy. An alternative development strategy could start by reconsidering the principles of self-reliance which would re-orient production regionally and give preference to "use value" instead of "exchange value" (Galtung 1976:6). This appears necessary to protect the natural environment, but it is also a social imperative. In a global or European environment hostile to changing the mode of production, such policies are difficult to achieve, especially if a country needs to act alone. 'Resilience against crises' may be the strongest argument. Currently, the European situation does not appear very stable. The structural problems of the global and European mode of production further disintegration and, for now, favour neo-nationalist and Neo-Fascist parties which continue the neoliberal EU policy by more authoritarian means (Becker 2018). Such parties are not interested in a change of the mode of production, but rather are supported by capital fractions that may perceive no other way of maintaining the status quo. Therefore, their proposals of heterodox economic policies may appear to be more acceptable (cf. Becker/Weissenbacher 2016).

Progressive alternatives can only attempt to use the narrow room to manoeuver as long as the international or EU structure appears unchangeable. Domestic capitalist and comprador classes will oppose policies which challenge the mode of production. Additionally, alternative regional and national policies need to be aware of nationalist traps. The geographer Edward Soja (1980:224) argued that "the transformation of capitalism can occur only through the combination and articulation of a horizontal (periphery vs. centre) and vertical (working class vs. bourgeoisie) class struggle, by transformation on both the social and spatial planes" (cf. Weissenbacher 2015, 2018). The imperatives of competition and competitiveness and the underlying perceptions of technological progress and innovation need to be challenged or interpreted anew, e.g. by taking up ideas from the self-reliance concept. Internalising externalities was, for Galtung (1976:12), one of the most important factors of self-reliance: "Much less is lost by reinventing something invented elsewhere already than by casting oneself in the role of the learner and imitator. In conventional terms: the research and development facilities may be clumsy – whatever that means – but they are one's own, as are the mistakes, and it is from own mistakes, not from those made by others, there is more to learn'.

1   I gratefully acknowledge that research for this paper was supported by funds from the Oesterreichische Nationalbank (Anniversary Fund, project number 17058). The article benefited from discussions with Joachim Becker, Predrag Ćetković, Daniel Grabner, and the comments by two anonymous reviewers.

2   This footnote is motivated by suggestions of one of the anonymous reviewers. It seems important to stress that the terminology has changed alongside the shifts in content in 'chain' research from commodity chains towards global commodity chains and global value chains. "By the early 2000s," writes Bair (2014:2), "the commodity chain terminology was frequently being used interchangeably with other constructs, such as global production networks (GPNs). In recent years, one such alternative nomenclature – global value chains (GVCs) – has become hegemonic, especially within more applied or policy-oriented studies of global industries. Global value chain analysis has even been taken up enthusiastically by international financial institutions [...]". Global commodity chains and global value chains "are analytically oriented towards the micro (individual firm) or meso (sector) level as opposed to the macro and holistic perspective characteristic of the world-system conceptualization of commodity chains" (Bair 2005:164). I will stick, therefore, to the original world-system terminology in this article: "World-systems theorists understand commodity chains as consisting not only of the steps involved in the transformation of raw materials into final goods, but also as webs connecting that set of productive activities with the social reproduction of human labor power as a critical input into this process. Additionally, world-systems theorists are most fundamentally interested in how commodity chains structure and reproduce a stratified and hierarchical world-system" (Bair 2005:155f.; see Bair 2009 and 2005 for a literature overview of the different strands of 'chain' literature).

3   Contrary to Karl Marx's 19th century expectations, the development of productive forces (labour/workers in combination with the means of production) has not (yet) lead to such conflicts with the relations of production (the economic material base with class relations between owners and not-owners of the means of production) that would change the social formation and the mode of production. TNC capitalism manages to fragment global workers even more (with highly polarised incomes), employs ever less wage labour due to high productivity (but accepts extreme labour-intensive conditions in the periphery), wastes resources (with the consequences for mankind), and establishes uneven consumption patterns. Since the relations of production are treated as 'given' in mainstream thinking, the 'development of the productive forces' experiences a "strange non-death" (to borrow a phrase from Colin Crouch 2011). Theodor Adorno (1972) had elaborated as early as 1968, shortly after the period Arrighi and Drangel consider transitional years (when industrial production ceased to be a core activity), the underlying issues of contemporary capitalism: "Late capitalism or industrial society?" It was "the current form of socially necessary appearance", he argued (Adorno 1972:368f.), "[t]hat productive forces and relations of productions are seen as one today and therefore one could readily design society from the productive forces". It was a necessary appearance for society, because it integrated formerly distinctive elements of the "so-

cial process", including people. Material production, distribution, consumption are administered in common, the boundaries of which become blurred: "All is one. The totality of mediation processes ['Vermittlungsprozesse'], truly of the exchange principle, produces another deceptive immediacy. It allows for the possible forgetting of differences and antagonisms, contrary to one's own perception, or to repress them from consciousness" (Adorno 1972:369). The ideology of core countries in late capitalism blocks the view at different development experiences (and narratives that might diverge from bottom-up capitalism as free market success story). Relations of production go beyond ownership of the means of production and include elements of the state and its administration. Adorno (1972:363) calls this the "role of the state as institutional capitalist ['Gesamtkapitalist']" which seems compatible with the symbiotic relationship between states and companies which Arrighi and Drangel talked about (above). The productive forces seem to resemble general technical rationality, and an appearance is thus created that "the universal interest is that in the status quo, and full employment is the ideal and not the liberation from dependent labor" (ibid). The relations of production have survived, argues Adorno (ibid), and have "continued to subjugate the productive forces. The signature of this age is the predominance of the relations of production over the productive forces, which have mocked the conditions for some time" (ibid).

References

Adorno, Theodor (1972 [1968]) Spätkapitalismus oder Industriegesellschaft? Einleitungsvortrag zum 16. Deutschen Soziologentag. In: Theodor Adorno: Soziologische Schriften I. Hrsg. von Rolf Tiedemann. Frankfurt/Main: Suhrkamp, 354-370. (= Gesammelte Schriften 8)

Arrighi, Giovanni (1985): Fascism to Democratic Socialism. Logic and Limits of a Transition. In: Arrighi, Giovanni (ed.): Semiperipheral Development. The Politics of Southern Europe in the Twentieth Century. Beverly Hills, London, and New Delhi: Sage, 243-279. (=Explorations in the World-Economy 5)

Arrighi, Giovanni (1990): The Developmentalist Illusion: A Reconceptualization of the Semiperiphery. In: William Martin (ed.): Semiperipheral States in the World-Economy. Greenwood Press: Westport, CT, 11-42.

Arrighi, Giovanni/Drangel, Jessica (1986): The Stratification of the World-Economy: An Exploration of the Semiperipheral Zone. In: Review 10 (1), 9-74. (=Anniversary Issue: The Work of the Fernand Braudel Center)

Arrighi, Giovanni/Silver, Beverly/Brewer, Benjamin (2003): Industrial Convergence, Globalization, and the Persistence of the North-South Divide. In: Studies in Comparative International Development 38 (1), 3-31. https://doi.org/10.1007/BF02686319

RUDY WEISSENBACHER

Bair, Jennifer (2005): Global Capitalism and Commodity Chains: Looking Back, Going Forward. In: Competition & Change 9 (2), 153-180. https://doi.org/10.1179/102452905X45382

Bair, Jennifer (2009): Global Commodity Chains: Genealogy and Review. In: Bair, Jennifer (ed.): Frontiers of Commodity Chain Research. Stanford: Stanford University Press, 1-34.

Bair, Jennifer (2014): Editor's Introduction: Commodity Chains in and of the World System. In: Journal of World-Systems Research 20 (1), 1-10. https://doi.org/10.5195/JWSR.2014.574

Becker, Joachim (2018): Neo-Nationalismus in der EU: sozio-ökonomische Programmatik und Praxis. Materialien zu Wirtschaft und Gesellschaft No. 179. Vienna: AK Wien.

Becker, Joachim, and Weissenbacher, Rudy (2014): Berlin Consensus and Disintegration: Monetary Regime and Uneven Development in the EU. In: Dymarski, Włodzimierz/Frangakis, Marica/Leaman, Jeremy (eds.): The Deepening Crisis of the European Union: The Case for Radical Change. Analysis and Proposals from EuroMemo Group. Poznań: Poznań University of Economics Press, 5-32.

Becker, Joachim, and Weissenbacher, Rudy (2016): Heterodoxy from the right: Economic policy concepts of the nationalist right in Europe. Euro Memo Group: 22nd Conference on Alternative Economic Policy in Europe. Coimbra, Portugal, 15.09.-17.09.

Becker, Joachim, Franziska Disslbacher, and Rudy Weissenbacher (2015): Zwischen Deutschland und Osteuropa: Österreichs neue Mittellage. In: Beigewum (ed.): Politische Ökonomie Österreichs. Kontinuitäten und Veränderungen seit dem EU-Beitritt. Wien: Mandelbaum, 132-155.

Chase-Dunn, Christopher (ed.) (1982): Socialist States in the World System. Beverly Hills: Sage.

Chenery, Hollis (1960): Patterns of Industrial Growth. American Economic Review 50 (4), 624–654.

Crouch, Colin (2011): The Strange Non-Death of Neoliberalism. Cambridge and Malden: Polity

ECB – European Central Bank (2015): Real convergence in the euro area: evidence, theory and policy implications. In: ECB Economic Bulletin 5, 30-45.

ECB – European Central Bank: Statistical Data Warehouse, http://sdw.ecb.europe.eu

EU Commission (ed.) (n/y): AMECO database. http://ec.europa.eu/economy_finance/ameco/user/serie/SelectSerie.cfm (Sept. 8, 2017)

Eurostat (ed.) (n/y1): Glossary:Purchasing power standard (PPS). Brussels, http://ec.europa.eu/eurostat/statistics-explained/index.php/Glossary:Purchasing_power_standard_(PPS) (Sept. 8, 2017)

Eurostat (ed.) (n/y2): Glossary:Purchasing power parities (PPPs). Brussels, http://ec.europa.eu/eurostat/statistics-explained/index.php/Glossary:Purchasing_power_parities_(PPPs) (Sept. 8, 2017)

Flassbeck, Heiner/Spiecker, Friederike (2011): The Euro - Story of Misunderstanding. In: Intereconomics 46 (4), 180-187. https://doi.org/10.1007/s10272-011-0381-8

Galtung, Johan (1976): Self-Reliance: Concept, Practice and Rationale. In: Transcend International, https://www.transcend.org/galtung/papers/Self-Reliance%20-%20Concept,%20Practice%20and%20Rationale.pdf (May 23, 2017)

Garcia-Bernardo, Javier/Fichtner Jan/Takes, Frank W./Heemskerk, Eelke M. (2017): Uncovering Offshore Financial Centers: Conduits and Sinks in the Global Corporate Ownership Network. In: Scientific Reports 7, https://doi.org/10.1038/s41598-017-06322-9

Hopkins, Terence, and Wallerstein, Immanuel (1977): Patterns of Development of the Modern World-System. In: Review 1 (2), 11-145.

Kirby, Peadar (2010): Celtic Tiger in Collapse. Explaining the Weaknesses of the Irish Model. Second Edition. Basingstoke: Palgrave-Macmillan. https://doi.org/10.1057/9780230278035

Lange, Peter (1985): Semiperiphery and Core in the European Context: Reflections on the Postwar Italian Experience. In: Arrighi, Giovanni (ed.) (1985): Semiperipheral Development. The Politics of Southern Europe in the Twentieth Century. Beverly Hills, London, and New Delhi, 179-214. (=Explorations in the World-Economy 5)

Maier, Gunther/Tödtling, Franz,/Trippl, Michaela (2006): Regional- und Stadtökonomik 2. Regionalentwicklung und Regionalpolitik. 3., aktualisierte und erweiterte Auflage. Wien and New York: Springer.

Monfort, Philippe (2008): Convergence of EU regions. Measures and evolution. Brussels: European Union (=Directorate-General for Regional Policy 1/2008).

OECD (n.y.) database, outward activity of multinationals by country of location - ISIC Rev 4, and population. http://stats.oecd.org (Sept. 8, 2017)

Soja, Edward (1980): The Socio-Spatial Dialectic. In: Annals of the Association of American Geographers 70 (2), 207-225. https://doi.org/10.1111/j.1467-8306.1980.tb01308.x

Stöllinger, Roman (2016): Structural Change and global value chains in the EU. In: Empirica 43 (4), 801-829. https://doi.org/10.1007/s10663-016-9349-z

UNCTAD (ed.) (2013): World Investment Report 2013. Global Value Chains: Investment and Trade for Development. New York and Geneva.

UNCTAD (ed.) (2016): World Investment Report 2016. Investor Nationality: Policy Challenges. New York and Geneva.

UNCTAD (ed.) (2017a): World Investment Report 2017. Investment and the Digital Economy. New York and Geneva.

UNCTAD (ed.) (2017b): World Investment Report 2017: Annex Tables. http://unctad.org/en/Pages/DIAE/World%20Investment%20Report/Annex-Tables.aspx, October 13, 2017.

Wallerstein, Immanuel (1979): The Capitalist World-Economy. New York: Cambridge University Press.

Wallerstein, Immanuel (1984): The Politics of the World-Economy. New York: Cambridge University Press.

Wallerstein, Immanuel (1985): The Relevance of the Concept of Semiperiphery to Southern Europe. In: Giovanni Arrighi (ed.): Semiperipheral Development: The Politics of Southern Europe in the Twentieth Century. Berverly Hills: Sage, 531-539.

Weissenbacher, Rudy (2005): Jugoslawien. Politische Ökonomie einer Desintegration. Wien: Promedia.

Weissenbacher, Rudy (2007): Historical Considerations of Uneven Development in East Central Europe. In: Joachim Becker/Weissenbacher, Rudy (eds.): Dollarization, Euroization and Financial Instability. Central and Eastern European Countries between Stagnation and Financial Crisis? Marburg: Metropolis, 35-83.

Weissenbacher, Rudy (2008): Keeping Up Appearances: Uneven Global Development in a System of Structural Imbalances. In: Journal für Entwicklungspolitik XXIV (4), 78-121. https://doi.org/10.20446/JEP-2414-3197-24-4-78

Weissenbacher, Rudy (2015): Periphere Integration und Desintegration in Europa: Zur Aktualität der „Europäischen Dependenzschule". In: Journal für Entwicklungspolitik XXXI (3), 86–111. https://doi.org/10.20446/JEP-2414-3197-31-3-86

Weissenbacher, Rudy (2018): Peripheral integration and disintegration in Europe: the 'European dependency school' revisited. Journal of Contemporary European Studies 26 (1), 81-98. https://doi.org/10.1080/14782804.2017.1302875

Weissenbacher, Rudy (forthcoming monography): The Core-Periphery Divide in the European Union: a Dependency Perspective.

Wickham, James (2012): After the party's over: the Irish employment model and the paradoxes of non-learning. In: Lehndorff, Steffen (ed.): A triumph of failed ideas. European models of capitalism in the crisis. Brussels: ETUI, 59-77.

Young, Andrew, Matthew Higgins, and Daniel Levy (2008): Sigma Convergence versus Beta Convergence: Evidence from U.S. County-Level Data. In: Journal of Money, Credit and Banking, 40 (5), 1083-1093. https://doi.org/10.1111/j.1538-4616.2008.00148.x

ABSTRACT *Produktion und Handel werden international in großem Ausmaß von transnationalen Konzernen (TNK) organisiert. TNK verschwinden in der Betrachtung aber oft hinter Güterketten, die wiederum Möglichkeiten für eine nachholende Entwicklung durch Industrialisierungsprozesse zu eröffnen scheinen. Aber ist diese Einschätzung gerechtfertigt? Dem Dependenzparadigma folgend haben Giovanni Arrighi und Jessica Drangel die Güterkettenforschung, wie sie von der Weltsystemforschung vorgestellt wurde, angepasst und interpretiert. Ihre Forschungsergebnisse legen nahe, dass die Organisation von industrieller Produktion innerhalb der eigenen Jurisdiktion seit den 1960er Jahren nicht mehr zur Charakteristik von Zentrumsländern gehörte. Stattdessen behielten Zentrumsländer ihren Status, indem sie die globalen Güterketten kontrollierten. Die Leiter der internationalen Arbeitsteilung zu erklimmen war nur innerhalb der Sphäre der Peripherie und der Semiperipherie möglich, dies führte zu industrieller Konvergenz ohne ,Entwicklung'.*

Der Beitrag möchte zeigen, dass diese Beobachtungen auch für die heutige EU zutreffen. Er schlägt dafür eine Zentrum-(Semi-)Peripherie-Typologie vor und argumentiert, dass der Industrialisierung in den (semi-)peripheren EU-Ländern keine ,Entwicklung' (in der Sprache der EU: Konvergenz und Kohäsion) gefolgt sei: Die Leiter scheint keine oberen Sprossen zu haben. Auch EU-Zentrumsländer haben an Manufakturproduktion eingebüßt, bewahren aber ihren Status durch die Kontrolle der Güterketten. Vom Standpunkt des Dependenzparadigmas aus bedeutet ,Entwicklung' die Überwindung der kapitalistischen Produktionsweise. Kleine erste Schritte der Realpolitik könnten versuchen, das Wettbewerbsparadigma (dominiert durch TNK) herauszufordern und damit die existierenden Produktions- und Konsummuster (aus sozialen und ökologischen Gründen) infrage zu stellen.

Rudy Weissenbacher
Vienna University of Economics and Business
rweissen@wu.ac.at

Tables

	1960–69	1970–79	1980–89	1990–99	2000–09	2010s*
Germany#	99	93	84	67	61	63
USA	99	86	72	63	51	47
USA, Germany =100	74	68	64	70	60	55

Table 1: Share of manufacturing industry (UVGM) in all branches (UVGo) - Gross value added at current prices, ECU/Euro, for the USA and Germany (1960=100 and Germany=100)

Source: Own calculations based on data from the AMECO-database: http://ec.europa. eu/economy_finance/ameco/user/serie/SelectSerie.cfm

Note: Germany#: before 1991: Western Germany

2010s*: Germany: 2010-2016, USA: 2010-2014; averages over decades. For detailed information on data see Table 4.

Country	1960–69	1970–79	1980–89	1990–99	2000–09	2010–18
Bulgaria*	...	...	...	22	30	37
Romania	...	...	...	21	29	44
Croatia*	...	...	...	36	46	46
Latvia	...	...	...	28	40	50
Poland**	...	...	...	32	42	52
Hungary****	...	...	...	38	47	52
Lithuania***	...	...	...	28	42	56
Estonia****	...	...	...	28	45	57
Greece	56	77	69	68	77	57
Slovakia****	...	...	...	38	49	60
Portugal	38	46	46	61	67	60
Czech Rep.	...	...	...	57	63	64

Slovenia	...	...	...	58	70	65
Cyprus	...	...	...	68	75	67
Malta**	...	...	...	59	65	68
Spain	56	64	59	69	82	72
Italy	73	79	83	92	93	78
UK	90	79	73	84	97	85
France	76	83	82	89	95	86
Finland	67	73	79	82	98	90
Belgium	81	87	86	96	102	95
Germany#	100	100	100	100	100	100
Ireland	57	58	55	73	101	101
Austria	79	87	88	99	105	101
Sweden	104	100	94	95	107	101
Denmark	92	89	85	93	104	103
Netherlands	95	96	87	99	115	104
Luxembourg	99	102	115	154	166	143

Table 2: Gross national income (GNI) at current prices per capita (PPS), Germany=100 (average over decade)

Source: Own calculations based on data from the AMECO-database: http://ec.europa. eu/economy_finance/ameco/user/serie/SelectSerie.cfm

*Note: Data sorted by last decade, Germany=100; # Before 1991: Western Germany. Grey: Enlargements from EU15 to EU28; * 1990-1999: Average of 1995-1999, ** 1990-1999: Average of 1991-1999, *** 1990-1999: Average of 1993 and 1995-1999, ****1990-1999: Average of 1993-1999*

Country	1960–69	1970–79	1980–89	1990–99	2000–09	2010–18	Total
Bulgaria	x	x	x	P	P	P	P
Romania	x	x	x	P	P	P	P
Croatia	x	x	x	P	P	P	P
Latvia	x	x	x	P	P	P	P

RUDY WEISSENBACHER

Poland	x	x	x	P	P	P	P
Hungary	x	x	x	P	P	P	P
Lithuania	x	x	x	P	P	P	P
Estonia	x	x	x	P	P	P	P
Greece	P	SP	SP	SP	SP	P	P
Slovakia	x	x	x	P	P	P	P
Portugal	P	P	P	SP	SP	P	P
Czech Rep.	x	x	x	SP	SP	SP	SP
Slovenia	x	x	x	SP	SP	SP	SP
Cyprus	x	x	x	SP	SP	SP	SP
Malta	x	x	x	SP	SP	SP	SP
Spain	P	P	P	SP	SP	SP	SP
Italy	SP	SP	C	C	C	SP	SP
UK	C	SP	SP	C	C	C	C
France	SP	C	C	C	C	C	C
Finland	SP	SP	SP	C	C	C	C
Belgium	SP	C	C	C	C	C	C
Germany	C	C	C	C	C	C	C
Ireland	P	P	P	SP	C	C	C
Austria	SP	C	C	C	C	C	C
Sweden	C	C	C	C	C	C	C
Denmark	C	C	C	C	C	C	C
Netherlands	C	C	C	C	C	C	C
Luxembourg	C	C	C	C	C	C	C

Table 3: Core – Semiperiphery – Periphery Typology for EU28

Source: Own calculations based on data from the AMECO-database: http://ec.europa. eu/economy_finance/ameco/user/serie/SelectSerie.cfm

Note: Countries sorted by last decade, Germany=100 (cf. Table 2); before 1991: Western Germany; Grey: enlargements countries post-EU15; Bold letters: Czech Republic, Slovenia, and Malta could be counted in the periphery in 1990-1999 as could Belgium in the core in 1960-1969, but this would not change the overall assessment. For all the other bold letters, see explanations above.

Country	1960–69	1970–79	1980–89	1990–99	2000–09	2010–16
Cyprus5	...	...	...	44	34	22
Luxembourg3	...	...	68	57	40	24
Greece	40	51	52	50	45	41
UK	...	66	62	70	52	44
Malta5	...	...	...	88	71	49
France	68	65	63	68	61	50
Netherlands1	70	66	59	70	62	52
Latvia6	...	...	...	84	59	56
Portugal	68	68	75	79	67	59
Spain	...	...	75	76	71	60
Denmark2	56	55	60	70	66	61
Belgium8	...	82	75	85	78	63
Croatia5	...	...	...	82	72	64
Italy8	70	79	80	86	79	69
Estonia4	...	...	...	84	74	70
Sweden	...	78	77	88	92	76
Finland	65	77	83	100	111	77
Austria	78	78	75	85	89	83
Poland6	...	...	...	91	81	83
Lithuania5	...	...	...	80	84	86
Slovakia4	...	...	...	98	102	95
Slovenia7	...	...	...	118	105	98
Germany*	100	100	100	100	100	100
Hungary7	...	...	...	94	97	101
Romania9	...	...	...	110	103	104
Czech Rep.	...	...	...	105	112	112
Ireland	...	...	...	96	108	116

Table 4: Share of manufacturing industry (UVGM) in all branches (UVGo) - Gross value added at current prices, ECU/Euro (Germany=100)

Source: Own calculations based on data from the AMECO-database: http://ec.europa. eu/economy_finance/ameco/user/serie/SelectSerie.cfm

*Note: * Before 1991: Western Germany; data sorted by last decade; grey: enlargements countries post EU15. Strictly adhering to a three-tier system (upper three quintiles of Germany=100), the middle frame distinguishes a typology of industrialised countries (higher than 80), semi-industrialised countries (61-80), and low industrialised countries: (60 and lower)*

Data limitations: 1: 1960s=1969, 2: 1966-1969, 3: 1985-1989, 4: 1993-1999, 5: 1995-1999, 6: 1992-1999, 7: 1991-1999, 8: 2010-2015, 9: 1995-1999, 2010-2014; No data for Bulgaria

Gross value added equals output valued at basic prices less intermediate consumption at purchasers' prices. Gross value added includes consumption of fixed capital. Manufacturing industry: Nace rev.1 D

	Number of TNC in Top 100	Foreign Assets %	Foreign Sales %	Employees Abroad %
Belgium	1	3	1	2
Denmark	1	0	1	1
Finland	1	1	1	1
France	11	10	9	9
Germany	11	11	15	13
Ireland	2	2	0	0
Italy	2	3	2	0
Luxembourg	1	1	1	1
Netherlands	1	1	0	1
Spain	3	3	2	2
Sweden	1	0	1	1
United Kingdom	15	17	15	12
United States	22	21	24	27

Table 5: Share of EU TNC among 100 Largest Global Non-Financial TNC
Source: UNCTAD (2017b): Table 24, own calculations.

On the Limitations of Industrial Policies in TNC Capitalism

	1990–1999	2000–2009	2010–2016
Bulgaria	-595.24	-19056.63	-43345.96
Romania	-1423.14	-31590.49	-72085.86
Croatia	-262.50	-14337.67	-23913.29
Latvia	-458.11	-5597.61	-12578.15
Hungary	-10154.44	-52034.75	-60952.14
Poland	-8534.47	-90845.12	-170623.57
Lithuania	-637.04	-7246.16	-12473.87
Estonia	-666.34	-6952.50	-12806.53
Greece	-7423.81	-10170.25	9612.03
Portugal	-14320.44	-32534.04	-57807.89
Slovakia	-1459.03	-28161.84	-46512.01
Czech Rep.	-6755.58	-62795.21	-107341.74
Slovenia	-1463.79	-3108.21	-5075.04
Cyprus	20.62	-6708.76	-5359.88
Malta	-719.35	-22528.09	-92523.92
Spain	-56565.26	-51117.99	-31076.89
Italy	35121.94	43683.87	148084.58
UK	101842.27	575667.92	310964.46
France	96530.24	280272.64	567068.56
Finland	8184.80	29257.22	40365.78
Belgium	ND	-16182.21	-10206.43
Germany	**183788.03**	**174897.44**	**513821.46**
Austria	-5708.61	-3849.20	40069.82
Ireland	-30192.18	-68977.77	66824.28
Sweden	37129.34	37989.00	57957.92
Denmark	2259.21	15081.68	78419.82
Netherlands	54800.11	152340.07	380215.60
Luxembourg	ND	-5384.47	-4847.05

Table 6: Net FDI Stock, Average Over Decades in Millions of Current US Dollar and per capita (Germany =100)

Sources: FDI data from: UNCTAD: World Investment Report, http://unctad.org/en/ Pages/DIAE/FDI%20Statistics/World-Investment-Report-(WIR)-Annex-Tables.aspx; average over decade as given; Population data from: Eurostat: Population Main Table,

DI_PC 1990–1999 Germany = 100	FDI_PC 2000–2009 Germany = 100	FDI_PC 2010–2016 Germany = 100	GNI_PC 2010–18^e Germany =100
-3	-116	-94	37
-3	-69	-57	44
-3	-156	-89	46
-8	-116	-98	50
-43	-242	-97	52
-10	-112	-71	52
-8	-102	-66	56
-20	-240	-153	57
-31	-44	14	57
-63	-147	-87	60
-12	-247	-136	60
-29	-288	-161	64
-32	-73	-39	65
1	-430	-100	67
-85	-2649	-3444	68
-63	-56	-11	72
27	36	39	78
78	450	77	85
74	217	142	86
71	263	117	90
ND	-73	-14	95
100	**100**	**100**	**100**
-32	-22	74	101
-370	-789	228	101
187	198	95	101
19	131	220	103
158	442	357	104
ND	-551	-141	143

http://ec.europa.eu/eurostat/web/population-demography-migration-projections/popu-
lation-data/main-tables; averages over decades, last decade: 2010-17; France: popula-
tion for mainland plus Corsica, average of 2010-2013; Grey: EU enlargments post EU15.
Sorted by GNI per capita 2010-18.

Note: e: 2017&18 estimates

JOURNAL FÜR ENTWICKLUNGSPOLITIK XXXIV 3/4-2018, S. 108–142

JULIA EDER, ETIENNE SCHNEIDER
Progressive Industrial Policy – A Remedy for Europe!?

ABSTRACT *Since the global economic and financial crisis, industrial policy has enjoyed a stunning revival. In the face of the structural imbalances in the European Union, different sides have proposed industrial policy as a way to overcome the crisis and to reduce unequal development. Left forces elaborated concepts of 'progressive' industrial policy, mainly with a post-Keynesian orientation. However, does this orientation make industrial policy genuinely progressive? After introducing the key rationales and proposals, this paper makes three specific contributions to the lively current debate on progressive industrial policy: (1) adding the dimension of politics, power relations and hegemony to the discussion of progressive industrial policy; (2) starting the process of substantiating buzzwords of the current debate, such as ecological sustainability, labour and democratic participation, and gender-sensitivity and (3) taking into account the question of core-periphery relations within the EU and what can be learned from debates on the Global South. We conclude that progressive industrial policy may constitute a remedy for Europe, but that the development of a genuinely progressive industrial policy on a regional scale faces multiple difficulties. In many respects, the national and sub-regional level still seems to leave more room for manoeuvre than on the EU level.*

KEYWORDS *progressive industrial policy, Euro crisis, uneven European development, Collective Self-Reliance, social-ecological transformation*

1. The resurgence of industrial policy

Industrial policy has experienced a stunning resurgence in public debate over the past 10 years (Warwick 2013, Rodrik 2008, Plank/Staritz 2013), and was promoted to the top of the EU agenda (European Commission 2014a, 2017a, Ambroziak 2017). Industrial policy played a pivotal role in post-war economic and development policy and has continued to do so, albeit less visibly, and with a different focus, in most countries of the Global North and in the so-called Newly Industrialized Countries in the Global South. However, with the rise of neoliberalism, industrial policy was vigorously ostracised from public discourse in most countries of the Global North, and effectively banned in many parts of the Global South under structural adjustment and Washington Consensus policies. From the neoliberal perspective, industrial policy became synonymous with discretionary, pro-active, interventionist, partly even 'proto-socialist' economic policy, which 'distorts' efficient and self-regulating market allocation, making it highly prone to 'government failure' (Stiglitz et al. 2013: 6).

Probably the most important reason for the remarkable resurgence of industrial policy is the experience of the economic crisis (Warwick 2013: 10f.): Overall, highly financialised economies were hit harder by the crisis than economies with a strong industrial base (Becker/Jäger 2010, Rehfeld/Dankbaar 2015: 496). Whereas in the EU in the 2000s, for instance, the real estate and financialisation-based 'Spanish Model' with its high growth rates (López Hernández/Rodriguez 2010) had been considered as a role model, as opposed to Germany, reckoned to be the 'sick man of Europe' in the 1990s, the exact opposite perception prevails now. Along these lines, while the desirability of visions such as that of a 'postindustrial society' have been increasingly called into question, recent studies re-emphasise long-held, but temporarily ousted, arguments that the industrial sector is both more innovative and provides on average higher wages than in the often-precarious service sectors (Rehfeld/Dankbaar 2015: 497). Moreover, in light of the search for a new capitalist development model, the industrial sector is perceived as a potential source for growth and employment in face of widespread economic stagnation (Warwick 2013: 7), prompting the European Commission to actively aim at increasing the industrial sector's share of GDP in the EU from 15 to 20%. At the same time, growing world market competition from China and other emerging economies has led to a rethinking of the significance of retaining industrial capacities in the European core economies (Warwick 2013: 7). Finally, yet importantly, the industrial policy has resurfaced as a transition policy towards sustainability, such as in the German 'Energiewende' strategy (i.e. the 'turn' towards renewable energies) (Rehfeld/Dankbaar 2015: 494).

Against this background, a great number of works have been published on the revival of industrial policy. In some of them, a call for 'progressive' industrial policy has been put forward and actively supported by various left-wing organisations and think tanks. A particular concern for these contributions are industrial policy strategies that aim to overcome economic asymmetries and uneven development in Europe. However, this call for progressive industrial policy may at the same time be surprising, as industrial policy has been met with various reservations by the Left. For one thing, industrial policy has been considered unfit to address the ecological crisis, as this would require not 'more', but 'less' industry (Thie 2013). It has also been doubted that industrial policy could – in the current context of rapid technological innovation and digitalisation – still contribute to significantly increase full-time employment opportunities in the manufacturing sector. Moreover, from a feminist perspective, industrial policy might be associated with the goal of maintaining and expanding Fordist-type, male-breadwinner employment relations in the industrial sector while disregarding female workers in the service and care sector.

Yet, in our view, these reservations tend to misinterpret the scope and function of industrial policy and the manufacturing sector as such. Indeed, industrial policy is not synonymous with (re-)industrialisation, i.e. an expansion of the manufacturing sector *per se*. Rather, it refers to policies intentionally aiming to promote *structural change* in the manufacturing sector. Instead of obstructing strategies to address the ecological crisis, an industrial policy which promotes a profound structural change of the manufacturing sector is indispensable for any meaningful social-ecological transformation that seriously tackles currently unsustainable forms of production. Secondly, any progressive policy which aims at expanding and improving public social infrastructure (such as in the health and care sector and also in the area of public transport) needs to channel resources from other sectors into these areas. As a result, if an industrial policy is gender-sensitive (see below), upgrading social and care service on the one hand and fostering industrial development on the other hand are not mutually exclusive, but rather support each other. Most importantly, however, industrial policy arguably provides the crucial instruments to overcome import

Julia Eder, Etienne Schneider

dependencies, which lie at the heart of both global inequality and the prevailing economic asymmetries between core and periphery in Europe.

Thus, the emerging debate on 'progressive industrial policy' in Europe is highly important. However, our impression is that the notion 'progressive' has generally been poorly defined. As a result, a range of different approaches use the tag 'progressive'. Therefore, this paper addresses the question: What makes industrial policy actually progressive? After introducing the key rationales and proposals in the lively current debate on progressive industrial policy, we attempt to make three specific contributions: (1) adding the dimension of *politics, power relations and hegemony* to the discussion of progressive industrial policy (section 3); (2) starting to fill out buzzwords in the current debate, including terms such as ecological sustainability, labour and democratic participation and gender-sensitivity with content (section 4); and (3) taking into account the question of core-periphery relations within the EU and what can be learned from debates on the Global South, for example, regarding strategic protectionism and peripheral cooperation (section 5). Thereby, we also problematise the trade-offs which might arise out of (possibly) conflicting objectives, particularly between job creation through industrial growth vs. social-ecological transformation, as well as between reducing dependencies in core-periphery relations on the one hand vs. technological catch-up on the other.

A necessarily brief remark on the definition of industrial policy: despite a variety of very broad understandings of industrial policy which are particularly prevalent in the Global North and define virtually any intentional, targeted economic policy as industrial policy, it seems more instructive to use a narrower definition of industrial policy here. This understanding is more common in the Global South and restricts the term to policies predominantly and intentionally aiming to promote structural change in the *manufacturing* sector.

2. What is progressive industrial policy in Europe?

The current debate on progressive industrial policy in Europe is shaped, on the one hand, by proposals from trade union organisations, particularly by proposals from the European Trade Union Confederation on industrial policy (ETUC 2015, 2017) and the German Trade Union Confederation's call for a "Marshall Plan for Europe" (DGB 2012). On the other hand, various publications by other left-wing organisations and think tanks, such as the Rosa Luxemburg Foundation, Euromemo or *transform!* have been explicitly calling for "alternative" (transform!europe 2015), "left" (Gauthier/Benatouil 2014, see also Ramírez/Benatouil 2014) or "progressive" industrial policy (Pianta et al. 2016; Rosa Luxemburg Foundation 2017) for the European Union. In these interventions and proposals, industrial policy is generally considered – if understood, designed and implemented in a progressive way – as a powerful and promising economic policy alternative to the dominant austerity-driven crisis management, capable of rebalancing the prevailing imbalances within the EU and the Eurozone as well as of reducing the weight of the financial sector vis-à-vis the so called real economy (ETUC 2017: 3, Benatouil 2017: 23).

An EU-wide investment plan, financed by institutions such as the European Investment Bank (EIB) and the EU Structural Funds, forms the cornerstone of a progressive industrial policy agenda in many proposals (Gauthier/Benatouil 2014: 5f.; transform!europe *2015*). So far, these proposals do not significantly go beyond the already existing Juncker Plan and the EU Commission's proposals, only insofar as they call for the allocation of more resources to the industrialisation programme, lower interest rates for long-term investment and/or a better coordination with national programmes (Troost 2017, DGB 2012).

A more significant point of departure from the existing European investment strategy is, first, the call for investment in 'green' production, which figures prominently in the current debate on progressive industrial policy. This includes investment in energy-efficiency and renewable energies (particularly transmission and distribution networks) (DGB 2012), as well as the "setting up of a European value chain for e-mobility" to promote European industrial leadership and European champions in these (and other) sectors (ETUC 2017: 4, see also Diem25 n.d.: 9), and even calls for a re-localisation of production (Benatouil 2017: 22).

Secondly, many proposals advocate a European investment strategy with the explicit goal of reducing imbalances between different regions and countries in Europe, i.e. "to strengthen productivity growth through strategic industrial policies in the countries of the EU periphery" in an attempt to "rebuild productive capacity and to improve the competitiveness of the deficit countries" (Euromemo 2017: 13). Although not explicitly spelled out in most proposals, this would require the fostering of new industrial capacities, the diversification of production, and the establishment of inter-sectoral and inter-industrial linkages, particularly in the de-industrialised Southern European periphery (cf. Whitfield et al. 2015: 5).

Thirdly, many proposals point to the crucial role played by labour in industrial policy. This does not only include an emphasis on the significance of pay rises as a demand factor in industrial policy or calls for a stricter protection of the EU Single Market against so-called dumping methods (ETUC 2017). It also refers to job preservation and workers' participation in the transition towards 'green' production and digitalisation (ETUC 2017: 3, see also ETUC 2011, Benatouil 2017: 22). These proposals call for the combination of workers' participation with a 'democratic' industrial policy, i.e. an industrial policy where strategic decisions are made based on "democratic consulting" (Benatouil 2017: 21).

In the context of this ongoing debate, the most comprehensive and detailed proposal so far for progressive industrial policy in Europe was put forward by Pianta et al. (2016) in their study *What is to be produced – The Making of a New Industrial Policy for Europe* for the Rosa Luxemburg Foundation. Pianta et al. (2016: 25ff.) present a decalogue for progressive industrial policy, which encompasses: 1) static efficiency (optimal use of the available resources); 2) dynamic efficiency (establishment of new sectors with the favoured growth potential); 3) democracy and power diffusion; 4) the design of appropriate technologies; 5) restriction of the role of the financial sector; 6) disarmament; 7) support of employment; 8) improvement of ecological sustainability; 9) fair distribution of the benefits; and 10) balancing unequal regional development in Europe.

The underlying policy rationale is to increase demand and to advance structural change of economy and society in order to achieve the ecological transition, to reach a balance between public and private activities, and to foster European cohesion. Pianta et al. propose that activities in the fields of environment and energy, knowledge and information and computer technologies (ICTs), as well as in health and welfare, should be prioritised. For this purpose, they suggest traditional tools of industrial policy, mainly based on strong state activity. Publicly owned or controlled enterprises and organisations play a key role, while state institutions fund the industrial policy projects. Along these lines, public R&D complements the public support of dynamic firms as well as public procurement programmes, and the creation of an appropriate institutional context is pivotal (Pianta et al. 2016: 28ff.).

Many of these suggestions are very valuable. Still, we think that the presented proposals and concepts have weaknesses regarding three main points: 1) They neglect questions of hegemony and balance of forces which shape and sustain industrial policies; 2) the role of labour, as well as the exact scope and processes of social-ecological transformation and democratic inclusion are not defined – gender sensitivity in particular is hardly ever mentioned; and, lastly, 3) the question of how to treat (unequal) world and regional market integration and the inner-European dependency relations (selective delinking? peripheral cooperation?) is either omitted or inadequately accounted for. In the remaining article, we will discuss each of these points in detail.

3. Social relations of forces and hegemony – The politics of industrial policy

Probably one of the most decisive deficits in the current debate on progressive industrial policy is the lack of sensitivity to the *politics* of industrial policy. For instance, while Pianta et al. (2016: 25) critically discuss "opaque connections between economic and political power" which reduce "democratic spaces", and point to the importance of the balance of power, they do not specifically address the question of how various fractions of capital (and labour) struggle to assert their respective interests through industrial policy strategies carried out by the state and embedded into relations of hegemony. Thus, many of the proposals advanced in the debate on progressive industrial policy are indeed highly important, but these proposals will remain ultimately ineffective if they are conceived in a vacuum outside of social relations of forces and hegemony, as Whitfield et al. (2015) and Raza et al. (2016) in particular convincingly argued.

As much as industrial policy is a question of economics, it is also a question of politics and specific constellations of class compromise – particularly in the case of progressive industrial policy, which aims at profound structural transformations of the economy and thus necessarily triggers conflicts between social classes and different factions of capital (Raza et al. 2016: 4). As a rule of thumb, "the more targeted the policy is and therefore the easier it is to identify the winners and the losers, the more immediate conflict it is likely to provoke" (Chang/Andreoni 2016: 28). Therefore, for progressive industrial policy to be more than an idealistic 'wish list', it has to take into account three pivotal, necessarily rather abstract – because highly variegated across specific contexts – aspects, which comprise the politics of industrial policy.

First, the given production system of an economy (country or region) and its international embeddedness implies (though not entirely determines) a specific configuration of societal interests and capital fractions (Raza et al. 2016). Accordingly, various fractions of capital can be differentiated according to their base of income (industry, finance, trade...) and according to their degree of internationalisation and dependence on foreign capital (Poulantzas 1978[1974], Sablowski 2010a). Through employment relations, the fractionation of capital corresponds with a fractionation of labour. Thus, different economic structures predispose different political alliances, which either endorse or oppose industrial policy in its general or specific forms. For instance, in an economy predominantly based on the extraction and export of natural resources, the economically dominant capital factions will either seek to block industrial policy which changes the economic structure and subsequently diminishes their economic power altogether, or they will push in the direction of an extraction-based industrial policy and industrialisation (such as oil refineries).

Secondly, the state as the driving force is not an independent social institution outside of the broader societal relations of forces but, as Poulantzas famously argued, a specific material "condensation of a relationship of forces between classes and class fractions" (2000[1978]: 132). This core tenet of materialist state theory implies that industrial policy is neither determined by the self-interest of politicians or civil servants, as argued by neoliberal critics of industrial policy, nor by a Weberian rational-legal bureaucratic rule, such as in the Development State literature (Whitfield et al. 2015: 7, Evans 1995). Rather, the state, as the strategic, highly selective terrain for the formulation and implementation of industrial policy, condenses the relation of forces between various economic and political forces, such as capital fractions, fractions of labour, political parties, civil society actors (social movements, faith-based institutions, media, NGOs), and the state bureaucracy and international organisations and donors (such as the IMF) (Raza et al. 2016: 6).

Based on a materialist state-theoretical approach to industrial policy, two decisive strategic questions arise: first, which alliances between key social actors and stakeholders are both congruent and strong enough to support progressive industrial policy? And, secondly, how can the selectivity of the state be altered so that industrial policy bodies are capable of withstanding and mediating the severe social conflicts which inevitably arise (Chang/Andreoni 2016: 28ff.)? Currently, such a progressive alliance would need to be forged by trade unions, Left parties and NGOs, social movements, and even partially capital in specific branches of industry. However, the notion that the state is a material condensation of a relationship of forces does not imply that industrial policy is merely a reflection of the existing social relations of forces. While these relations set up a corridor for options, progressive industrial policy can be pivotal in successively changing the relations of forces through targeted interventions which, for instance, weaken the basis of accumulation of individual capital fractions and change the overall economic incentive and ownership structure. To this end, at least, specific state apparatuses which carry out these industrial policy interventions need to attain and defend, as Peter Evans (1995) famously argued, "embedded autonomy". This means that they dispose over in-depth knowledge of industrial sectors and production but are not prone to being captured by specific capital fractions and clientelistic networks, thus forming so called "pockets of efficiency" within the state[1].

Lastly and *thirdly*, however, the effectiveness and success of progressive industrial policy is not just a question of 'pockets of efficiency' (although they might be an important entry point) or 'political settlements' between ruling elites, as argued by the Political Survival of Ruling Elites approach (Khan 2010). Rather, it is ultimately a question of societal hegemony, i.e. broadly shared norms, values, attitudes and ideas, underpinned by a broad material compromise, which sustains a specific model of economic development[2] (Opratko 2014, Raza et al. 2016: 8). Broad societal and ultimately hegemonic support for industrial policy strategies which aim at far-reaching transformations is, in turn, a crucial precondition for an industrial policy which is *coherent* with other components of economic policy. The importance of coherence in industrial policy has been particularly stressed in institutionalist approaches, emphasising that industrial policy targets need to be consistent with a variety of other fields, such as education policies, exchange rate policies, monetary policy, trade policies, interest rate policy, infrastructure policies, energy policy, technology policies, financial policies (particularly de-financialisation), as well as policies aiming at care relations and service sectors related to industrial production (Chang/Grabel 2004: 74f.; Cimoli et al. 2008: 10; Pianta et al. 2016: 73). Moreover, redistributive policies need to make sure that industrial policy, mostly supply-side focused, is sustained by an adequate and corresponding development of effective demand (Chang/Andreoni 2016: 25ff.).

On the regional level, such as in the European context, the set of actors becomes even more complex, and power relations shift towards actors who can organise their interests across borders. Bob Jessop (2012: 5f.) argues that social struggles characterise region building. In this process, different groups try to push their preferred strategy in the regional integration project (according to their own interests). This finds expression on the institutional level. Regional integration typically leads to the establishment of a new level of decision making which surpasses the nation states. While intergovernmental bodies are still composed of national government representatives, supranational ones – such as the European Commission – have no direct link to them. The institutional structures of regional integration projects – and specifically the weight of supranational structures and actors in relation to national and intergovernmental bodies and actors – are highly relevant for the relation of forces between different classes and class fractions. For example, a bias towards executive bodies facilitates the exercise of influence through lobby groups, compared to democratically elected representatives. In general terms, the political influence of labour organisations is in an inferior position compared to (export-oriented and financial) capital groups, which seek to promote their favoured accumulation strategy in the region (Becker 2006: 12ff.; 23). The EU represents a particularly advanced expression of these processes of transnationalisation and internationalisation that alter the overall selectivity of the state in favour of capital (cf. Sandbeck/Schneider 2014). Along these lines, the EU has been theorised as a "second order condensation of societal power relations" (Bieling /Brand 2015: 193), i.e. a supranational layer of condensation shaped by national as well as supra- and transnational forces which rebounds on the first order condensation on the national terrain of EU member states. As a result, policy space for progressive alternatives is severely restricted, not only economically, but also politically and legally, especially in countries of the European periphery (see also section 5).

The implementation of a progressive policy programme in the EU would consequently require the strengthening of labour interests relative to capital interests on the European level. Therefore, trade unions would need to become key players as mediating organisations, because "industrial policy could (...) only be progressive as long as it allows and contributes to labour empowerment" (Durand 2017: 11). Durand (2017: 10) argues – referring to the Global South – that even well-designed progressive industrial policy programmes are prone to fail if labour autonomy is not sufficiently developed, because this is a necessary precondition to pressure the capital side. We argue that this also holds for the European Union. However, a further problem in this context relates to the highly diverse picture of labour organisations, whose relations reflect, *inter alia*, the centre-periphery relations in Europe. In reference to Schmalz and Dörre (2014), those differences could be analysed according to the diverging institutional, organisational, structural and associative power of particular trade unions in the bigger set of European industrial relations. However, due to the lack of space, we cannot provide such an analysis here. We will therefore focus on the most important basis for the implementation of progressive industrial policy at the EU level: the creation of transnational solidarity.

While successful European transnational solidarity practices have sporadically surged (Bieler 2014), Las Heras (2015, 2018) discusses several problems related to their emergence, of which the "predominance of national and local micro-corporatist interests in opposition to a cross-country solidaristic 'European identity'" is specifically relevant (Las Heras 2015: 101f.). Particularly in European core countries, such as Germany and Austria, cross-class alliances in the form of corporatist arrangements manage to push so called national interests at the expense of workers' solidarity along the value chain. As Becker et al. (2015: 92) highlight, there was, particularly in the wake of the recent global financial and economic crisis, no basis for efficient Europe-wide labour action, for example, against the implementation of austerity measures in Greece. Arguably, progressive industrial policy on a European level would require active productive reconstruction and transformation in the Southern, Eastern and South-Eastern European peripheries in different forms (see for this, Landesmann/ Stöllinger 2018). However, such policy reforms, particularly the establishment of sizeable transfer mechanisms, are rather unlikely if those who account for the bulk of tax revenues under current distribution settings, i.e. workers from the core countries, do not support them. Still, we agree with Bieler (2014: 122) who defends a dialectical, not deterministic approach towards transnational solidarity: "Whether different labour movements engage in relations of transnational solidarity is not pre-determined by the structuring conditions of the capitalist social relations of production, but ultimately depends on the outcome of class struggle." Trade unions could act as drivers and mediators of strategies of industrial conversion, but in order to do so they would need to overcome obstacles to the transnational coordination of their actions, as well as to start to organise effective public campaigns promoting alternatives to austerity (Schmalz/Dörre 2014: 234).

4. Crosscutting issues: ecological sustainability, democratic participation, labour issues, and gender-sensitivity

Several crosscutting issues are at the core of progressive industrial policy: (i) ecological sustainability, (ii) democratic participation, (iii) labour issues and (iv) gender-sensitivity. However, it is far from clear in the current debate what these buzzwords precisely mean.

(i) As mentioned above, one of the reasons for the comeback of industrial policy is the rising awareness that a fundamental structural transformation, particularly of the industrial sector, is required in order to tackle the looming ecological crisis (Rehfeld/Dankbaar 2015: 494). Along these lines, the notion of 'green' industrial policy has even made its way into the mainstream debate (see f.i. Rodrik 2014, SGIP 2016). In which way, then, is ecological sustainability a defining principle of progressive industrial policy as opposed to conventional approaches?

In many instances, 'green' industrial policy refers to strategies to foster 'green growth' and to build a 'green competitive advantage', i.e. to establish lead sectors in sustainable technology in world market competition (Rodrik 2014: 473, Europe 2020 (2010): 12). In this sense, 'green' industrial policy can be regarded as part of the 'Green Economy' debate (Brand/ Wissen 2014) that promises "techno-scientific solutions" (Butzko/Hinterberger 2017: 28): electric mobility, agro-fuels and other renewable energy sources are promoted as new promising fields for capital accumulation and economic growth in light of an increasingly stagnant global capitalism. Against this background, the mainstream understanding of 'green' industrial policy aims at correcting 'market failures' which inhibit the full potential of the 'Green Economy', such as R&D externalities, particularly concerning 'green' technologies, or the inadequate representation of 'ecological costs' in market-generated prices and incentives identified in the neoclassical ecological economics debate (Rodrik 2014: 470f., SGIP 2016: 15f., Lütkenhorst et al. 2014: 10ff., Binder et al. 2001). The entire promise of reconciling growth with sustainability rests, however, on an ultimately flawed 'fantasy of dematerialisation', i.e. the assumption that economic growth, particularly in the manufacturing sector, can be decoupled from material resource use. While a relative decoupling through more efficient technology is of course possible and, indeed, desirable, an absolute decoupling is arguably impossible in face of the exponential nature of growth and the ineluctable materiality of production[3] as well as so called rebound-effects[4] (Jackson 2009).

Considering this inherent impossibility of 'sustainable growth', progressive industrial policy must therefore aim at a profound *social-ecological transformation* (Butzko/Hinterberger 2017), which needs to be more profound and disruptive than a gradual transition into a so-called 'Green Economy'. As Ulrich Brand (2016) argues, however, the term 'transformation' itself is highly blurry and builds the conceptual foundation of a new 'critical orthodoxy' which acknowledges the severity of the ecological crisis and the need for comprehensive transformation (see for example IPCC 2014: 3), without, however, adequately taking into account the "structural obstacles to far-reaching transformation processes" such as "the ongoing expansion of the production and consumption of unsustainable commodities" and "a focus on economic growth at almost any cost" (Brand 2016:

Julia Eder, Etienne Schneider

25). In terms of industrial policy, these structural obstacles particularly include the difficulties of restructuring so-called 'brown' industries such as the automotive industry, and of disempowering the well-entrenched capital fractions behind them. Along these lines, while some of the instruments discussed under 'green' industrial policy are, of course, relevant for progressive industrial policy in order to promote sustainable technologies and associated patterns of industrial production, at least as important for progressive industrial policy are strategies to *disrupt* existing pathways of industrial production and associated norms of consumption (Lütkenhorst et al. 2014, Sablowski 2010b). These industrial policy interventions need to go hand in hand with complementary structural policies (regarding energy infrastructure, transport systems and settlement patterns). A particular challenge for progressive industrial policy is that such a profound restructuring not only devalues extensive amounts of capital already invested into existing paths of industrial production, but also endangers employment in a variety of sectors and therefore potentially provokes resistance by workers and trade unions. What is crucial, therefore, are comprehensive strategies of *industrial conversion* (Candeias 2011, Röttger 2011, Blöcker 2014). These need to include social compensation for workers, programmes of retraining and redeployment, welfare state and unemployment benefits, as well as an improvement of qualitative components of living standard, such as work time reduction, biographical security and less alienating forms of work (Chang/Andreoni 2016: 32).

(ii) The call for 'democratic' industrial policy in the debate on progressive industrial policy is at least as vague as the call for an ecological dimension. Indeed, Pianta et al. (2016: 25) argue in favour of "the use of public action for opening up new spaces for democratic practices in the deliberation of common priorities, decision making processes and in action aimed at reshaping economic activities". Furthermore, they state that "democratic participation, representation and power diffusion" should become basic principles for the governance of institutions responsible for industrial policy, as well as for the elaboration and implementation of such a policy. However, they do not specify further which shape this could take. In this regard, the emerging discussion about progressive industrial policy could benefit from the rich debates about economic democracy (Demirović 2007, Vilmar/Sattler 1978). While Holcombe (2011: 3) argues that industrial policy favours capital interests whereas economic democracy has a bias towards the working class, we do not necessarily see these as opposites. However, progressive industrial policy would not only have to promote economic democracy at company level, for instance by making targeted support for specific industries conditional upon the introduction and expansion of micro-level democratic elements, such as co- and workers' self-determination (Hirschel/Schulten 2011). For industrial policy to be truly democratic, the meso-economic design of industrial policy itself would have to be designed democratically. This would, of course, require a complex process of priority determination, as was, for instance, already envisioned and discussed in depth in the debate on democratic investment planning and investment control in the 1970s (Zinn 1976).

(iii) In recent years, trade unions and other labour organisations have increasingly emphasised the potential of industrial policy to create jobs and to foster favourable working conditions (AK/ÖGB 2015; ETUC 2015; ITUC 2016; Nübler 2011). Considering that the labour movement has its roots in different branches of industrial production, and that, in many European countries, trade unions are still anchored there, this is not astonishing (Schmalz/Dörre 2014: 218). However, the neoliberal tide, as well as the decline of employees in manufacturing due to technological progress and offshoring, have weakened their influence in Europe (Frege/Kelly 2008: 181; Nachtwey 2017). Curiously, trade unions have shown signs of revitalisation in the wake of the recent economic and financial crisis (see, for example, Schmalz/Dörre 2014). Due to this recent recovery and their strong presence in different industry branches, they are in a suitable position to influence industrial policy elaboration and implementation according to labour interests. In addition, other labour organisations, such as the International Labour Organisation (ILO), are engaged in the topic. In a report for ILO, Nübler (2011: 20ff.) criticised that the role of employment was barely discussed in conceptions of industrial policy. Furthermore, Nübler pointed to empirical research, which concluded that labour market institutions – such as trade unions – played an important role in the creation of sound working conditions. Along similar lines, a position paper of the Austrian Chamber of Labour and the Austrian Trade Union Confederation (2015: 7) claimed that industrial policy should contribute to

JULIA EDER, ETIENNE SCHNEIDER

the overriding goal of high-quality and well-paid jobs based on a sustainable mode of production.

In this context, one major goal of progressive industrial policy needs to be the preservation or creation of jobs. However, even an ambitious progressive industrial policy would nowadays not be able to provide full time jobs for all unemployed and underemployed people in Europe. Moreover, considering ecological constraints, progressive industrial policy would need to carefully select the branches of industry in which it strives for the promotion of employment opportunities through industrial growth. At the same time, it would need to determine others which should fade out of production (congruent with the objective of social-ecological transformation). Clearly, this is where labour and ecological issues potentially collide. Therefore, we need trade unions as mediating actors, which ensure that workers are not left behind. In this respect, it would be reasonable to include the goal of worktime reduction in manufacturing (as well as in the economy as a whole) in the debate on progressive industrial policy.

Furthermore, progressive industrial policy should aspire to the improvement of working conditions. However, research showed that different forms of economic upgrading, to which industrial policy often aims, do not automatically imply social upgrading for the workers (Barrientos 2011: 323f.). This accounts for other industrial policy measures, too. In our view, the promotion of public ownership of the means of production – besides the support of cooperatives – as suggested by Pianta et al. (2016: 31f.; 79f.), is crucial in this context. More specifically, and going beyond Pianta et al., we argue that the public ownership or control of companies in key sectors facilitates benchmark-setting processes concerning high labour standards. Moreover, the accomplishment of best practice guidelines concerning working conditions should become a precondition for the eligibility for support through industrial policy programmes. However, public ownership also becomes very relevant when we talk about the distribution of the benefits of industrial policy. As Pianta et al. (2016: 79f.) argue, a big share of public ownership prevents the general public from financing structural change while the profits remain in just a few hands.

(iv) Finally, yet importantly, if we ask who benefits from industrial policy, it is crucial to introduce a gender dimension to our analysis. Macro and meso-economic policies are often perceived as being 'gender-neutral'.

This also accounts for industrial policy, the most prominent advocates of which (Chang 2013, Cimoli et al. 2008, Rodrik 2008; 2014, Stiglitz et al. 2013) do not discuss gender relations in manufacturing. Likewise, the current debate in the European Left on progressive industrial policy does not dedicate much attention to this topic. However, for the design of progressive industrial policy, it is important to bear in mind that industrial policy measures affect women and men differently, due to a variety of reasons. The most obvious reason lies in the distribution of the male and female labour force in the European Union across sectors. In 2015, according to the International Labour Organization (2017), 77% of employees in manufacturing were male. This share has barely changed since 2000, when it was 75%. However, the share of female entrepreneurs in manufacturing reached in 2012 only 20%, as reported by the European Commission (2014b: 96). Thus, positive and negative effects of strategic industrial policy directly affect far more men than women. Furthermore, the membership composition of industrial trade unions, which still tend to be mainly comprised of male, white, full time workers (Bieler 2014: 123), could exacerbate the inclusion of the gender dimension in industrial policy formulation.

However, exclusively setting the aim of increasing the female share of employees in manufacturing provides no solution on its own. This is due to the processes of devaluation – expressed, *inter alia*, in decreasing wages and prestige – which researchers have discovered to set in when industries feminise (Aulenbacher 2010: 150). Furthermore, technological conditions of production are drivers of (de-)feminisation (Tejani and Milberg 2016: 31ff.; 45f.). For instance, technological upgrading within labour-intensive industries – that is, the technical rationalisation of the production process – was in most countries around the world the driver of defeminisation in manufacturing (Kucera/Tejani 2014: 570; 578f.). Apparently, employers preferred male workers for technologically more sophisticated jobs. Tejani and Milberg (2016: 45f.) assume this is due to gender norms, which designate men as being more apt for such jobs. However, they add that women might also lack on-the-job training and/or the necessary skills (partially due to pre-market discrimination in education). In Europe, these findings deserve special attention in regard to increasing digitalisation and the evolution of Industry 4.0.

Julia Eder, Etienne Schneider

In the light of those findings, the call for 'gender-sensitive' industrial policy has intensified (ITUC 2016: 2; Seguino et al. 2010: 15; UNIDO 2015: 6). Nevertheless, concrete suggestions appear rather disappointing considering the current state of research. Seguino et al. (2010: 15) suggest the stimulation of productivity growth in female-dominated industries, the promotion of strategic industries, which can provide good wage opportunities for male and female workers, and the encouragement of full employment through demand-side management policies. We argue, however, that those initiatives are not sufficient in view of the dynamics described above. Additional measures could prescribe that firms or branches only qualify for support through industrial policy under certain circumstances (as it is the case with ecological standards). Such criteria could encompass a low/decreasing gender wage gap on the firm or industry level, a trend to feminisation or – at least – a stable share of female workers on the branch level, the requirement of a specific share of women in leading positions on the firm level, the provision of childcare facilities in the firm, and so on.

However, several obstacles complicate the implementation of such measures. For example, it is striking that it is usually easier for transnational corporations to comply with such requirements due to their size and available budget than for small and medium enterprises. Moreover, the enforcement of feminisation would lead to the displacement of male workers in the context of a stagnating or shrinking manufacturing sector, which would further undermine the emergence of workers' solidarity. Arguably, progressive industrial policy should not aggravate conflicts between different groups of workers. Therefore, such policy would require the call for wage equality across sectors so that non-manufacturing jobs become more attractive. Furthermore, it would be crucial to coordinate (gender-sensitive) industrial policy with other policies in the framework of a broader development strategy, which also considers the reproductive sphere, particularly, the care economy.

5. World and regional market integration

While all cross-cutting issues have in common the fact that they are undertheorised and highly-controversial, an arguably even larger blind spot concerns the analysis of core-periphery dependency relations inside Europe and strategies to reduce and eventually overcome them. While the industrial policy literature has frequently problematised the subordinated integration of peripheral regions of the Global South into the capitalist world market along industrial value chains (e.g. Barrientos et al., Gereffi and Rossi 2011; Chang/Andreoni 2016: 42ff.), this has rarely been the case for the European Union. Interestingly, also in left-wing publications, the current debate does not mainly revolve around the highly delicate question of appropriate degrees of the regional and international insertion of the European periphery. Progressive approaches to industrial policy, such as Pianta et al. (2016), do indeed problematise the divergence between centre and periphery in the EU, and advocate EU Structural Funds and cohesion policy. However, they do not challenge as such the integration process of peripheral European economies into the orbit of the dominant production systems of core countries (particularly Germany and, to a lesser extent, France).

Becker et al. (2015: 85ff.) problematise this integration process and point to three major phases of de-industrialisation for the Southern European periphery: First, the establishment of the European Single Market in 1993 intensified the asymmetric relations in the European Union. On the one hand, the subordinate integration of the Southern periphery into the European division of labour reduced the economic links between the peripheral economies and has since increasingly led to an economic orientation towards the core. On the other, the liberalisation of cross-border movement of goods, services, workforce and capital in the EU eroded the weaker industrial production systems, particularly in the Southern Periphery (see also Schneider 2017: 27ff.; Secchi 1982). Moreover, the introduction of the Single Market simultaneously restricted the room for manoeuvre for industrial policy, especially via EU competition policy (Buch-Hansen/Wigger 2011; Landesmann/Stöllinger 2018: 27-28). This led to a partial deindustrialisation of those countries (Becker et al. 2015: 87). In a second stage, the introduction of the Euro brought devastating effects for the Southern periphery. The common currency deprived them of the option to use monetary policy (devaluation) to increase their competitiveness, which led to a further decline of industrial capacities. The third phase started with the economic and financial crisis, which significantly decreased industrial production in these countries even further. Compared to the pre-crisis level (2007), industrial production had only reached 77.7% in Spain, 78.1% in Greece and 83.8% in Portugal by 2017 (Sablowski et al. 2018). This asymmetric economic integration has deeply transformed the class relations in the core as well as in the periphery. While it strengthened export-oriented capital fractions in the core countries and – through corporatist arrangements – also labour in these sectors, Otto Holman (1996) has shown that this process was supported and actively pursued by transnationally oriented fractions of capital in the peripheries, especially those of finance capital. Through FDI, fractions of labour in the periphery have also benefitted from European economic integration, even though regional integration has in general led to an erosion of industrial production capacities in these countries.

Our following arguments, for several reasons, focus specifically on the Southern European periphery. First, they are the longest members of all peripheral EU countries. Second, they have no socialist legacy like the Central and Eastern European Countries (CEE), which included a specific type of industrial development during socialism and a peculiar transition to capitalism. Lastly, the problems connected to deindustrialisation are currently most pressing in the South of Europe: Simonazzi et al. (2013) and Landesmann and Stöllinger (2018: 19-23) show that, while the Viségrad countries[5] in particular constitute the lower tiers of supply chains stretching to the production systems of the core countries (especially Germany), the Southern periphery is increasingly marginalised within European economic relations. Hence, how can progressive industrial policy contribute to change the peripheral status of Southern European countries?

Considering the current situation, we identify two potential ways to overcome the imbalances on the European level in a progressive way. The first one would be a comprehensive European solution in the form of a transfer union. Several post-Keynesian scholars and activists have already raised this proposal (see section 1 of this paper). The support of the Southern periphery would consist of significant transfer payments to support structural change of their economies towards partial re-industrialisation. Strategic industrial policy would represent a key element of such a proposal. Crucially, this approach does not question the integration of peripheral economies into the Single Market and the world market as such, and, consequently, does not consider partial delinking from the core countries as a viable option, especially for smaller economies. In our view, there are two major problems associated with this. First, such a proposal would need the decisive support of the core countries (of capital and labour alike) to set up a transfer union. Currently, we see no indications that this is or will be the case, even in the long term (Schneider/Syrovatka 2017). Secondly, the prevailing dependency relations not only damaged the formerly existing industrial capacities in the past; they will also constrain future re-industrialisation strategies (Becker et al. 2015: 92), especially as industries are usually not competitive in the beginning, and need protection until they blossom (Chang/Andreoni 2016: 15). The European Single Market, however, impedes such strategic protectionism. Furthermore, the common currency restricts the room for manoeuvre of the periphery. Under such conditions, the countries of the Southern peripheries would find it at the very least difficult to develop new industries, even if transfer payments were significantly increased.

Bearing this in mind, we think it is crucial to dedicate more attention to the question of protectionism from a left perspective in order to formulate more far-reaching strategies (for the differences between left-wing and right-wing protectionism see Komlosy 2017). While the spread of neoliberalism discredited the use of trade barriers as a policy tool (around the world), right-wing forces in the United States and in the European Union have recently come back to the issue. In May 2017, the newly elected French president Macron introduced the topic of smart protectionism in public discourse (essentially directed against the growing Chinese influence in Europe; Chassany 2017). The Left, by contrast, has so far hesitated to start a discussion about the advantages and disadvantages of protectionist measures in Europe. In our view, however, this is indispensable. It would constitute a way of fundamentally reversing the central lines of the current debate on a 'multi-speed' Europe, which foresees that core and peripheries develop the European integration project at different paces.

　　　　　　Julia Eder, Etienne Schneider

While the integration model of a 'multi-speed' Europe currently discussed cannot represent a progressive alternative, it is already an informal reality in economic and political terms. Consequently, the crucial question is whether the 'multi-speed' concept can be converted into a progressive proposal by framing it in a new way. If the call for 'multi-speed' integration were to recognise the diverging levels of economic development in the European Union and allow the peripheries to 'curb the pace' of integration in order to protect their economies in strategic sectors, it could reduce the asymmetric relations and, thereby, mitigate the current crisis. Drawing on the language of the prominent concept of 'pockets of efficiency', this could take the form of 'pockets of protectionism' for peripheral economies within the Single European Market. However, this option would require a change in EU legislation – specifically regarding the rules of the Single Market – and, therefore, the support of the core countries.

The second proposal would therefore require us to go into a more radical direction, because it seeks to reduce dependency relations through different degrees of delinking from the core countries, accompanied by the reinforcement of links between the peripheral countries – for instance, among Southern European economies where progressive forces are currently significantly stronger than in the European core economies. Crucially, this proposal does not advocate a return to the nation-states and national development strategies. Rather, it advocates a *different form* of regional integration that aspires at overcoming dependency by creating new solidary relations of cooperation among the peripheral economies. Such an approach could be developed based on the controversial and wide-ranging debate concerning the relation between (semi-)decoupling from core countries or (sub)regions and industrial development, which took place during the 1960s and 1970s between different protagonists of the developing countries. Notwithstanding its various highly diverging positions, the debate converged on the overarching agreement that the attainment of a certain amount of independence from the core countries was necessary to overcome destructive dependency relations.

The key objective of their reflections at this time was to reach 'self-reliant development' on the national level, i.e. a development without reliance on other countries for basic needs goods, as well as 'Collective Self-Reliance' on the regional and interregional level. Representatives of the Non-Aligned Movement (NAM 1976), Yugoslavian researchers and policy makers, as well as some scholars of the Latin American 'dependency school' and of the World System Theory referred to this concept. The first two groups sought to increase their country's or region's autonomy towards the core through the establishment of more intense relations with other countries at the same development level. This included, for instance, the advocacy of strategic protectionist measures, the implementation of common industrial policy measures, and the proposal to establish joint enterprises and technical cooperation. However, representatives of the second group (particularly from the dependency approach) such as Samir Amin, Johan Galtung and Dieter Senghaas, who were also in favour of South-South Cooperation, emphasised that only delinking from the world market (respectively, the core countries) would permit self-reliant development for peripheral countries (Amin 1981: 535; Fischer 2016; Galtung 1983: 47ff.; Kahn 1978: 23ff.).

While the persecution of 'self-reliant development' in terms of comprehensive delinking does not seem a viable strategy for any smaller peripheral country in the current stage of globalisation due to globalised or regionalised production structures (be it in Europe or outside), we think that the idea of a closer cooperation among the peripheral states merits some more attention. While regional or *Collective* Self-Reliance (CSR) has overwhelmingly remained a theoretical concept, establishing such links among peripheries in order to complement the relations with the core countries could be of crucial importance for European peripheries. In economic terms, a partial reconstruction of industrial capacities in the Southern European sub-region, supported through strategic protectionist measures, could become the goal. In political terms, a multi-vector orientation could allow for the maintenance of more flexible relations with different countries, also outside the EU.

This approach has several advantages over the current dynamics dominating EU integration. A partial re-regionalisation of production would perfectly harmonise with the goal of social-ecological transformation, because it shortens transportation routes (although it is also less efficient than using economies of scale). Successful productive reconstruction would also reduce the European peripheries' vulnerability in global crises. Regional (or in Europe sub-regional) cooperation in the framework of CSR could create a balance between diversification on the national level and the regionalisation of industrial capacities, which cannot be economically organised on a national scale (Becker et al. 2015: 91; 93). In Latin America, the regional integration projects of the Bolivarian Alliance for the Peoples of Our America (ALBA-TCP 2009) sought – without much success, however – to establish such production capacities based on the creation of new regional value chains (Eder 2016).

To be sure, CSR-inspired cooperation projects, which are composed exclusively of less developed countries, face many problems in practice which do not exist in other cases, such as the lack of technological capacities and financial limitations (Eder 2016: 106ff.). From this perspective, the integration with a dominant economy bears several advantages: it allows for technology transfer, support in the construction of industrial capacities, the coordination of research and development activities, and so on. This is also why we defend strategic protectionism instead of complete delinking. However, this would require that the dominant economy supports the less developed economies in setting up proper industrial production without concomitantly integrating them into the lower ranks of existing value chains to its own benefit. Arguably, this would necessitate labour mobilisation or at least the support of labour institutions from core countries for such a project (e.g. in the form of a solidary transfer union instead of currently dominant neo-mercantilist orientations in the core). At the same time, at least parts of the dominant capital fractions would need to support such a strategy. In practice, this would require building a new capital-labour-consensus to reach a more balanced development in Europe, which to us seems rather unlikely under current power relations.

However, as argued in section 2, the prevailing relations of forces and selectivities on the EU level foreclose such an option in the short and medium term. Moreover, if the peripheral economies are not allowed to protect themselves and to at least partially erect trade barriers for goods produced in stronger economies, catch-up development is rather unlikely (Becker et al. 2015: 93). Considering these severe problems, and recalling what we have discussed in chapter 2, it would arguably be easier to create progressive alliances on the national scale than on the supranational level to implement *inter alia* a progressive industrial policy. To be sure, such an alliance would face severe resistance from transnationally oriented capital and potentially even fractions of labour in the periphery which have so far mostly benefitted from transnationalisation. Its success would therefore crucially depend on the support from the labour movement in the core. Nonetheless, by promoting the strategic use of FDI inflows and strategic protectionist measures for infant industry development, such an alliance on the national and – following the CSR approach – on the sub-regional level, could be the basis for a progressive industrial policy strategy which is ultimately more viable then the presently dominant call for progressive industrial policy on an EU-wide scale.

6. Concluding remarks

In this paper, we argued that industrial policy must address three key issues in order to be progressive. First, the successful formulation and implementation of an industrial policy programme not only requires an understanding of given economic structures. It also needs to focus on the question of which relations of forces between various class fractions correspond with specific economic models, how they express themselves in terms of hegemony as well as within the state, and how they can be shifted while at the same time forged into a compromise between diverging interests. In this regard, progressive industrial policy is not merely reformist but transformative. Second, progressive industrial policy should not (solely) be restricted to economic growth, but should consider questions of distribution, as well as crosscutting issues such as gender-sensitivity, social-ecological transformation and democratic participation. Lastly, and presumably most controversially, progressive industrial policy transcends the goal of deeper transnational market integration by means of the elimination of trade barriers and the fixation on regional and/or international competitiveness. It challenges the existing hierarchical division of labour by allowing the reconstruction of specific key sectors through strategic protectionism and selective dissociation from the core countries. This could be part of a progressive 'multi-speed' Europe, which concedes 'pockets of protectionism' to the peripheral economies.

Julia Eder, Etienne Schneider

The recent proposals by the European Union point into a very different direction (Wigger 2018). Instead of financing an industrial policy strategy to reduce economic imbalances and social inequality in Europe, the European parliament and the Council of the European Union released a "proposal for a regulation on establishing the European Defence Industrial Development Programme" (EDIDP) in June 2017 (European Commission 2017b). This relates to the "capability window" of the European Defence Fund, the launch of which the Commission announced in the same communication. All proposals are part of the European Defence Action Plan, a political project to revitalise the European integration process along new geopolitical ambitions to counteract looming disintegration tendencies in the EU. The EDIDP officially aims at increasing "competitiveness and innovative capacity of the EU defence industry, including cyber defence" (European Parliament 2017). While it does not fund the actual production of weapons and other military equipment, it heavily supports research and development in this area with a budget of 500 million to (up to) one billion Euro per year (European Commission 2017b: 6; European Parliament 2017).

In conclusion, the current debate on progressive industrial policy strategies in Europe is of crucial importance, but their prospects for implementation in the short and medium term are dire. However, in order to move beyond crucial, but merely defensive, struggles against industrial policy as an instrument to increasingly militarise the EU, it is pivotal to continue to develop and refine progressive concepts for industrial development (see also Wigger 2018: 11-13). To forge political alliance for their implementation will presumably be, as we have argued, easier inside individual nation states and on the sub-regional level, especially in light of the current influence of powerful capital groups on, and the specific selectivity of the EU level. In those alliances, the Left needs to spur the struggle for a more profound transformation of the production system along the lines outlined above. Difficult as this will be, such an alliance would be not only a desirable, but also a feasible strategy in the medium term to promote a progressive, social-ecological productive reconstruction which effectively challenges the looming rift between core and periphery in Europe.

Acknowledgement

Editing of this article was financially supported by the Faculty of Social Sciences at the University of Vienna.

1 This is particularly crucial in the public banking sector. The Brazilian Development bank is commonly referred to as a prototypical example of such a 'pocket of efficiency' in the public banking sector (Evan 1995: 61)

2 For instance, a social-ecological conversion of the German automotive industry would be impossible without also challenging automobility on the level of everyday practices and symbolic meanings (such as the car as a symbol of status and freedom).

3 For instance, the electric car is often heralded as a sustainable alternative to the present form of mobility. Yet, while the energy used by electric cars might come from renewable sources, the finitude of resources necessary to build these cars, especially its batteries, make it impossible to envision a 'sustainable', i.e. resource neutral, growth of the electric car market.

4 The so-called rebound effect refers to the phenomenon that increases in efficiency make production cheaper, which ultimately encourages higher consumption.

5 Other parts of the Eastern periphery of the EU, the Baltic countries as well as Bulgaria and partly Romania, are more similar to the Southern periphery as they exhibit similar characteristics of de-industrialisation and passive financialisation (Becker 2012).

References

Aulenbacher, Brigitte (2010): Arbeit und Geschlecht – Perspektiven der Geschlechterforschung. In: Aulenbacher, Brigitte et al. (Hg.): Soziologische Geschlechterforschung. Wiesbaden: VS Verlag für Sozialwissenschaften, 141-155. https://doi.org/10.1007/978-3-531-92045-0_8

Austrian Chamber of Labour (AK)/Austrian Trade Union Confederation (ÖGB) (2015): Industriepolitik für Beschäftigung und langfristigen Wohlstand. Der Blick der ArbeitnehmerInnen auf den produzierenden Sektor in Österreich. Position Paper, June 2015. https://media.arbeiterkammer.at/PDF/Industriekonzept_23.6.2015.pdf, 7.12.2016.

ALBA-TCP (2009): Action Plan for Trade Development in the Joint Development Economic Zone of the ALBA-TCP. http://alba-tcp.org/en/contenido/action-plan-economic-zone-alba-tcp, 29.08.2016.

Ambroziak, Adam A. (ed., 2017): The New Industrial Policy of the European Union. Contributions to Economics. Cham: Springer International Publishing.

Amin, Samir (1981): Some Thoughts on Self-reliant Development, Collective Self-reliance and the New International Economic Order. In: Grassman, Sven/ Lundberg, Erik (eds.): The World Economic Order: Past & Prospects. London: Palgrave Macmillan, 534-552. https://doi.org/10.1007/978-1-349-16488-2_16

Barrientos, Stephanie/Gereffi, Gary/Rossi, Arianna (2011): Economic and social upgrading in global production networks: A new paradigm for a changing world. In: International Labour Review 150(3–4), 319-340. https://doi.org/10.1111/j.1564-913X.2011.00119.x

Becker, Joachim (2006): Metamorphosen der regionalen Integration. In: Journal für Entwicklungspolitik 22(2), 11-44. https://doi.org/10.20446/JEP-2414-3197-22-2-11

Becker, Joachim/ Jäger, Johannes (2010): Development Trajectories in the Crisis in Europe. In: Journal of Contemporary Central and Eastern Europe 18(1), 5-27. https://doi.org/10.1080/09651561003732488

Becker, Joachim (2012): Blindstellen: ungleiche Entwicklung und ungleiche Mobilisierung in der EU. In: Prokla 42(3), 467-476. https://doi.org/10.32387/prokla.v42i168.303

Becker, Joachim/Jäger, Johannes/Weissenbacher, Rudy (2015): Uneven and dependent development in Europe. The crisis and its implications. In: Jäger, Johannes/Springler, Elisabeth (ed.): Asymmetric Crisis in Europe and Possible Futures: Critical Political Economy and post-Keynesian perspectives. London/ New York: Routledge.

Benatouil, Maxime (2017): No alternative politics of European integration without a progressive European industrial policy. In: Rosa Luxemburg Foundation (ed.): Progressive Industrial Policy for the EU? Outmanoeuvring Neoliberalism. Brussel: Rosa Luxemburg Foundation Brussels, 17-24.

Beigel, Fernanda (2015): Das Erbe des lateinamerikanischen Dependentismo und die Aktualität des Begriffs der Abhängigkeit. In: Journal für Entwicklungspolitik 31(3), 11-38. https://doi.org/10.20446/JEP-2414-3197-31-3-11

Binder, Manfred/ Jänicke, Martin/ Petschow, Ulrich (eds., 2001): Green Industrial Restructuring. Berlin/Heidelberg: Springer.

Bieler, Andreas (2014): Transnational Labour Solidarity in (the) Crisis. In: Global Labour Journal 5 (2), 114-133. https://doi.org/10.15173/glj.v5i2.1154

Bieling, Hans-Jürgen/ Brand, Ulrich (2015): Competitiveness or Emancipation? Rethinking Regulation and (Counter-)Hegemony in Times of Capitalist Crisis. In: Albritton, Robert/Badeen, Dennis/ Westra, Richard (ed.): The Future of Capitalism After the Financial Crisis. The Varieties of Capitalism Debate in the Age of Austerity. London: Routledge, 184-204.

Blöcker, Antje (2014): Arbeit und Innovationen für den sozial-ökologischen Umbau in Industriebetrieben. Düsseldorf: Hans Böckler Stiftung.

Brand, Ulrich (2016): Transformation as a New Critical Orthodoxy. The Strategic Use of the Term Transformation Does Not Prevent Multiple Crises. In: GAIA 25/1(2016), 23–27. https://doi.org/10.14512/gaia.25.1.7

Brand, Ulrich/ Wissen, Markus (2014): Strategies of a Green Economy, contours of a Green Capitalism. In: Van der Pijl, Kees (ed.): Handbook of the International Political Economy of Production. Northhampton: Edward Elgar, 508-523.

Buch-Hansen, Hubert/ Wigger, Angela (2011): The Politics of European Competition Regulation: A Critical Political Economy Perspective. RIPE Series in Global Political Economy. New York: Routledge. https://doi.org/10.4324/9780203828526

Buczko, Christina/Hinterberger, Fritz (2017): Progressive industrial policy and the challenge of socio-ecological transformation. In: Rosa Luxemburg Foundation (ed.): Progressive Industrial Policy for the EU? Outmanoeuvring Neoliberalism. Brussel: Rosa Luxemburg Foundation Brussels, 25-36.

Candeias, Mario (2011): Konversion – Einstieg in einer öko-sozialistische Reproduktionsökonomie. In: Candeias, Mario/ Rilling, Rainer/ Röttger, Bernd/ Thimmel, Stefan (eds.): Globale Ökonomie des Autos. Mobilität, Arbeit, Konversion. Hamburg: VSA, 253-274.

Chang, Ha-Joon (2013): Comments on "Comparative Advantage: The Silver Bullet of Industrial Policy" by Justin Lin and Célestin Monga. In: Stiglitz, Joseph E./Lin, Justin (eds.): The Industrial Policy Revolution I. The Role of Government Beyond Ideology. New York: Palgrave Macmillan, 39-42. https://doi.org/10.1057/9781137335173_3

Chang, Ha-Joon/ Andreoni, Antonio (2016): Industrial Policy in a Changing World: Basic Principles, Neglected Issues and New Challenges. In: Cambridge Journal of Economics 40 Years Conference. Cambridge.

Chang, Ha-Joon/ Grabel, Ilene (2004): Reclaiming Development. An Alternative Economic Policy Manual. London/New York: Zed Books.

Chassany, Anne-Sylvaine (2017): Macron wants tougher EU on trade and foreign investment. In: Financial Times, 11.05.2017. https://www.ft.com/content/38e98f94-359b-11e7-99bd-13beb0903fa3, 18.01.2018.

Cimoli, Mario/ Dosi, Giovanni Dosi/ Stiglitz, Joseph E. (eds., 2008): Industrial Policy and Development. The Political Economy of Capabilities Accumulation. Oxford: Oxford University Press.

Council of the European Union (2017): Europäische Verteidigung: Rat legt Standpunkt zur vorgeschlagenen Verordnung zur Einrichtung des Europäischen Programms zur industriellen Entwicklung im Verteidigungsbereich (EDIDP) fest. Press Release. 12.12.2017. http://www.consilium.europa.eu/de/press/press-releases/2017/12/12/european-defence-council-agrees-its-position-on-the-proposed-regulation-establishing-the-european-defence-industrial-development-programme-edidp/pdf, 13.01.2017.

Demirović, Alex (2007): Demokratie in der Wirtschaft. Positionen, Probleme, Perspektiven. Münster: Westfälisches Dampfboot.

Deutscher Gewerkschaftsbund (DGB) (2012): A Marshall Plan for Europe. Proposal by the DGB for an economic stimulus, investment and development programme for Europe. Berlin.

Diem25 (n.d.): The EU will be democratised. Or it will disintegrate! Manifesto.

Durand, Cédric (2017): Toward a Progressive Rejuvenation of Industrial Policy. Brussels: Rosa Luxemburg Foundation Brussels. http://www.rosalux. eu/publications/global-progressive-industrial-policy-an-alternative-for-more-social-justice/?tx_wwcore_pagelist%5Bevent%5D=&tx_wwcore_pagelist%5Baction%5D=show&tx_wwcore_pagelist%5Bcontroller%5D=Page& cHash=ac4857123b7ae7db1aa4613af412e4d8, 02.01.2018.

Eder, Julia Theresa (2016): Trade and Productive Integration in ALBA-TCP – A systematic comparison with the corresponding agendas of COMECON and NAM. In: Journal für Entwicklungspolitik 32(3), 91-112. https://doi. org/10.20446/JEP-2414-3197-32-3-91

EuroMemorandum (2017): The European Union: The Threat of Disintegration. http://www2.euromemorandum.eu/uploads/euromemorandum_2017.pdf, 2.9.2017.

Europe 2020 (2010): A European strategy for smart, sustainable and inclusive growth. Brussels: European Commission.

European Commission (2014a): For a European Industrial Renaissance. Brussels.

European Commission (2014b): Statistical Data on Women Entrepreneurs in Europe. Brussels.

European Commission (2017a): Investing in a smart, innovative and sustainable Industry. A renewed EU Industrial Policy Strategy. Brussels.

European Commission (2017b): Proposal for a Regulation of the European Parliament and of the Council establishing the European Defence Industrial Development Programme aiming at supporting the competitiveness and innovative capacity of the EU defence industry. COM(2017)294, 7.6.2017, 2017/0125 (COD). Brussels.

European Parliament (2017): Europe as a stronger global actor. European defence industrial development programme. http://www.europarl.europa.eu/legislative-train/theme-europe-as-a-stronger-global-actor/file-european-defence-industrial-development-programme, 18.01.2018.

European Trade Union Federation (ETUC) (2011): Resolution on Industrial policies and worker participation. Brussels: ETUC.

European Trade Union Federation (ETUC) (2015): Climate change, the new industrial policies and ways out of the crisis. Brussels: ETUC.

European Trade Union Congress (ETUC) (2017): ETUC position paper. A renewed EU industrial policy – ETUC reaction. Brussels: ETUC.

Evans, Peter (1995): Embedded Autonomy. States and Industrial Transformation. Princeton: Princeton University Press.

Fischer, Karin (2016): Collective self-reliance: failed idea or still a valuable contribution worth considering? Conference Paper. https://www.researchgate.net/publi-

cation/304019955_Collective_self-reliance_failed_idea_or_still_a_valuable_
contribution_worth_considering, 5.9.2017.

Galtung, Johan (1983): Self-Reliance: Beiträge zu einer alternativen Entwicklungsstrategie. Munich: Minerva.

Gauthier, Elisabeth/Benatouil, Maxime (2014): Left Industrial Policy. Productive
Transformation for Europe. Vienna: transform! Report.

Hirschel, Dierk/ Schulten, Thorsten (2011): Mit Wirtschaftsdemokratie aus der
Krise? Gewerkschaftliche Debatten über einen notwendigen Kurswechsel
nach der Krise. In: Meine, Hartmut/Schumann, Michael/Urban, Hans-Jürgen
(eds.), Mehr Wirtschaftsdemokratie wagen! Hamburg: VSA, 86–97.

Holman, Otto (1996): Integrating Southern Europe. EC Expansion and the Trans-
nationalization of Spain. London: Routledge.

International Labour Organization (ILO) (2017): Employment by sector -- ILO
modelled estimates, May 2017. www.ilo.org/ilostat-files/Documents/Excel/
MBI_33_EN.xlsx, 16.01.2018.

IPCC (2014): Climate Change 2014: Synthesis Report. Geneva.

International Trade Union Federation (ITUC) (2016): ITUC Statement to the 14th
UNCTAD Conference. https://www.ituc-csi.org/IMG/pdf/ituc_statement_
to_the_14th_unctad_conference_en.pdf, 20.4.2017.

Jackson, Tim (2009): Prosperity Without Growth. Economics for a Finite Planet.
London: Sterling, VA. https://doi.org/10.4324/9781849774338

Jessop, Bob (2012): Dynamics of Regionalism and Globalism: A Critical Political
Economy Perspective. http://www.ritsumei.ac.jp/acd/re/k-rsc/hss/book/pdf/
vol05_02.pdf, 17.12.2016.

Khan, Khushi M. (1978): "Collective Self-Reliance" als Entwicklungsstrategie für
die Dritte Welt. In: Khan, Khushi M./Matthies, Volker (eds.): Collective Self-
Reliance: Programme und Perspektiven der Dritten Welt. München/London:
Weltforum Verlag, 1-26.

Khan, Mushtaq (2010): "Political Settlements and the Governance of Growth-
Enhancing Institutions. London: School of Oriental and African Studies.

Komlosy, Andrea (2017): Karneval der Geopolitik. Das Zentrum verordnet sich
Protektion. In: Kurswechsel 3, 26-41.

Kucera, David/Tejani, Sheba (2014): Feminization, Defeminization, and Structural
Change in Manufacturing. In: World Development 64, 569–582. https://doi.
org/10.1016/j.worlddev.2014.06.033

Landesmann, Michael/Stöllinger, Roman (2018): Structural Change, Trade and
Global Production Networks: An 'Appropriate Industrial Policy' for Peripheral
and Catching-Up Economies. Wiiw Policy Notes and Reports, No. 21, May
2018. https://doi.org/10.1016/j.strueco.2018.04.001

Las Heras, Jon (2015): Framing Labour Strategies in the European Automotive
Industry: Any Inflexion Point Ahoy? In: Wirtschaft und Management (Band
22: Europe in Crisis: Challenges and Scenarios for Cohesion). Vienna: University of Applied Sciences bfi Vienna, 95-111.

JULIA EDER, ETIENNE SCHNEIDER

Las Heras, Jon (2018): International Political Economy of Labour and collective bargaining in the automotive industry. In: Competition & Change 22(3), 313-331. https://doi.org/10.1177/1024529418764350López Hernández, Isidro/ Rodriguez, Emmanuel (2010): The Spanish Model. In: New Left Review 54(69), 5-29.

Lütkenhorst, Wilfried/ Altenburg, Tilman/ Pegels, Anna/ Vidican,Georgeta (2014): Green Industrial Policy: Managing Transformation under Uncertainty. Bonn: Discussion Paper Deutsches Institut Für Entwicklungspolitik, 28/2014.

Mamede, Ricardo/Mira Godinho, Manuel/Corado Simões, Vítor (2014): Assessment and challenges of industrial policies in Portugal. In: Teixeira, Aurora A. C./ Silva, Ester/ Mamede, Ricardo (eds.): Structural Change, Competitiveness and Industrial Policy. Painful lessons from the European periphery. London: Routledge, 258-277.

Nachtwey, Oliver (2017): Die Abstiegsgesellschaft. Über das Aufbegehren in der regressiven Moderne. 6. Auflage. Berlin: Suhrkamp Verlag, 181-233.

Non-Aligned Movement (NAM) (1976): Aktionsprogramm für wirtschaftliche Zusammenarbeit. Fünfte Konferenz der Staats- und Regierungschefs der blockfreien Länder in Colombo, August 1976. In: Khan, Khushi M./Matthies, Volker (eds., 1978): Collective Self-Reliance: Programme und Perspektiven der Dritten Welt. München/London: Weltforum Verlag, 171-194.

Nübler, Irmgard (2011): Industrial Policies and Capabilities for Catching up: Frameworks and Paradigms. ILO Employment Working Paper No. 77. Geneva: International Labour Organization.

Opratko, Benjamin (2014): Hegemonie. Politische Theorie nach Antonio Gramsci. Münster: Westfälisches Dampfboot.

Pianta, Mario/Lucchese, Matteo/Nascia, Leopoldo (2016): What is to be produced? The making of a new industrial policy in Europe. Brussels: Rosa Luxemburg Foundation Brussels.

Plank, Leonhard/ Staritz, Cornelia (2013): Renaissance der Industriepolitik – Irr- oder Königsweg? In: Kurswechsel 3/2013: 74–91.

Poulantzas, Nicos (1978 [1974]): Classes in Contemporary Capitalism. London: Verso.

Poulantzas, N. (2000 [1978]): State, Power, Socialism. London: Verso.

Prebisch, Raúl (1974): Informe reservado al Secretario General de las Naciones Unidas sobre los recursos excedentes del petróleo y el Nuevo Orden Económico Mundial http://repositorio.cepal.org/handle/11362/32934, 7.8.2017.

Ramírez Pérez, Sgfrido/ Benatouil, Maxime (2014): From Industrial Policy to a European Productive Reconstruction. Vienna: transform!europe Discussion Paper No. 3.

Raza, Werner/Staritz, Cornelia/Grumiller, Jan (2016): Framework to Assess Institutional Setups for Industrial Policies. Vienna: Austrian Foundation for Development Research (ÖFSE).

Rehfeld, Dieter/ Dankbaar, Ben (2015): Industriepolitik. Theoretische Grundlagen, Varianten und Herausforderungen. In: WSI-Mitteilungen 7/2015, 491-499.

Rosa Luxemburg Foundation (2017) (ed.): Progressive Industrial Policy for the EU? Outmanoeuvring Neoliberalism. Brussels: Rosa Luxemburg Foundation Brussels Office.

Rodrik, Dani (2008): Normalizing Industrial Policy. Washington: International Bank for Reconstruction and Development/The World Bank, Commission on Growth and Development Working Paper Nr. 3.

Rodrik, Dani (2014): Green Industrial Policy. In: Oxford Review of Economic Policy 30 (3), 469–91. https://doi.org/10.1093/oxrep/gru025

Röttger, Bernd (2011): Betriebliche Konversion. In: Candeias, Mario/ Rilling, Rainer/ Röttger, Bernd/ Thimmel, Stefan (eds.): Globale Ökonomie des Autos. Mobilität. Arbeit. Konversion. Hamburg: VSA, 241-252.

Sablowski, Thomas (2010a) Widersprüche innerhalb der Bourgeoisie und der Staat bei Poulantzas. In: Demirovic, Alex/ Adolphs, Stephan/Karakayali, Serhat (eds.): Das Staatsverständnis von NicosPoulantzas. Baden-Baden: Nomos. https://doi.org/10.5771/9783845221038-189

Sablowski, Thomas (2010b): Konsumnorm, Konsumweise. In: Historisch-Kritisches Wörterbuch des Marxismus 7/II. Hamburg: Argument Verlag, 1642-1654.

Sablowski, Thomas/ Schneider, Etienne/ Syrovatka, Felix (2018): Zehn Jahre Krise. Regulation des Lohnverhältnisses und ungleiche Entwicklung in der Europäischen Union. In: Prokla 48(3), forthcoming.

Sandbeck, Sune/ Schneider, Etienne (2014): From the Sovereign Debt Crisis to Authoritarian Statism: Contradictions of the European State Project. In: New Political Economy 19(6), 847-71. https://doi.org/10.1080/13563467.2013.861411

Schmalz, Stefan/Dörre, Klaus (2014): Der Machtressourcenansatz: Ein Instrument zur Analyse gewerkschaftlichen Handlungsvermögens. In: Industrielle Beziehungen 21(3), 217-237.

Schneider, Etienne (2017): Raus aus dem Euro – rein in die Abhängigkeit? Perspektiven und Grenzen alternativer Wirtschaftspolitik außerhalb des Euro. Hamburg: VSA.

Schneider, Etienne/Syrovatka, Felix (2017): Die Zukunft der europäischen Wirtschaftsintegration. Blockierte und wachsende Asymmetrie zwischen Deutschland und Frankreich. In: Prokla 47(4), 653-673. https://doi.org/10.32387/prokla.v47i189.62

Secchi, Carlo (1982): Impact on the Less Developed Regions of the EEC. In: Seers, Dudley/ Vaitsos, Constantin/ Kiljunen, Marja-Liisa (eds.): The Second Enlargement of the EEC. The Integration of Unequal Partners. London/ Basingstoke, 176- 89. https://doi.org/10.1007/978-1-349-16760-9_10

Seguino, Stephanie/ Berik, Günseli/ Meulen Rogers, Yana van der (2010): An Investment that pays off. Promoting Gender Equality as a Means to Finance Development. Friedrich-Ebert-Stiftung. http://www.gendermatters.eu/

resources_documents/UserFiles/File/Resourse/Promoting_gender_equality_as_a_means_to_finance_development.pdf, 25.4.2017.

Stiglitz, Joseph E., Justin Yifu Lin, and Celestin Monga. (2013): The Rejuvenation of Industrial Policy. Washington: The World Bank Policy Research Working Paper 6628. https://doi.org/10.1596/1813-9450-6628

Strategic Green Industrial Policy (SGIP) (2016): Practitioner's Guide. UNEP, ILO, UNDP, UNIDO, UNITAR.

Tejani, Sheba/Milberg, William (2016): Global Defeminization? Industrial Upgrading and Manufacturing Employment in Developing Countries. In: Feminist Economics 22(2), 24-54. https://doi.org/10.1080/13545701.2015.1120880

Thie, Hans (2013): ‚Mehr Industriepolitik' ist im ökologischen Zeitalter die falsche Formel. In: Kurswechsel 3/2013, 86-91.

transform!europe (2015): Towards Europe's Productive Transformation – an Emergency For an Alternative Industrial Policy. Vienna: transform! Discussion Paper 1/2015.

Troost, Axel (2017): Industrial policy for Europe – a topic for the political left? In: Rosa Luxemburg Foundation (ed.): Progressive Industrial Policy for the EU? Outmanoeuvring Neoliberalism. Brussel: Rosa Luxemburg Foundation Brussels, 77-84.

UNIDO (2015): Gender Equality and Empowerment of Women Strategy, 2016-2019. https://www.unido.org/fileadmin/user_media/PMO/GC.16/GC.16_8_E_Gender_Equality_and_Empowerment_of_Women_Strategy__2016-2019.pdf, 5.1.2018.

Vilmar, Fritz/Satller, Karl-Otto (1978): Wirtschaftsdemokratie und Humanisierung der Arbeit. Systematische Integration der wichtigsten Konzepte. Köln/Frankfurt am Main: Europäische Verlagsanstalt.

Warwick, Ken (2013): Beyond Industrial Policy. OECD Science, Technology and Industry Policy Papers, No. 2. Paris: OECD Publishing.

Whitfield, Lindsay/ Therkildsen, Ole/ Buur, Lars/ Kjaer, Anne Mette (2015): The Politics of African Industrial Policy. A Comparative Perspective. Cambridge: Cambridge University Press. https://doi.org/10.1017/CBO9781316225509

Wigger, Angela (2018): The new EU industrial policy: authoriarian neoliberal structural adjustment and the case for alternatives. In: Globalizations. https://doi.org/10.1080/14747731.2018.1502496

Zinn, Karl Georg (1976): Investitionskontrollen und –planung. In: Sarrazin, Thilo (ed.): Investitionslenkung. „Spielwiese" oder „vorausschauende Industriepolitik"? Bonn/Bad Godesberg, 15-24.

ABSTRACT *Die globale Wirtschafts- und Finanzkrise hat die Diskussion über Industriepolitik neu belebt. Angesichts der strukturellen Ungleichgewichte in der Europäischen Union wurde Industriepolitik von verschiedenen Seiten als Weg aus der Krise und zur Reduzierung ungleicher Entwicklung ins Spiel gebracht. Von linker Seite wurden Konzepte für eine „progressive" Industriepolitik mit mehrheitlich post-keynesianischer Orientierung erarbeitet. Aber inwiefern ist eine Industriepolitik mit dieser Orientierung tatsächlich ‚progressiv'? Nach einer Einführung in die Schlüsselannahmen und -vorschläge in der Diskussion über progressive Industriepolitik leistet der Artikel drei spezifische Beiträge zu dieser lebendigen Debatte: Erstens erweitern wir die aktuelle Debatte um die Dimension der politischen Durchsetzungsfähigkeit (politics) sowie Fragen zu Machtbeziehungen und Hegemonie. Zweitens beginnen wir, häufig verwendeten Schlagwörtern der aktuellen Debatte wie ökologische Nachhaltigkeit, ArbeiternehmerInnenbeteiligung und demokratische Partizipation sowie Geschlechtersensibilität einen konkreteren Inhalt zu geben. Und drittens diskutieren wir vor dem Hintergrund der Zentrum-Peripherie-Beziehungen innerhalb der EU, was die aktuelle Debatte von Erfahrungen aus dem Globalen Süden lernen kann. Unsere Schlussfolgerung ist, dass progressive Industriepolitik zwar einen Ausweg aus der ungleichen europäischen Entwicklung darstellen kann, dass aber die Ausarbeitung und Umsetzung einer tatsächlich progressiven Industriepolitik auf europäischer Ebene vor enormen Schwierigkeiten steht. In vielerlei Hinsicht lässt die nationale oder subregionale Ebene nach wie vor mehr Spielraum als die supranationale.*

Julia Eder
Institute of Sociology, Johannes Kepler University Linz
julia_theresa.eder@jku.at

Etienne Schneider
Department of Political Science, University of Vienna
etienne.schneider@univie.ac.at

Journal für Entwicklungspolitik XXXIV 3/4-2018, S. 143–172

Anita Pelle, Sarolta Somosi
Possible Challenges for EU-Level Industrial Policy: Where Do Potentials for Policy Improvement in Central and Eastern European Countries Lie?

Abstract *Regarding the issue of industrial policy in the 21st century, we are facing fundamental changes, including the servitisation of industry, the potential in upskilling and upgrading, the process of digital transformation, and the evolution of value webs and complex business ecosystems. In industry within the EU, we can identify internal differences: in principle, the EU is divided into a core and a periphery or, possibly, several peripheries.*

How will EU member states cope with these challenges? How is the EU-level industrial policy strategy likely to affect member states' (relative) positions? Is there policy-level differentiation? If so, how does it work; if not, what are the implications?

Keywords *industrial policy, European Union, servitisation of industry, Industry 4.0, manufacturing*

1. Introduction

In contrast to trade and competition policies, the European Economic Community (EEC) and then the European Union (EU) have never had a supranational industrial policy declared by primary EU law. Even so, there have from time to time been attempts at EEC/EU level to shape European industry through policy. In the early times of European integration, the widespread approach was strong interventionism, but at the national level. However, after the gloomy 1970s the approach had to be reviewed and, slowly, the structural and regulatory approach has gained relevance

and prevalence in European industrial policies (Grabas/Nützenadel 2013), leading to the current set of EU industrial policy priorities (EU 2018):
- fostering competitiveness;
- encouraging innovation;
- promoting sustainable and socially responsible businesses;
- promoting access to resources, including finance, skilled labour, energy, and raw materials;
- a well-functioning internal market;
- ensuring a business-friendly environment;
- supporting internationalisation of businesses;
- providing support for the protection of intellectual property rights.

Evidently, not only the attitudes and tools of European industrial policy have changed throughout the decades, but the EEC/EU, the global economy, and industry itself as well. The 1973 enlargement, with the accession of the United Kingdom, was perhaps the first moment to shed light on the consequences of industrial change on regional economic development, and on the social situation of the working class losing ground. At that time, textiles, coal and steel, and shipbuilding were considered so-called sensitive industries in Europe that needed special attention and care (Molle/ Van Mourik 1987, Puslecki 2003).

The accession of the Southern European countries (Greece in 1981, Spain and Portugal in 1986) to the EEC posed a slightly different challenge to the European policy framework: regarding industrial specificities, these countries had been characterised by a significant relative technological backwardness and limited access to markets in comparison with the existing member states of the EEC, due to the lack of a liberal democratic system in these countries at that time (Acemoglu/Robinson 2012).[1] Accordingly, the need for economic and social cohesion was accentuated in the Single European Act of 1986. Nevertheless, the industrial policy approach of the time did not handle the convergence issue as a priority, neither at the European nor at the national levels; instead, these goals were hoped to be reached by the Community's reformed regional and structural policies, in the first place. Accordingly, and also because regional policy was the prior source of Community funding as European industrial policy has never disposed over financial resources, the industrial policy aspect was inserted into regional policy.

ANITA PELLE, SAROLTA SOMOSI

In 1988, among the five objectives of the reformed common regional policy, Objective 2 was aimed at "converting regions seriously affected by industrial decline". In the 1989-1993 period, the major beneficiary countries were the United Kingdom (ECU 2 billion; 35.5% of population), Spain (ECU 1.5 billion; 22.2%) and France (ECU 1.2 billion; 18.3%), followed by Greece, Ireland and Portugal. Objective 2 remained for the 1994-1999 period as well, covering 60.6 million (16.3%) of the EEC population at that time. Then, in the 2000-2006 period, the objective was recalibrated with the aim of "supporting the economic and social conversion of areas facing structural difficulties", but still supporting projects, mainly in the fields of enhancing the productive environment (with a special attention to small and medium-sized enterprises), and physical regeneration, often of earlier industrial sites (Goulet 2008). From 2007 onwards, namely in the 2007-2013 and 2014-2020 programming periods, the terms "industrial decline" and "structural change" no longer appear in the regional development policy documents, but competitiveness and employment come into focus instead (EC Regulation No 1083/2006, EU Regulation No 1303/2013). This shift was in line with the most recent change in the general approach to industry in Europe: that a horizontal (vs. sectoral) and more integrated policy setting should be applied, and that "[t]he Community's structural crisis is reflected in the unacceptably high level of unemployment" (ESC 1993:9), so the structural issue should be tackled in parallel with addressing (un)employment.

Another challenge driven by the enlargement of the EU was that posed by the post-socialist new member states (NMSs) after 2004. The system change from socialism to capitalism had brought about a drastic decline of industrial production and the collapse of numerous firms in these countries, independent of whether shock therapy had been applied (Kornai 1994). Although industrial sectors had, by the time of the accession of these countries, largely been transformed through the massive FDI-inflows following the transition from planned to market economies (Benacek et al. 2000), considerable structural and other deficiencies have remained. In fact, the segments of the global value chains located in the region have mainly been the lower ones, with paradoxical effects: while the incoming FDI has considerably contributed to the rather smooth and successful transformation of these countries from planned to market economies in economic terms, it has at the same time had negative unintended social side-effects (Szelényi 2014) and has over time contributed to the preservation of these countries' peripheral or semi-peripheral status in Europe and the world (Nölke/Vliegenthart 2009, Farkas 2011), even if there are examples of fragile but beneficial changes in subsidiaries of multinationals in the region (Szalavetz 2016a, Szalavetz 2016b): job creation, enhanced industrial and human competences and capacities, access to new and/or wider markets, and in certain cases even development activities established at these firms. The fragility arises from the fact that these activities are less embedded locally and thus easily move on to other locations. In this respect, the "stickiness" of jobs (Von Hippel 1994, Hira 2009, Finegold/McCarthy 2010) also matters. The term "sticky" in relation to jobs refers to workplaces that are less likely to be relocated by multinationals along competitiveness considerations.

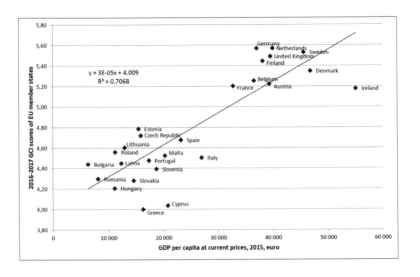

Figure 1: GDP per capita (2015, euro) and competitiveness (2016-2017, GCI score) of EU member states

Source: own edition based on Eurostat and World Economic Forum data

Note: Luxembourg is missing as an outlier (in GDP per cap. terms)

ANITA PELLE, SAROLTA SOMOSI

As regards the global context, the emerging economies in Asia and other continents have gradually appeared as ever more serious competitors, especially to the less developed parts of the European industrial base. As these latter segments tend to concentrate in the Southern and Eastern peripheries of the EU and the Eurozone, the challenge has taken on a regional aspect. In fact, most integrated European value chains are concentrated in the pre-2004 EU15 countries; however, intra-firm trade between Western European parent firms and their subsidiaries in Eastern NMSs account for between 20 and 70 per cent of total trade between these regions, so the significance of the Eastern NMSs for the EU15 countries varies greatly. Recently, Central and Eastern Europe (CEE) has mostly maintained its position as an offshoring destination, while such activities have been considerably withdrawn from Southern Europe, and China has become a preeminent reshoring destination for Europe-based multinationals. As a result, the performance of the Central and Eastern, and the Southern peripheries of the EU have more or less levelled off (Marin et al. 2017), which is also traceable in their GDP/capita and competitiveness levels (Figure 1). The global economic and financial crisis, and especially its consecutive wave in the Eurozone periphery with the sovereign debt crisis, has only aggravated these problems further and has rendered the prospects of the Southern Eurozone periphery gloomier still (Rangone/Solari 2012, Vihriälä/Wolff 2013, Gambarotto/Solari 2015). EU industry was largely affected by the crisis, though these effects were uneven across EU member states (Table 1).

	2007	2008	2009	2010
EU28	2 326 019.6	2 315 606.5	2 046 711.4	2 204 121.5
Belgium	60 182.1	59 011.5	53 592.0	57 549.2
Bulgaria	6 315.3	6 472.0	6 767.5	6 723.2
Czech Republic	39 718.9	45 520.1	40 385.4	42 390.1
Denmark	40 373.7	42 068.7	35 907.0	38 651.3
Germany	603 159.0	601 607.0	522 487.0	600 439.0
Estonia	2 881.8	2 922.3	2 439.4	2 838.5
Ireland	40 151.2	37 507.2	39 225.0	37 080.2
Greece	26 863.9	27 176.3	25 825.2	22 367.5
Spain	176 905.0	183 870.0	167 465.0	169 978.0
France	261 725.0	256 635.0	241 546.0	243 780.0
Croatia	7 463.3	7 983.5	7 656.5	7 830.4
Italy	296 524.5	296 233.8	259 929.2	270 579.4
Cyprus	1 382.2	1 387.4	1 395.4	1 426.8
Latvia	2 890.2	3 107.9	2 639.1	2 902.3
Lithuania	5 676.6	6 258.1	5 148.0	5 856.6
Luxembourg	3 584.9	3 185.0	2 346.2	2 660.7
Hungary	22 873.3	23 249.3	19 748.0	21 514.7
Malta	811.5	920.6	837.1	893.6
Netherlands	100 563.0	104 723.0	92 601.0	95 149.0
Austria	60 864.9	61 029.0	56 837.8	58 433.6
Poland	69 319.7	80 146.6	70 409.7	78 540.1
Portugal	26 829.4	26 032.6	25 064.8	26 594.2
Romania	29 001.9	32 044.6	28 512.7	35 434.7
Slovenia	8 375.8	8 582.3	7 466.6	7 651.0
Slovakia	15 187.2	17 054.5	14 065.3	16 167.3
Finland	46 329.0	45 596.0	35 893.0	38 495.0
Sweden	75 684.8	72 150.1	57 443.9	74 758.1
United Kingdom	294 432.6	262 881.1	222 581.8	237 339.1

Table 1: Industry value added (gross) in the EU and its member states, current prices, million EUR, 2007-2016

2011	2012	2013	2014	2015	2016
294 138.5	2 324 323.2	2 332 994.9	2 403 117.1	2 570 550.8	2 590 206.3
58 694.7	58 205.9	58 506.3	59 251.4	61 829.0	63 551.3
8 277.5	8 370.0	8 225.7	8 428.2	9 209.9	10 130.6
45 664.6	45 044.1	43 701.8	45 855.1	48 753.0	51 038.1
40 304.5	41 916.1	41 763.2	42 047.3	42 478.9	44 755.4
635 684.0	650 111.0	652 498.0	684 476.0	711 692.0	728 603.0
3 265.3	3 355.3	3 612.5	3 825.1	3 790.4	3 788.0
41 313.9	40 773.6	40 866.4	43 419.4	94 454.5	93 318.2
22 016.4	21 570.5	21 790.8	21 492.5	21 047.4	20 971.3
171 651.0	165 568.0	163 944.0	165 854.0	176 484.0	181 210.0
254 065.0	258 467.0	263 767.0	267 166.0	278 030.0	279 973.0
8 043.6	8 043.6	7 816.8	7 810.9	7 936.1	8 186.7
273 890.8	267 781.0	267 973.3	270 480.9	278 865.9	288 616.1
1 297.0	1 246.6	1 146.7	1 090.3	1 171.2	1 197.0
3 176.9	3 379.0	3 337.0	3 265.0	3 369.1	3 477.5
6 930.7	7 493.0	7 449.4	7 630.4	7 575.0	7 709.9
2 705.8	2 673.3	2 942.2	3 251.0	3 345.4	3 476.1
22 202.1	21 909.0	22 184.7	23 446.1	25 633.1	25 752.3
870.8	817.5	842.5	862.5	890.2	930.5
99 481.0	101 456.0	99 658.0	95 277.0	96 515.0	96 214.0
61 443.0	63 655.2	64 132.3	65 533.6	66 936.6	67 205.3
84 251.3	88 346.6	87 081.6	92 405.4	99 714.6	100 099.7
25 587.6	24 991.3	25 399.5	26 488.0	28 753.0	29 464.9
37 958.7	33 486.1	36 344.3	38 020.6	38 591.7	39 084.8
8 041.9	8 095.1	8 346.6	8 812.7	9 092.0	9 479.9
17 009.0	17 504.0	17 050.9	18 362.7	18 773.0	19 753.2
38 340.0	35 286.0	35 983.0	36 313.0	37 341.0	37 615.0
80 214.4	79 748.9	79 465.1	77 357.8	74 424.2	76 359.2
41 676.3	264 909.3	267 421.0	285 194.5	323 877.2	298 782.2

Source: Eurostat (code: nama_10_a10)

Obviously, industry itself looks very different from what it was like decades ago. Technological advancements, with special regard to the evolution and spread of information and communication technologies (ICT), have genuinely transformed the industrial sector as a whole. Similarly, the recent servitisation of manufacturing has been influential. In fact, both in the global sphere and in Europe, various regions have achieved various levels of success (or failure) in adapting to these changes. In this article, we argue that this has not depended solely on local, national and European intentions and wisdom, but that history and path-dependence also play a role. EEC/EU industrial (and, in part, other) policy actions have also influenced the status of the member states, just as have done the national institutional settings.

2. The various challenges that policy is facing

The basis of any discussion of EU industry and policy includes conceptual and methodological questions, starting with what is (and what is not) considered as industry at present. In our view, the most relevant conceptual issue is the relation between (business) services and (classical) industry. We by no means should neglect the quality-type changes, most of which are rooted in the ongoing technological transformation.

2.1 Conceptual-methodological challenges

We can ask what industry is in our days, and how it is changing with the technological and organisational advancements. The servitisation of developed industry is a prevalent phenomenon. Vandermerwe and Rada (1988) described it as the process of adding value to what is offered to the customer through bundles of goods, services, support, knowledge and self-service. Although the concept is not new (see also Levitt 1972 and 1976), economic literature recognised it rather late: the number of papers referring to servitisation as a noteworthy issue grew only after 2003 and, more significantly, since 2009 (Hou et al. 2013). In Veugelers' (2013) approach, the emphasis is on manufacturers providing solutions rather than products to customers, which leads to the blurring of the boundaries between manufacturing and services.

Anita Pelle, Sarolta Somosi

Despite the already documented service paradox (Gebauer et al. 2005, Gebauer et al. 2012, Visnjic Kastalli/Van Looy 2013), namely that when some companies face difficulties in relation to servitisation, it may even result in their declining performance, competition is intensifying in the service content added to products. Global trade integration might further enhance competition in higher value-added activities where European industries have traditionally had a comparative advantage (EC 2014). In their study, Brax and Visintin (2017:17) define different types or levels of servitisation as "conceptually different, generic value constellations". The value of a final manufacturing product embodies, directly and indirectly, value added created by services provided either domestically or abroad. This shows the relevance of services for manufacturing production – and, on the other hand, the role of manufacturing as a carrier function for (business) services. Visnjic Kastalli and Van Looy (2013), but also Lee et al. (2016), examined whether services are provided integrated in a business model as an inseparable strategic complement to products, or only as an add-on asset. They found that, in this latter case, the companies may more likely outsource services either domestically or abroad to specialised service providers.

With this increase in the share of services in manufacturing, we must review how we measure industry's performance. As stated by ECSIP (2014), manufacturing has to be defined in a broader sense, considering all activities related to the production of manufactured final products. This is how the manufacturing value chain is calculated (by means of input-output analysis). A huge difference appears along the different methods, though. When considering the share of manufacturing in the contribution to the global final demand of manufactured products, the EU27, in the classical industry perspective, reached 16% in 2011, yet, in the value chain perspective, 22% of value added was generated in the EU. Moreover, within the manufacturing value chain, about 40% of value added was generated by service activities (ECSIP 2014). Therefore, caution is called for in respect to (any) figures, and in-depth quality analyses seem inevitable.

Across EU member states, the shares in value chains correlate positively with the shares of manufacturing in GDP. What is more problematic, from a dynamic perspective, is that countries which have lost shares in manufacturing value added to GDP (i.e. the Southern Eurozone members who were also tendentiously more affected by the latest crisis [Mazzucato 2015]), could only partly compensate the loss through further contributions to the manufacturing value chain by providing corresponding business services. A deeper change is nowadays affecting heavily industrialised countries.

The growing complexity of modern manufacturing, resulting from the application of new technologies, has also increased the service content of many manufactured goods (Miozzo/Soete 2001). Infrastructural and knowledge-intensive activities that were previously classified as manufacturing are now considered as service. The higher the degree of complexity of an economy, the tighter the linkage between the production of services and the demand for these from manufacturing industry.

Innovation and value creation themselves are being transformed in fundamental ways, further blurring the distinction between manufacturing and services. Services can be categorised relative to their position in the value chain as upstream services, including activities such as R&D[2] and design; core (production) services including supply management, production and process engineering and other technical services; and downstream (market) services, mainly distribution and after-sales maintenance (ECSIP 2014). These are all manifestations of the servitisation of manufacturing; what is common to them is that they all contribute to EU manufacturers' international competitiveness through comparative advantages. Through these advancements, EU industry seems to be able to reverse the decline in industrial export market shares and in the share of industry in total value added (EC 2017). As a matter of fact, this can only be achieved through innovation and industrial upgrading, which appear to be a must for the EU, as emerging economies such as China are becoming competitors in the higher value added segments as well.

2.2 Technology-driven advancements in industry

The fourth industrial revolution, or Industry 4.0, is widely discussed in current literature (Manyika et al. 2013, Bloem et al. 2014, Schwab 2016, Smit et al. 2016, Hallward-Driemeier/Nayyar 2018). We hereby refer to the latest technological changes led by advanced digitalisation (e.g. cloud technology or the Internet of Things), automation and robotisation (e.g. near-autonomous machines and vehicles), 3D printing (i.e. tailor-made produc-

ANITA PELLE, SAROLTA SOMOSI

tion becoming ever more feasible and profitable) and advanced bio- and nanotechnology (offering new materials and processes to regular industrial activities), by this umbrella expression. As for organisational innovation, we consider upskilling and upgrading, the complex process of the digitalisation of organising work (from design to after-sales services), the evolution of value webs (instead of the classical value chains) and, again, rather complex business ecosystems (Kelly/Marchese 2015), often across borders, as the most relevant ones.

This ongoing and recently quite accelerated transformation of the technological environment of manufacturing opens up new potentials. Enhanced efficiency may change the recently worsening trends of production effectiveness (Kovács 2017a). Advantages of digitalisation appear even in unexpected areas such as greening (the transition to a more environmentally friendly economy), or the shift to the circular economy (where lifecycles of products do not end as waste but are put in circulation again in one way or another) (Kovács 2017b). However, commitment is also a necessary condition. An additional appearance of the usage of Industry 4.0 techniques, due to real-time operability, interoperability and modularity, could be the almost just-in-time adaptation to market demands and needs (Hermann et al. 2015).

Value can also be added through the creative innovative capacities triggered by Industry 4.0. Lee et al. (2013) pointed out that the most important effect on manufacturing is the improvement of predictive manufacturing systems that contribute to the development of predictive analytics to mitigate uncertainties, including unreliable downstream capacity, unpredictable variation of raw materials or parts in terms of delivery, quantity and quality, market and customer demand fluctuation, incomplete product design due to the lack of accurate estimation of product state during production and usage, and may even meet requirements like waste reduction (to achieve greener production) and work reduction (to realise leaner production).

Industry 4.0 requires answers and strategies on three fronts: business, government and regulation, and the population itself (Andor 2018). There are huge differences among industrial sectors in how they are affected by ICT. We can define three big groups: ICT-user industries (e.g. the packaging sector, biochemistry and biotechnology, eco-friendly industries, logistics); ICT-producer industries; and non-ICT-intensive industries. How an ICT-intensive industry can prosper is highly dependent on absorptive and diffusive capabilities, jointly referred to as readiness (Kovács 2017a).

According to the above mentioned effects of the latest industrial revolution, we found an analogy with Dudley's (2010) thoughts: the present technological environment of manufacturing and digitalisation may appear as a general purpose technology (GPT), as it does not offer the final solutions either in industry or in other areas of life, but provides the tools to properly select and achieve our new targets.

2.3 The presence and nature of intra-EU differences

If we take a look at EU industry, we can identify intra-EU differences. In principle, the EU is divided into a core that is characterised by structural competitiveness, and a periphery or, possibly, several peripheries, that can be described by constrained cost competitiveness and where the moderate innovators and innovation followers of the EU are are found (EU 2017).

We have already discussed the increasing service content of manufacturing. Now the question is how the EU member states perform at the level of integration of services in manufacturing. They can decide to either add it in-house or through ordering buy-in services sourced from service providers. In case of the latter, this may have a local/domestic or an international origin. The two cases appear differently in statistical accounts: in the former case it will be included in manufacturing value added, while in the latter it will appear as service (UNIDO 2013, Lanz/Maurer 2015).

Nevertheless, the changes in the service content are not uniform: some countries remain relatively specialised in manufacturing (Germany, Austria and V4[3]/CEE countries), others specialise more in business services (UK, the Netherlands, Belgium and France), while the remaining regions (Baltics, Southern Europe) face a decline in manufacturing because of a less favourable manufacturing base, paired with a failure to improve specialisation in business services. This specialisation pattern within the EU (Figure 2) can be explained by relative differences of productivity growth in manufacturing and services, and wage drift across sectors. Other factors also seem to play a role (e.g. agglomeration and scale effects, FDI patterns, evolution of production linkages, industrial and economic history). Moreover, manufacturers in larger countries can rely on a more substantial base of domestically supplied services that realise economies of scale, while those in smaller countries need to rely more on foreign-sourced business services (ECSIP 2014). And, of course, the service providers of larger countries benefit also from the integrated internal market of the EU. Even so, potential barriers to cross-border trade in services and international manufacturing-services linkages are a relevant policy issue, even where legislation is rather up to date and Industry 4.0 is likely to increase tradability in the EU.

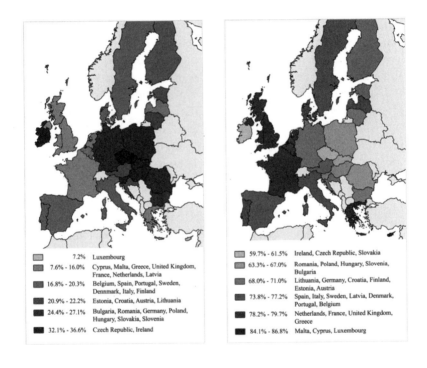

Figure 2: Share of industry (left) and services (right) in gross value added (2016, %)
Source: own edition with Openheatmap based on Eurostat data (code: nama_10_a10)

Among those actors that represent the innovative base of manufacturing, we find a vast majority (99.2%) of small and medium sized enterprises (SMEs) producing just 45% of value added, mostly in the services sector. The majority of SMEs in the post-2004 NMSs are younger, less experienced and are often farther from the technological frontier, with weaker technological capacities than their counterparts in the EU15. In addition, ca. 75% of European SMEs are concentrated in five sectors (in descending order): wholesale and retail trade, manufacturing, construction, business services, and accommodation and food services.[4] Regarding manufacturing, SMEs account for 59% of employees, 45% of value added and 39% of sales (Vladimirov 2017). Regarding employment, it is the case that particularly young firms in knowledge-intensive services based in business-friendly environments had large job creation capacities (Muller et al. 2015), while some peripheral countries (namely Ireland, Malta, Greece and Spain) stood out both in terms of annual growth in the number of enterprises (Ireland and Malta: over 5%, Greece and Spain: ca. 4%) and in employment (Malta: ca. 5%, Greece: ca. 4%, Spain and Ireland: over 3%) in 2015 (Muller et al. 2016:15), which is in part due to the previously harsh situations in these countries, although this had resulted in low base year values.

When looking at SMEs in the post-2004 NMSs, we can see that their general economic and institutional environment is less sophisticated. The industrial structures differ in terms of technology, and in innovation and absorption capacities (Vladimirov 2017). Therefore, setting unique standards (levelling the playing field) for SMEs all across Europe may well reproduce or even deepen the existing inequalities (Borbás 2014:101). The European Commission had already noted that "differences in innovation performance in the EU have started to increase, signalling a possible halt to convergence in Member States' innovation performance" (EC 2013a:5). However, the specific action plans to address the problems of SMEs in this peripheral region have yet to be drafted. One strategy that SMEs may follow is clustering. Successful participation in a cluster requires a minimum level of social capital and confidence embedded in social relations – but this is precisely what is lacking in many NMSs. SMEs in these countries are therefore less willing to collaborate. According to Karaev et al. (2007), there is not much empirical evidence of successful clustering in post-socialist economies.

As stated above, FDI played a major role in the early transition from socialism to capitalism. This has had positive (possibility to join global value chains [GVCs] and benefit from knowledge spillover) and negative (competitive pressure) impact on local SMEs (Drahokoupil/Galgóczi 2015). In GVCs, there is always scope for functional upgrading. SMEs' chances for that depend on their absorptive capacity and the institutional environment. As stated earlier, these are relatively weak in NMSs. Staritz and Plank (2013) are highly critical in respect of multinationals' investments in transition economies, as these companies' strategic interests (exploitation of low costs) fundamentally contradict long-term local interests (upskilling and upgrading). Evidence shows that the sought-for upgrading is not happening, in fact quite the contrary: domestic value added in gross exports declined in most NMSs in the 1955-2011 period (Bierut/Kuziemska-Pawlak 2016). At the country level, Germany is definitely a "headquarter economy" (where multinationals' headquarters and core development activities are located) vis-à-vis the NMSs, which may thus be condemned to remain "factory economies" (providing location for lower value-added subsidiaries) in the longer run as well (Baldwin 2012: 13-14, Szalavetz 2017, Vladimirov 2017, Stöllinger et al. 2018). Also, local SMEs tend to have difficulties in becoming suppliers to multinationals and thus enter GVCs (Vladimirov 2017). The EU has in fact limited power to intervene in these processes – but let us take a look at policy.

3. The policy level

Industrial policy (IP) can be described as government efforts to encourage the development of some parts of, or the entire, industrial sector. Bianchi and Labory (2006) define IP as a set of governmental measures aimed at guiding the structural transformation of an economy to improve a country's industrial performance. Rodrik (2007) claims that IP is well designed if it eventually maximises its potential to contribute to economic growth while minimising the risk of generating waste and rent-seeking. Pianta et al. (2016) have recently authored a comprehensive report on a progressive IP for Europe that "should favour the evolution of knowledge, technologies and economic activities in directions that improve economic performance, social conditions and environmental sustainability" (Pianta et al. 2016:30). To that end, a considerable role is to be devoted to the public sector in the forms of publicly owned firms, public investment banks and public-private partnership, public R&D and publicly financed support to dynamic publicly owned firms, and public procurement.

3.1 The state of affairs in EU-level industrial policy strategies and actions

As was mentioned at the beginning of this article, the horizontal approach was introduced in the EU, as of the mid-1990s, in order to find answers to revealed global challenges. The new approach involved the theory of clusters and the recognition of the importance of GVCs. The main goal was to create an environment favourable to industrial development, and to overcome the negative effects of deindustrialisation (Pitelis 2006). In addition, attention has been devoted to SME development as well. This focus has been strengthened under the Competitiveness of Enterprises and Small and Medium-sized Enterprises (COSME) programme and Horizon 2020. However, despite the horizontal approach, some sectoral aspects are still visible today: instead of textiles, steel and shipbuilding, we can see steel, space and defence industries handled independently, with an increased emphasis (EC 2017). A 2002 EU policy paper saw the Eastern enlargement as a major source of opportunities for industries both in the EU15 and NMSs (EC 2002).

In the European policy discourse the earlier sector-related industrial policy itself is increasingly focusing on competitiveness, and thus the policy has been largely replaced by competitiveness policy and enterprise policy (Vladimirov 2007). In parallel, the EU has experienced significant changes in the importance of the manufacturing sector in terms of its contribution to GDP and employment, asserting that "Europe needs to reverse the declining role of industry in Europe for the 21st century. This is the only way to deliver sustainable growth, create high-value jobs and solve the societal challenges that we face" (EC 2012:3). In 2014 the European Commission confirmed its commitment to reindustrialisation by setting the objective of increasing industry's contribution to GDP to 20% by 2020 (EC 2014). Veugelers and Batsaikhan (2017) argue that this is rather pointless as a target in itself since there can be many structural and/or historical reasons for the actual share of industry in GDP. Also, the absolute and relative value-added capabilities of the industrial (i.e. the technological level) and services (i.e. sophisticated business services vs. low-wage services like tourism) sectors of countries have an effect on the overall composition of GDP.

Most recently, in September 2017, the European Commission released "A renewed EU Industrial Policy Strategy" (EC 2017). The strategy reaffirms the importance of industry to economic prosperity in Europe. To that end, EU industry's ability to adapt to and embrace technological change is key. Nevertheless, the Commission admits that the responsibility lies with companies, as upgrading is their task to undertake. The strategy sees policy's main roles in promoting improved regulation carried out with the involvement of stakeholders. Among these, we can find advocates of other EU policies (single market, sustainability, investment, digitalisation) along with representatives of industry and business, as well as member states, regions, cities, social partners and the civil society.

3.2 Policy implications of the challenges

Importantly, we find that, despite the evident and rather persistent intra-EU differences in industrial performance and development prospects, no explicit policy approach and/or tool at EU level can be detected that would further the mitigation of these. Accordingly, the main questions that arise are the following: How will the various EU member states cope with the identified challenges? How is EU-level industrial policy strategy likely to affect member states' (relative) positions?

Revitalising manufacturing requires a specific focus on increasing SME productivity and value added. However, policy design is also challenged by lower economic growth, narrowing financial leeway and so a lower amount of capital for productive investments (Mauro-Zilinsky 2016), factors which altogether mean a narrowed policy leeway.

Lower economic growth also contributes to growing inequalities, which is a barrier to the diffusion of both technological and non-technological innovations. This may also undermine the political stability of a society (Milanovic 2016). If the EU does not take into consideration the obvious differences between member states, then the revolutionary effects of Industry 4.0, due to the interference between the member states, may in fact further deepen the gap between them (Kovács 2017b).

4. Conclusions and policy recommendations

Taking into consideration the aspects reviewed by this article, servitisation appears important to focus on, since the closer the relationship between industrial production and highly-skilled service sectors, the more 'sticky' jobs are likely to evolve. Thus the performance of manufacturing could be improved through policies that support the development of business services activities and their quality, and vice versa. Regarding smaller member states, improved access to foreign business service suppliers could be a policy objective. But that would seem to matter for the manufacturing core (headquarter) countries as well, since they could benefit from enhanced competition among business service suppliers. The possibility of internationalisation of business services is also relevant for those countries that are becoming more and more specialised in such services. All in all, there is an increasing need for cross-border flows of services within Europe, and so further steps towards integration should be undertaken (the services directive, reinforcing the internal market, a digital single market). Although these steps should be taken with caution, as they should by no means lead to more uneven development across Europe.

Reshaping of industrial policy should include answers to the fundamental question as to what the EU's objective(s) in relations to industry should be (as the 20% target is highly contentious). Also, who will take the lead? The EU is governed by its member states and these latter obviously have diverse interests stemming from their varying (relative) situations and positions. In what way shall the "smart, innovative and sustainable industry" (EC 2017) be secured across the EU?

Stehrer et al. (2016) talk about smart specialisation, which is a bottom-up approach in discovering regions' strengths, resources and latent comparative advantages, according to which selected industrial activities may be promising for certain regions. Landesmann (2015) also recommends that industrial policy formulation and execution must take place at all levels (regional, national and supra-national). However, we must admit that, even with the involvement of local stakeholders, the problem of picking a winner persists: an unavoidable feature of any active innovation and industrial policy is that the most promising areas or industries somehow have to be selected, with all the associated risks and consequences. When deciding, we can only hope that the positive results outperform the negative outcomes. As regards the question of leadership, Pianta (2015:143) says that "individual EU countries are too small to develop an industrial policy that could be effective in the current context of globalisation." Therefore, EU industrial policy also has the task of reconciling member states' interests, as well as public and private interests.

Once EU targets are set, the next issue is how to sell the vision to key stakeholders. Private actors of industry are key players, as they provide a high share of industrial R&D&I[5] expenditures (Veugelers 2015). Nevertheless, this growing involvement of private stakeholders in policy design should target the previously mentioned locally active multinational enterprises as well as their (potential) local SME partners. Compared to a selective and determined progressive industrial policy, such solutions may be more successful in the longer run due to the efforts undertaken to harmonise various interests. For enterprises (particularly SMEs) in NMSs, improving their participation in policy decisions is crucial but definitely requires a mix of measures specifically addressing their local challenges (Vladimirov 2017), rather than anticipating their contribution to a single policy instrument. For these enterprises, policies targeting SMEs' entrepreneurial culture and trust development, improving technological readiness, clustering, and joining GVCs in prospective ways (i.e. with upgrading in sight, see Szalavetz [2016c]) are needed.

Another issue at stake is firms' participation within the newly evolving transnational/global digital ecosystems. National and EU industrial policy measures should include actions that promote such advancements across the EU. The general purpose technology (GPT) character of Industry 4.0 is another opportunity for firms that policy can enhance. This may hold promises also for NMSs that are currently playing roles of factory economies. Nevertheless, the integration of value creating activities cannot be confined to production: cyber-physical systems integrate the whole value chain (or web).

As changes are profound and fast, policy actions must show flexibility and must provide possibilities for interim intervention if deemed necessary. One major benefit of Industry 4.0 is advanced data science – something that policy should also embrace. Policy design could also outreach to areas such as education and training. Also, the allocation of funds and resources should take place rapidly and dynamically. The presented challenges require flexible adaptation but, in reality, they may still be too slow for financial sector preferences. These are the cases where the states' role comes into the picture (Mazzucato 2013). Could the EU actually play the role of Mazzucato's (2013) entrepreneurial state? In financial terms, definitely not, for the time being. Kovács (2017b) in fact recommends for the EU to take up relevant industrial projects ignored by the financial sector for reasons of unprofitably long return periods. The public sector's involvement may also be justified in the compensation of SMEs. We consider these cases as the very space where the progressive industrial policy approach is relevant and desired.

The role of an "appropriate institutional context" (Pianta et al. 2016:34) is also mentioned in relation to progressive IP, but not discussed in detail. On the other hand, Berglof (2016), applying the Neo-Schumpeterian framework in which the three core assumptions are that long-run growth is driven by innovation, innovation results from entrepreneurial activities, and creative destruction is critical, warns that state capacity largely determines the success of industrial policy. We find this latter observation crucial, as it implies that progressive IP cannot be universal.

Some less considered advantages also arise from the widespread usage of Industry 4.0 techniques in the applied policy instruments themselves. For an example, the earlier grey or black economies[6] can be whitened/controlled due to greater transparency and investigation techniques, and the additional tax incomes may be channelled into further developments in the economies' technological readiness (Kovács 2017b).

Timing and sequencing of policy actions should also be subject of consideration; a systemic approach is needed in this respect. Industrial policy should match a wider development policy framework and be in line with business preferences. At this point we emphasise innovation policies and just mention that, as state aid is an area of EU competition policy, it is thus connected to industrial policy and state aid law, and its enforcement can also be scrutinised from this perspective (Aghion/Akcigit 2017).

Innovation appears both in the horizontal and in the sector-specific approaches of the EU's current industrial policy context. Innovation can be stimulated by various external (institutional and business environment) and internal (company capabilities in terms of knowledge, human capital and absorptive capacity) conditions (Bianchi/Labory 2006). Accelerating the catching-up process of countries that are farther from the technology frontier firstly requires effective industrial upgrading and then improving the adoption (or absorption) of new technologies and skills development, rather than immediate innovations (Veugelers 2015). A dual support is needed, both for innovation itself and for building innovation capabilities (Vladimirov 2017). More attention should be paid to stimulating the quality of human capital formation and supporting firms' incentives to adopt new technologies, everywhere tailored to local needs. This suggests a need for the development of customised policies and not simply the mechanical application of a general EU-level policy approach (Reid 2011).

In fact, the 2017 Innovation Union Scoreboard (EU 2017) reveals that EU innovation performance as a whole has improved, especially thanks to human resources, an innovation-friendly environment, own-resource investments, and attractive research systems; however, if we check the details, there is no significant improvement in human resources in favour of NMSs, and their distance from innovation leaders has not narrowed. Education has enormous responsibility in improving humans' innovation absorption capacities, their entrepreneurial motivations, lifelong learning, and the utilisation of Industry 4.0 as a general purpose technology (GPT). According to Kovács (2017a), the national educational systems do not yet comply with the challenges of the digital era, or at least not to the same extent. To many firms, employees and their skills are the most valuable assets. As workers (both high and lower skilled) are less mobile than companies, and as technological capabilities are embodied in them, they represent a unique locational advantage which makes a firm's activity less transferable to other locations. Overall, more coherence needs to be realised among industry, industrial policy, education, and the labour market. Such advancement could trigger a virtuous circle: well-designed policies implemented by a capable EU may enhance the quality and readiness of the human resources and the supportive nature of the business environment, which would then yield improved industrial performance that may serve as a form of reassurance, and thus provide feedback to the design of future policies. This could also be a way to cope with the challenge that the speed of technological change raises, both for policy and the economy.

We agree with Stehrer et al. (2016) that there should be at least a national/regional focus on individual industries (referred to as smart specialisation earlier), since the present state of technological readiness and future prospects vary considerably across the EU. This consideration is entirely in line with endogenous growth theory (Aghion/Howitt 1998) and progressive industrial policy (Pianta et al. 2016). Landesmann and Stöllinger (2018) have developed an "appropriate industrial policy" specifically for catching-up European economies. They emphasise the vulnerability of these countries and also point out the contradiction between a European "level playing field" and the "heterogeneity" of the catching-up economies (Landesmann/Stöllinger 2018:10).

The sectoral perspective also holds the possibility of specific policy recommendations. The so-called sunset industries where the EU does not have comparative advantages (e.g. the textile and leather industry, the electrical and optical equipment industry) and industrial sectors where substantial comparative advantages exist (e.g. machinery, transport equipment, or chemical industries) should be handled differently. Besides national or possibly regional goals adjusted to the local strengths and potentials, other horizontal measures (e.g. educational and vocational training, R&D policies, or the completion of the single market) may complement them. Thus the sectoral perspective should be accompanied by an EU-level effort to foster value-added generation capabilities all across the EU (Kovács 2017b) – again, tailored to national and local needs and particularities at the level of specific actions.

Certainly, a one-size-fits-all type policy approach is not a solution; it is not realistic, not feasible and, even if everybody upgrades relative to their past performance, differences will still persist. Nevertheless, industrial policy strategies and actions remain important for the EU. Accordingly, in our view, sophistication and differentiation are where possible solutions lie, combined with the upskilling and upgrading of the very policy itself, both in terms of design and implementation.

Acknowledgements

This research was supported by the project nr. EFOP-3.6.2-16-2017-00007, titled Aspects on the development of intelligent, sustainable and inclusive society: social, technological, innovation networks in employment and digital economy. The project has been supported by the European Union, co-financed by the European Social Fund and the budget of Hungary.

1   The 1995 enlargement was insignificant in this respect.
2   R&D: Research and Development
3   The abbreviation V4 refers to the four Visegrad countries: Poland, Czech Republic, Slovakia, Hungary.
4   The four sectors outside manufacturing all belong to the overall services (tertiary) sector.
5   R&D&I: Research and Development and Innovation. In 2013, the EU expanded its R&D policy into R&D&I policy.
6   Grey economy: pursuit of economic activities that are legal but are not executed legally, e.g. tax is not or not fully paid. Black economy: pursuit of illegal economic activities which therefore have to be executed without the oversight of public authorities and, consequently, no taxes are paid.

References

Acemoglu, Daron/Robinson, James A. (2012): Why Nations Fail: The Origins of Power, Prosperity and Poverty. New York: Crown Publishers.

Aghion, Philippe/Akcigit, Ufuk (2017): Innovation and growth: the Schumpeterian perspective. In: Blundell, Richard et al. (Eds.): Economics without borders. Economic research for European policy challenges. Cambridge: Cambridge University Press, 29-72. https://doi.org/10.1017/9781316636404.003

Aghion, Philippe/Howitt, Peter (1998): Endogenous growth. Cambridge, MA: MIT Press.

Andor, László (2018): A digitalizáció és a munka világa. Mi várható a robotforradalom után? [Beyond the Robot Revolution: Digitalisation and the World of Work]. Magyar Tudomány [Hungarian Science] 179(1), 47-54. https://doi.org/10.1556/2065.179.2018.1.5

Baldwin, Richard (2012): Global supply chains: why they emerged, why they matter, and where they are going. In: CTEI Working Papers CTEI-2012-13, Geneva: The Graduate Institute, Centre for Trade and Economic Integration.

Benacek, Vladimir/Gronicki, Miroslaw/Holland, Dawn/Sass, Magdolna (2000): The determinants and impact of foreign direct investment in Central and Eastern Europe: A comparison of survey and econometric evidence. Transnational Corporations 9(3), 163-212.

Berglof, Erik (2016): European Industrial Policy – Tapping the Full Growth Potential of the EU. In: New Growth for Europe – On Investment, Crisis Management and Growth Potential, Forum, Intereconomics 51(6), 335-340. https://doi.org/10.1007/s10272-016-0631-x

Bianchi, Patrizio/Labory, Sandrine (2006): From 'old' industrial policy to 'new' industrial development policies. In Bianchi, Patrizio/Labory, Sandrine (Eds.): International handbook on industrial policy. Cheltenham: Edward Elgar, 3-27. https://doi.org/10.4337/9781847201546.00008

Bierut, Beata K./Kuziemska-Pawlak, Kamila (2016): Competitiveness and export performance of CEE countries. In: NBP Working Paper, 248, Warsaw: Economic Institute.

Bloem, Jaap/van Doorn, Menno/Duivenstain, Sander/Excoffier, David/Maas, René/van Ommeren, Erik (2014): The Fourth Industrial Revolution: Things to Tighten the Link Between IT and OT. Groningen: Sogeti VINT.

Borbás, László (2014): Supporting SMEs in Central-Eastern Europe, Management, Enterprise and Benchmarking - In the 21ST Century, Budapest. https://kgk.uni-obuda.hu/sites/default/files/05_Borbas.pdf, 20.12.2017.

Brax, Saara A./Visintin, Filippo (2017): Meta-model of servitization: The integrative profiling approach. Industrial Marketing Management 60(1), 17-32. https://doi.org/10.1016/j.indmarman.2016.04.014

Drahokoupil, Jan/Galgóczi, Béla (2015): Introduction. Foreign Direct Investment in Eastern and Southern European countries: still an engine of growth? In: Galgóczi Béla/Drahokoupil, Jan/Bernaciak Magdalena (Eds.): Foreign investment in Eastern and Southern Europe after 2008: Still a lever of growth? Brussels: ETUI, 19-35.

Dudley, Leonard (2010): General Purpose Technologies and the Industrial Revolution. Papers on Economics and Evolution, 1011. Jena: Max Planck Institute of Economics.

EC (2002): Industrial Policy in an Enlarged Europe. COM(2002) 714 final. Brussels: European Commission.

EC (2012): A stronger European industry for growth and economic recovery. Industrial policy communication update, COM(2012) 582 final. Brussels: European Commission.

EC (2013a): Industrial competitiveness of EU member states: some progress made, but many challenges still lay ahead, 25 September 2013. MEMO/13/816, Brussels: European Commission.

EC (2013b): Towards Knowledge Driven Reindustrialisation, European Competitiveness Report. Commission Staff Working Document SWD (2013) 347 final, Brussels: European Commission.

Anita Pelle, Sarolta Somosi

EC (2014): For a European industrial renaissance, COM(2014) 12 final. Brussels: European Commission.

EC (2017): Investing in a smart, innovative and sustainable Industry. A renewed EU Industrial Policy Strategy, COM(2017) 479 final. Brussels: European Commission.

ECSIP Consortium (2014): Study on the relation between industry and services in terms of productivity and value creation. Final report. Within the Framework Contract for Industrial Competitiveness and Market Performance – ENTR/90/PP/2011/FC

ESC (1993): Growth, Competitiveness and Employment. Brussels: Economic and Social Committee.

EU (2017): European Innovation Scoreboard 2017. Luxembourg: European Union.

EU (2018): Industrial Policy. Brussels: European Commission. https://ec.europa.eu/growth/industry/policy_en, 15.01.2018.

Farkas, Beáta (2011): The Central and Eastern European model of capitalism. Post-Communist Economies 23(1), 15-34. https://doi.org/10.1080/14631377.2011.5469 72

Finegold, David/McCarthy, John (2010): Creating a Sector Skill Strategy: Developing High-Skill Ecosystems. In: Finegold, David/Gatta, Mary/Salzman, Hal/Schurman, Susan J. (Eds.): Transforming the U.S. Workforce Development System: Lessons from Research and Practice. Champaign, IL: Labor and Employment Relations Association, 181-204.

Gambarotto, Francesca/Solari, Stefano (2015): The peripheralization of Southern European capitalism within the EMU. Review of International Political Economy 22(4), 788-812. https://doi.org/10.1080/09692290.2014.955518

Gebauer, Heiko/Fleisch, Elgar/Friedli, Thomas (2005): Overcoming the service paradox in manufacturing companies. European Management Journal 23(1), 14–26. https://doi.org/10.1016/j.emj.2004.12.006

Gebauer, Heiko/Ren, Guang-Jie/Valtakoski, Aku/Reynoso, Javier (2012): Service-driven manufacturing: provision, evolution and financial impact of services in industrial firms. Journal of Service Management 23(1), 120–136. https://doi.org/10.1108/09564231211209005

Goulet, Rafaël (2008): EU Cohesion Policy 1988-2008: Investing in Europe's Future. Inforegio Panorama, 26.

Grabas, Christian/Nützenadel, Alexander (2013): Industrial Policies in Europe in Historical Perspective. WWWforEurope Working Paper, 15. http://www.foreurope.eu/fileadmin/documents/pdf/Workingpapers/WWWforEurope_WPS_no015_MS66.pdf, 20.12.2017

Hallward-Driemeier, Mary/Nayyar, Gaurav (2018): Trouble in the Making? The Future of Manufacturing-Led Development. Washington, DC: The World Bank.

Hermann, Mario/Pentek, Tobias/Otto, Boris (2015): Design Principles for Industrie 4.0 Scenarios: A Literature Review. Technische Universität Dortmund, Working Paper, 01/2015.

Hira, Ron (2009): A Policy Agenda for Offshoring. EPI Working Papers, 282, March. Washington, DC: Economic Policy Institute.

Hou, Jingchen/Neely, Andy (2013): Barriers of servitization: results of a systematic literature review. In: Proceedings of the Spring Servitization Conference. Cambridge: University Of Cambridge.

Karaev, Aleksandar/Koh, S. C. Lenny/Szamosi, Leslie T. (2007): The cluster approach and SME competitiveness: A review. Journal of Manufacturing Technology Management, 18(7), 818-835. https://doi.org/10.1108/17410380710817273

Kelly, Eamonn/Marchese, Kelly (2015): Supply chains and value webs. In: Canning, Mike/Kelly, Eamonn (Eds.): Business ecosystems come of age. Westlake, TX, USA: Deloitte University Press, 55-65.

Kornai, János (1994): Transformational Recession: The Main Causes. Journal of Comparative Economics, 19(1), 39-63. https://doi.org/10.1006/jcec.1994.1062

Kovács, Olivér (2017a): Az ipar 4.0 komplexitása – I. [The Complexity of Industry 4.0 – I.] Közgazdasági Szemle [Economic Review], 64(7-8), 823-851. https://doi.org/10.18414/KSZ.2017.7-8.823

Kovács, Olivér (2017b): Az ipar 4.0 komplexitása – II. [The Complexity of Industry 4.0 – II.] Közgazdasági Szemle [Economic Review], 64(9), 970-987. https://doi.org/10.18414/KSZ.2017.9.970

Landesmann, Michael A. (2015): Industrial Policy: Its Role in the European Economy. Which Industrial Policy Does Europe Need? Forum, Intereconomics, 50(3), 133-138.

Landesmann, Michael A./Stöllinger, R. (2018): Structural Change, Trade and Global Production Networks: An 'Appropriate Industrial Policy' for Peripheral and Catching-up Economies. Policy Note and Report 21, May. The Vienna Institute for International Economic Studies

Lanz, Rainer/Maurer, Andreas (2015): Services and global value chains – Some evidence on servicification of manufacturing and services networks. WTO Working Paper ERSD-2015-3, World Trade Organization.

Lee, Jay/Lapira, Edzel/Bagheri, Behrad/Kao, Hung-an (2013): Recent advances and trends in predictive manufacturing systems in big data environment. Elsevier, Manufacturing Letters 1, 38-41. Research Letters.

Lee, Sunghee/Yoo, Shijin/Kim, Daeki (2016): When is servitization a profitable competitive strategy? International Journal of Production Economics 173(3), 43-53. https://doi.org/10.1016/j.ijpe.2015.12.003

Levitt, Theodore (1972): Production-Line Approach to Service. Harvard Business Review, September. https://hbr.org/1972/09/production-line-approach-to-service , 15.12.2017

Levitt, Theodore (1976): The Industrialization of Service. Harvard Business Review, September. https://hbr.org/1976/09/the-industrialization-of-service, 15.12.2017

Manyika, James/Chui, Michael/Bughin, Jacques/Dobbs, Richard/Bisson, Peter/ Marrs, Alex (2013): Disruptive technologies: Advances that will transform life, business, and the global economy. McKinsey Global Institute, McKinsey & Company, e-book.

Marin, Dalia/Veugelers, Reinhilde/Feliu, Justine (2017): A revival of manufacturing in Europe? Recent evidence about reshoring. In: Veugelers, Reinhilde (Ed.): Remaking Europe: The new manufacturing as an engine for growth. Bruegel Blueprint Series 26. Brussels: Bruegel, 102-124.

Mauro, Paolo/Zilinsky, Jan (2016): Reducing Government Debt Ratios in an Era of Low Growth. Policy Brief, Peterson Institute for International Economics. https://piie.com/system/files/documents/pb16-10.pdf., 15.12.2017

Mazzucato, Mariana (2013): The Entrepreneurial State: Debunking Public vs. Private Sector Myths. London: Anthem Press.

Mazzucato, Mariana (2015): Innovation Systems: From Fixing Market Failures to Creating Markets. Which Industrial Policy Does Europe Need? Forum, Intereconomics, 50(3), 120-125. https://doi.org/10.21874/rsp.v66i4.1303

Milanovic, Branko (2016): Global Inequality: A New Approach for the Age of Globalization. Boston: Harvard University Press. https://doi.org/10.4159/9780674969797

Miozzo, Marcela/Soete, Luc (2001): Internationalization of Services, A technological Perspective. Technological Forecasting and Social Change, 67(2-3), 159-185. https://doi.org/10.1016/S0040-1625(00)00091-3

Molle, Willem/Van Mourik, Aad (1987): Economic Instruments of a Common European Foreign Policy. In: De Vree, Johan K./Coffey, Peter/Lauwaars, Richard H. (Eds.): Toward a European Foreign Policy: Legal, Economic and Political Dimensions. Dordrecht/Boston/Lancaster: Kluwer Academic Publishers, 165-192.

Muller, Patrice/Caliandro, Cecilia/Peycheva, Viktoriya/Gagliardi, Dimitri/ Marzocchi, Chiara/Ramlogan, Ronald/Cox, Deborah (2015): Annual report on European SMEs 2014 / 2015, SMEs start hiring again, SME Performance Review 2014/2015, Final report. Brussels: European Commission.

Muller, Patrice/Devnani, Shaan/Julius, Jenna/Gagliardi, Dimitri/Marzocchi, Chiara (2016): Annual Report on European SMEs 2015 / 2016, SME recovery continues, SME Performance Review 2015/2016, Final report. Brussels: European Commission.

Nölke, Andreas/Vliegenthart, Arjan (2009): Enlarging the varieties of capitalism: The emergence of dependent market economies and East Central Europe. World Politics 61(4), 670-702. https://doi.org/10.1017/S0043887109990098

Pianta, Mario (2015): What Is to Be Produced? The Case for Industrial Policy. In: Which Industrial Policy Does Europe Need? Forum, Intereconomics, 50(3), 139-145.

Pianta, Mario/Lucchese, Matteo/Nascia, Leopoldo (2016): What is to be produced? The making of a new industrial policy in Europe. Brussels: Rosa-Luxemburg-Stiftung.

Pitelis C. N. (2006) Industrial policy: perspectives, experience, issues. In: Bianchi, Patrizio/Labory, Sandrine (Eds.): International handbook on industrial policy. Cheltenham: Edward Elgar, 435-444. https://doi.org/10.4337/9781847201546.0 0034

Puslecki, Zdzislaw W. (2003): Trade Conflicts during the Multilateral Negotiations on the International Trade Liberalization. In: Nagel, Stuart S. (Ed.): Policy-making and Prosperity: A Multinational Anthology. Lanham, MD: Lexington Books, 79-100.

Rangone, Marco/Solari, Stefano (2012): From the Southern-European model to nowhere: the ecolution of Italian capitalism, 1976-2011. Journal of European Public Policy 19(8), 1188-1206. https://doi.org/10.1080/13501763.2012.709014

Reid, Alasdair (2011): EU innovation policy: one size doesn't fit all! In: Radosevic Slavo/Kaderabkova Anna (Eds.): Challenges for European innovation policy: Cohesion and excellence from a Schumpeterian perspective. Cheltenham: Edward Elgar, 112-149. https://doi.org/10.4337/9780857935212.00013

Rodrik, Dani (2007): One Economics, Many Recipes: Globalization, Institutions and Economic Growth. Princeton and Oxford: Princeton University Press.

Schwab, Klaus (2016): The Fourth Industrial Revolution. Geneva: World Economic Forum.

Smit, Jan/Kreutzer, Stephan/Moeller, Carolin/Carlberg, Malin (2016): Industry 4.0 Analytical Study. Brussels: European Parliament Policy Department.

Staritz, Cornelia/Plank, Leonhard (2013): Precarious upgrading' in electronics global production networks. Central and Eastern Europe: the cases of Hungary and Romania. In: Capturing the Gains, Working Paper, 31, Manchester: University of Manchester.

Stehrer, Robert/Leitner, Sandra/Marcias, Manuel/Mirza, Daniel/Stöllinger, Roman (2016): The Future Development of EU Industry in a Global Context. Research Report 409. The Vienna Institute for International Economic Studies.

Stöllinger, Roman/Hanzl-Weiss, Doris/Leitner, Sandra/Stehrer, Robert (2018): Global and Regional Value Chains: How Important, How Different? Research Report 427. The Vienna Institute for International Economic Studies.

Szalavetz, Andrea (2016a): Post-crisis development in global value chains: example of foreign investors' Hungarian subsidiaries. Working Paper, 219, Budapest: Centre for the Economic and Regional Studies Hungarian Academy of Sciences.

Szalavetz, Andrea (2016b): Global crisis and upgrading of MNCs' manufacturing subsidiaries: A case study of Hungary. Central European Business Review, 5(1), 37-44. https://doi.org/10.18267/j.cebr.143

Szalavetz, Andrea (2016c): Chronicle of a Revolution Foretold in Hungary – Industry 4.0 Technologies and Manufacturing Subsidiaries. Studies in International Economics, 2(2): 29-51.

Szalavetz, Andrea (2017): Industry 4.0 in 'factory economies'. In: Galgóczi, Béla/Drahokoupil, Jan (Eds.): Condemned to be left behind? Can Central and Eastern Europe emerge from its low-wage model? Brussels: ETUI, 133-152.

Szelényi, Iván (2014): Pathways from and Crisis after Communism – The case of Central Eastern Europe. Belvedere Meridionale, 26(4): 7-23. https://doi.org/10.14232/belv.2014.4.1

UNIDO (2013): Industrial Development Report 2013, Sustaining Employment Growth: The Role of Manufacturing and Structural Change. Vienna: United Nations Industrial Development Organization.

Vandermerwe, Sandra/Rada, Juan (1988): Servitization of business: Adding value by adding services. European Management Journal, 6(4), 314-324. https://doi.org/10.1016/0263-2373(88)90033-3

Veugelers, Reinhilde (2013): Trends, challenges and prospects for manufacturing in Europe. In: Veugelers, Reinhilde (Ed.): Manufacturing Europe's future. Bruegel Blueprint Series 21. Brussels: Bruegel, 7-47.

Veugelers, Reinhilde (2015): Do we have the right kind of diversity in innovation policies among EU Member States? Working Paper, 108, Vienna: Austrian Institute of Economic Research.

Veugelers, Reinhilde/Batsaikhan, Uuriintuya (2017): European and global manufacturing: Trends, challenges and the way ahead. In: Veugelers, Reinhilde (Ed.): Remaking Europe: The new manufacturing as an engine for growth. Bruegel Blueprint Series 26. Brussels: Bruegel, 24-52.

Vihriälä, Erkki/Wolff, Guntram B. (2013): Manufacturing as a source of growth for southern Europe: opportunities and obstacles. Manufacturing Europe's future. Bruegel Blueprint Series 21. Brussels: Bruegel, 48-72.

Visnjic Kastalli, Ivanka/Van Looy, Bart (2013): Servitization: Disentangling the impacts of services business model innovation on manufacturing frim performance. Journal of Operation Management 31(4), 169-180. https://doi.org/10.1016/j.jom.2013.02.001

Vladimirov, Zhelyu (2017): The EU industrial policy and SME development in Central and Eastern Europe. In: Galgóczi, Béla/Drahokoupil, Jan (Eds.): Condemned to be left behind? Can Central and Eastern Europe emerge from its low-wage model? Brussels: ETUI, 189-208.

Von Hippel, Eric (1994): "Sticky Information" and the Locus of Problem Solving: Implications for Innovation. Management Science, 40(4): 429-439. https://doi.org/10.1287/mnsc.40.4.429

Legal references

EC Regulation No 1083/2006 of 11 July 2006 laying down general provisions on the
European Regional Development Fund, the European Social Fund and the
Cohesion Fund and repealing Regulation (EC) No 1260/1999

EU Regulation No 1303/2013 of the European Parliament and of the Council of 17
December 2013 laying down common provisions on the European Regional
Development Fund, the European Social Fund, the Cohesion Fund, the European Agricultural Fund for Rural Development and the European Maritime and Fisheries Fund and laying down general provisions on the European
Regional Development Fund, the European Social Fund, the Cohesion Fund
and the European Maritime and Fisheries Fund and repealing Council Regulation (EC) No 1083/2006

ABSTRACT *Die Industriepolitik steht im 21. Jahrhundert vor grundle-
genden Veränderungen. Dazu zählen die Servitization der Industrie, Möglichkeiten zur Verbesserung und Modernisierung, die Prozesse der digitalen Transformation sowie die Entwicklung von Wertschöpfungsketten und komplexen
Geschäftsökosystemen. In der Industrie innerhalb der EU können wir interne
Unterschiede feststellen. Grundsätzlich ist die EU in einen Kern und in eine,
oder möglicherweise mehrere, Peripherien unterteilt.*

*Wie werden die EU-Mitgliedsstaaten diese Herausforderungen bewäl-
tigen? Wie wird sich die industriepolitische Strategie auf EU-Ebene voraus-
sichtlich auf die (relativen) Positionen der Mitgliedsstaaten auswirken? Wird
eine Differenzierung auf politischer Ebene stattfinden? Wenn ja, wie kann
diese funktionieren? Wenn nicht, was sind die Folgen?*

Anita Pelle
University of Szeged, Hungary
pelle@eco.u-szeged.hu

Sarolta Somosi
University of Szeged, Hungary
Somosi.Sarolta@eco.u-szeged.hu

Review-Essay

ARNO SONDEREGGER
Mandelas Hunderter

Stephan Bierling: Nelson Mandela: Rebell, Häftling, Präsident.
München: C.H. Beck, 2018, 416 Seiten, 24,95 Euro.

Anlässlich des hundertsten Geburtstags Nelson Mandelas, der im
Dezember 2013 in seinem sechsundneunzigsten Lebensjahr hochbetagt
verstarb, erschien 2018 im Münchner Verlag C.H. Beck eine Biographie. Eine so zeitnahe Einschätzung der Bedeutung eines Menschenle-
bens vorzunehmen ist immer eine schwierige Aufgabe. Festzustellen, was
von bleibender Relevanz sein wird und was nicht, ist umso schwieriger in
einem Fall wie dem von Nelson Mandela, dessen letzter Lebensabschnitt
mit einer epochalen Zäsur zusammenfiel. Dieser Einschnitt lässt sich einerseits an der Erosion und Auflösung des rassistischen Apartheidstaats seit
den 1980er Jahren festmachen, verursacht durch die Kombination innerer
systemischer Widersprüche, des zunehmenden Widerstands der Unter-
drückten und dem Ende des Kalten Kriegs. Andererseits lässt er sich an den
Bemühungen um ein neues Südafrika seit 1994 erkennen, in dem erstmals
alle Südafrikanerinnen und Südafrikaner gleiche Bürgerrechte besitzen
sowie Versöhnung und Herstellung von Chancengleichheit zu Leitprinzi-
pien künftiger Entwicklung ausgerufen wurden. Diese Epochenzäsur, die
sowohl global- als auch südafrikahistorisch spezifisch begründet werden
kann, fällt mit Mandelas Entlassung aus dem Gefängnis, nach 27jähriger
Inhaftierung, im Februar 1990 zusammen. Mandela war zu diesem Zeit-
punkt fast 72 Jahre alt.
    Nach den Wahlen im April 1994, die der *African National Congress*
(ANC) mit überwältigender Mehrheit gewann, bildete Mandela, nun 76,

die erste freie Regierung in der Geschichte Südafrikas – eines zunächst kolonialen Herrschaftsgebildes, das in den bis heute bestehenden Territorialgrenzen im Rahmen konkurrierender europäischer Imperialismen zu Beginn des 20. Jahrhunderts entstanden war. Mit der Gründung der Südafrikanischen Union im Jahr 1910 agierte dieses Gebilde als Commonwealth-Dominion bereits in wesentlichen Zügen autonom, 1931 erlangte es die gesetzgeberische Unabhängigkeit von Großbritannien. Ein Ende der Fremdherrschaft bedeutete solche Unabhängigkeit freilich nicht, die systemische Unterdrückung aller „nicht-weißen" Akteure im Land – also mehr als 90 Prozent der Gesamtbevölkerung – ging ungebrochen weiter. Mit der Durchsetzung der Apartheid-Politik nach dem Wahlsieg der burischen Nationalpartei 1948 wurde sie sogar in einer Weise systematisiert und juristisch abgesichert, wie es zuvor nur in Nazi-Deutschland praktiziert worden war.

Anders als die nationalsozialistische Herrschaft überdauerte die Apartheid in Südafrika vier Jahrzehnte. Einer der Erklärungsfaktoren ist die durchaus wohlwollende Unterstützung des Regimes durch die mächtigen Staaten der sogenannten „freien Welt", die im „weißen", industriell-kapitalistisch operierenden Südafrika ihr Bollwerk gegenüber benachbarten afrikanischen Befreiungsbestrebungen sahen. Von seinem 23. Lebensjahr an, als Mandela sich aus seiner ländlichen Umgebung löste, in der er eine von Missions- und Kolonialschule geprägte Ausbildung erfahren hatte, und sich nach Johannesburg verabschiedete (1941), befand er sich im konstanten Widerstand gegen die herrschende Ungerechtigkeit kolonial-rassistischer Unterdrückung. Er wurde wiederholt inhaftiert und auch anderweitig in seiner Bewegungsfreiheit eingeschränkt (mit „Bann" belegt). Mandela agierte in einer Vielzahl verschiedener Rollen: als Organisator von politischen Veranstaltungen und sozialen Netzwerktreffen; als Rechtsbeistand und Anwalt vor Gericht, mitunter als Zeuge, aber auch als Angeklagter; schließlich als strategischer Denker und führender Kopf des ANC, der unablässig daran arbeitete, Bündnisse mit anderen widerständigen Organisationen in Südafrika herbeizuführen.

Stephan Bierling, Politikwissenschaftler und Autor der vorliegenden Biographie, vermittelt seinen Leserinnen und Lesern keinen adäquaten Begriff von alldem. Er steht vielmehr völlig im Bann der späten Jahre Mandelas, des erfolgreichen Politikers und Staatsmannes, und seiner internationalen Wirkung, die er seit den 1990er Jahren unbestreitbar hatte und die weiterhin medienwirksam bespielt wird. Gleich zu Beginn bezeichnet er Mandela als „ein Rätsel" (S. 14) und hält dessen „Rätselhaftigkeit" (S. 14) für konstitutiv. Von daher ist es nur logisch, dass ihm Mandela auch das gesamte Buch hindurch ein Rätsel bleibt. Daraus ergibt sich jedoch ein ganz grundsätzliches Problem, unter der diese Biographie leidet: Bierling ist fasziniert vom beispiellosen politischen Erfolg dieses Mannes als Präsident Südafrikas von 1994 bis 1998 und seiner Rolle als international anerkannter *elder statesman* seither, aber er kann ihn sich nicht erklären. Zu sehr steht alles, wofür Mandela vor den 1980er Jahren steht – Widerstand, Opposition und Kampf –, im Gegensatz zu eigenen, positiv besetzten Werten des Autors. Von einer herrschaftskritischen Perspektive, in der sowohl die Geschichte Südafrikas – und der Welt – als auch der Werdegang Nelson Mandelas relativ leicht nachvollzogen werden könnten, ist Bierling bedauernswerterweise meilenweit entfernt.

Mit dem „Rebellen" Mandela, dem Widerständigen, dem Unangenehmen, dem Kämpfer für Gleichberechtigung der südafrikanischen Bevölkerungsmehrheit unter Bedingungen des in Politik, Wirtschaft und Gesellschaft diskriminierenden Rassenstaats, zu dem Südafrika spätestens mit der Einsetzung der Apartheid-Maßnahmen seit 1948 geworden war, weiß Bierling, das wird durch die Lektüre sehr rasch klar, wenig anzufangen. Kein Zweifel besteht für ihn daran, dass Mandela zu den „große[n] Staatsmänner[n]" zählt (S. 15); als Mittsiebziger also erscheint ihm Mandela groß und bedeutend, doch über die weitesten Teile seines Lebens bleibt er ihm suspekt und fremd. Und er unternimmt wenig Anstrengung, ihm nahezukommen.

Der Autor, in dessen Vita nichts darauf hindeutet, was ihn zum Biographen Mandelas prädestinieren würde, demonstriert Zeile für Zeile, dass er weder mit afrikawissenschaftlichen Konventionen noch mit Rassismusforschung noch mit einschlägigen historischen Praxen vertraut ist. Auch von der Geschichte Südafrikas hat er nur wenig Ahnung. Man stelle sich einen Biographen Hitlers vor – ohne Deutschkenntnisse, ohne Interesse an der deutschen und europäischen Geschichte, ohne klaren Begriff von Rassismus und ohne das Rüstzeug geschichtswissenschaftlichen Handwerks. Das Resultat könnte kaum desaströser sein als im vorliegenden Fall. Was um alles in der Welt bewegt einen Verlag zur Publikation eines derartig unzureichenden Machwerks? Das wirft Fragen danach auf, wie der Verlag C.H. Beck seine Autoren auswählt und welche Maßnahmen zur Qualitätssicherung er ergreift, doch ließe sich hier darüber nur spekulieren. Einige Beispiele müssen genügen, um die sich durch das ganze Buch durchziehenden Probleme zu veranschaulichen.

Dabei weiß man fast gar nicht, wo man beginnen soll, so viele falsche und/oder problematische Aussagen werden hier zum Teil innerhalb eines Satzes getätigt: „Die Mandelas gehörten zu den Thembus [sic!], einem der fünf Hauptstämme [sic!] des Xhosa-Volks [sic!], das seit dem Mittelalter [sic!] aus der Region der Großen Seen in der Mitte des Kontinents [sic!] in die Transkei [sic!] eingewandert sind. [...] In der Sprache der Ureinwohner [sic!], der Khoisan [sic!], bedeutet Xhosa »die wütenden Männer«. [...] [Mandelas Eltern,] Nosekeni oder Henry hatten wahrscheinlich Khoisan-Vorfahren, die man auch »Buschmänner« nennt [sic!], auf jeden Fall legen das Mandelas tiefhängende Augenlider [sic!], hohe Wangenknochen [sic!] und heller Teint [sic!] nahe" (S. 18f). Hier kann fast nichts unwidersprochen hingenommen werden. Es „stämmelt" und „völkelt" im unpräzise, aber naturalistisch und zeitlos inszenierten Habitat („Mitte des Kontinents", „Mittelalter"), und rassenkundliches Vokabular feiert fröhliche Urstände. Ein linguistisches Kunstwort (Khoisan) wird ethnisiert bzw. rassifiziert, und das gleich dazu auch noch falsch („Buschmänner" war die kolonial geprägte Bezeichnung für die Sammler-und-Jäger-Gemeinschaften der San, während die Rinder haltenden bzw. agrarisch wirtschaftenden Khoikhoi im kolonialrassistischen Kontext abwertend als „Hottentotten" bezeichnet wurden/werden.)

Was oberflächlich vielleicht als bloße sprachliche Unzulänglichkeit erscheinen könnte, erweist sich jedoch als grundsätzliche begriffliche Fehlleistung. Bierling nimmt Mandela und Südafrika ausschließlich durch die europäische Brille wahr. Unkritisch übernimmt er koloniale und Apartheid-Kategorien der Gruppenbildung und fasst sie auf, als wären sie naturgegeben und würden die vielschichtige soziale Realität Südafrikas im Entferntesten adäquat abbilden. So kann er für die 1860er Jahre für Südafrika von den „drei großen Bevölkerungsgruppen" (S. 23) phantasieren und damit Briten, Buren und „Afrikaner" meinen. Er erwähnt zwar, dass Letztere in „mehreren afrikanischen Königreichen" (S. 23) organisiert waren, erkennt aber nicht, dass sie nur aus europäischer Perspektive zur Gruppe

Arno Sonderegger

gebündelt wurden. „Dazu kamen die Inder [...]" (S. 23), eine vierte Größe also, die im südafrikanischen Kontext zu einer staatlich anerkannten Gruppe gefasst werden sollte, um sie auch ganz offiziell, *de jure* und nicht bloß *de facto*, zu diskriminieren.

Historisch akkurat zu sein, daran liegt dieser Biographie nichts. Den Oranje-Freistaat, die neben Transvaal zweite bedeutende Burenrepublik, tauft Bierling in „Transoranje" um. Das kurzlebige burische „Natalia", das von 1839 bis 1843 bestand, dann zur britischen Kolonie Natal wurde, wird bei Bierling erst 1877 britisch (S. 23). Den zweiten Burenkrieg zwischen Briten und Buren von 1899 bis 1902 als den „ersten antikolonialistischen Kampf der modernen Geschichte in Afrika" (S. 24) zu bezeichnen, spottet jeder Beschreibung. (Wenn zwei koloniale Akteure, Buren und Briten, gegeneinander Krieg führen, mag es gerade noch akzeptabel scheinen, das einen Kolonialkrieg zu nennen, weil er sich in einem kolonialen Raum abspielt, doch sind hier keine antikolonialen Kräfte am Werk. Diese weitere Überdehnung ist darum völlig abwegig.) Und da sind wir noch nicht einmal im 20. Jahrhundert.

Dort wird es freilich keinen Deut besser. Antikoloniale nationalistische Befreiungsbewegungen und ihre Persönlichkeiten werden als „Rebellenführer" etikettiert. Würde Bierling den von ihm offenbar hochgeschätzten George Washington, „Befreier, Gründer und Sinnstifter der Nation" (S. 12), solcherart bezeichnen? Wohl kaum. Doch Afrika ist in manchen Kreisen, die in Erinnerungen an *good old Europe* schwelgen (Bierling ist ein USA-Kenner), bekanntlich *„ein anderes Land"*. Und so liest der Afrikanist, der ich bin, mit Entsetzen angesichts der zur Schau getragenen Unkenntnis rezenter afrikanischer Geschichte und Arroganz den folgenden Satz: „Da viele afrikanische Rebellenführer von Julius Nyerere in Tansania über Kenneth Kaunda in Sambia und Robert Mugabe in Simbabwe nach ihrem Sieg gegen die weißen Kolonialherren ihr Land zugrunde richteten, ist das Verlangen nach einem schwarzen Superhelden in Afrika und im Westen so überwältigend, dass Mandelas tapfer ertragene Gefängnisjahre und seine titanenhafte Versöhnungspolitik alle anderen Aspekte seiner politischen Karriere und seines persönlichen Lebens überlagern" (S. 13). Nur minimales Wissen um die spätkoloniale und postkoloniale Geschichte dieser drei Länder ist nötig, um die Absurdität dieses Satzes zu erkennen, der drei völlig unterschiedlich agierende Politiker und

Regime der jüngeren afrikanischen Geschichte amalgamiert und ihnen, wider die geringste empirische Evidenz, konstatiert, ihre Länder zugrunde gerichtet zu haben. Es ist in etwa so, als wollte man schreiben: „Da die alliierten Regierungsklüngelspitzen von Franklin D. Roosevelt in den USA und Charles de Gaulle in Frankreich über Winston Churchill in Großbritannien und Josef Stalin in der UdSSR nach ihrem Sieg gegen die nationalsozialistische Herrenrasse ihr Land zugrunde richteten, ist das Verlangen nach einem weißen Superhelden in Europa und weltweit überwältigend." Bierlings Satz ist um keinen Deut weniger absurd. Doch enthält er leider eine nur allzu klar verständliche Botschaft: Afrikaner taugen nicht zur politischen Führung, und sie rufen allesamt nach dem starken Mann, dessen sie bedürftig sind.

Daneben erscheinen andere Ungereimtheiten im Text fast unbedeutend. Wiederholt werden südafrikanische schwarze Nationalisten etwa als „Afrikanisten" bezeichnet; sehr zur Verwunderung jener, die diesem Berufsstand im deutschen Sprachraum angehören. In diesem wie in manch anderen Zusammenhängen fehlt dem Autor offenkundig das Bewusstsein, dass nicht alles wortgetreu aus dem Englischen (oder anderen Sprachen) ins Deutsche (oder eine andere Sprache) übertragen werden kann, ohne seinen spezifischen Sinn zu verlieren und andere Bedeutungen anzunehmen. Für Kontextabhängigkeit hat er kein Gespür. Das erklärt die ständige Präsenz von „Stämmen" und „Häuptlingen" in seinem Text, die sich dort – gedankenlos, wie es scheint – tummeln. Doch die Gedankenlosigkeit ist die des Autors, nicht derjenigen, über die er zu schreiben meint. (Zur Klärung: „Tribe" ist mit „Stamm" meist inadäquat übersetzt, die Bedeutungen von „chief" und „Häuptling" sind nicht dieselben.)

Das Buch nähert sich Mandela von dessen Ende her, mit dem der Autor sympathisiert (dem Großen, Schönen und Reichen, wenn ich so sagen darf), und grenzt es scharf vom Großteil seines Lebens ab, dem Bierling wenig Sympathie und sehr viel Ablehnung entgegenbringt. Dem selbstbewussten Charme, mit dem Mandela als angehender Rechtsanwalt gegen Diskriminierung und staatliche Repression auftrat, kann er sich nicht völlig entziehen, was insbesondere seine Schilderungen des sogenannten Hochverratsprozesses gegen führende Mitglieder der *Congress Alliance* (einer „multirassischen" Allianz einschließlich des ANC) in den Jahren 1956/57 bis 1960 und des Rivonia-Prozesses 1963 bis 1964 verdeutli-

ARNO SONDEREGGER

chen. Doch machen dieselben Abschnitte auch klar, dass er kein bisschen mit den Grundüberzeugungen Mandelas übereinstimmt, und auch, dass ihm ein adäquates Verständnis der südafrikanischen Situation völlig fehlt.

Der südafrikanische Apartheidstaat scheint ihm ein Staat wie jeder andere zu sein, dem gegenüber bedingungslose Gehorsamspflicht besteht. Vor diesem Hintergrund werden strategische Aussagen und Zurückweisungen von Anklagepunkten im Prozessverfahren als „Lügen" Mandelas gedeutet und suggeriert, dies werfe begründete Zweifel an seiner Moralität auf. Denselben Effekt soll wahrscheinlich auch der wiederkehrende Hinweis auf dessen Eheprobleme und seine Affären in den 1950er Jahren erzielen (Mandela war dreimal verheiratet: mit Evelyn Mase, 1944–1958; mit Winnie Madikizela-Mandela, 1958–1997; schließlich mit Graça Machel, 1998–2013). Mandela im politischen Widerstand soll nicht nur als schlechter Staatsbürger, als Lügner und politischer Gewalttäter erscheinen, sondern auch als schlechter Ehemann, Ehebrecher und pflichtvergessener Familienvater gebrandmarkt werden. Eine durchsichtige Strategie, die private und öffentliche Sphären willkürlich vermengt, um ideologischen Urteilen, die unhaltbar sind, ein Hintertürchen offenzuhalten. Seriös ist das nicht. Eventuelles Fehlverhalten in persönlichen Belangen entwertet ein bestimmtes politisches Handeln und Denken ebenso wenig wie öffentliche politische Verirrungen ein solides Familienleben verhindern. Hier besteht keinerlei zwingender Zusammenhang.

Das Kommunisten-Bashing, das Bierling in bester Tradition des ideologischen Kalten Kriegers betreibt, mutet anno 2018 etwas sonderbar an, aber immerhin hat es Methode. Die Annäherung zwischen ANC und südafrikanischen Kommunistinnen und Kommunisten, zu der es infolge des Verbots der *Communist Party of South Africa* (CPSA) (und der „illegalen" Neugründung als *South African Communist Party* [SACP]) 1950 kam, ist für Bierling offenkundig ein Pakt mit dem Teufel. Mit Kommunisten ist kein Staat zu machen. Punkt. Egal unter welchen Bedingungen. Umso weniger, als diese Ideologie in solchen Kreisen bekanntermaßen jüdisch unterwandert ist: „In der 1921 gegründeten KP Südafrikas, die Ende der 1920er Jahre unter die direkte [sic!] und dauerhafte [sic!] Kontrolle Moskaus geriet, nahmen Juden stets leitende Funktionen ein" (S. 84). Er denkt dabei an die 1919 von Lenin begründete Dritte Internationale, die Kommunistische Internationale, die als Werkzeug der Weltrevolution dienen sollte, und unterschlägt, dass diese Organisation 1943 wieder aufgelöst wurde, auch weil ihr Scheitern in der Durchsetzung des sowjetischen Diktats an allzu vielen Orten sichtbar geworden war. Direkte, dauerhafte Marionetten Moskaus? Mit der historischen Wahrheit nimmt es der Autor nicht gerade genau.

Sogleich schließt er an, schießt er nach: „Fast alle KP-Führer [sic!]" – darunter subsumiert er sowohl jene der CPSA als auch der SACP, suggeriert also eine über Jahrzehnte dauernde essenzielle Kontinuität von den 1920ern an bis, ja bis wann eigentlich? – „verehrten Stalin, identifizierten sich kritiklos [sic!] mit sowjetischen Positionen und warfen Abweichler aus der Partei, waren nicht frei von Paternalismus gegenüber Nicht-Weißen [sic!] und Frauen [sic!] und beschäftigten schwarze Dienstmädchen und Gärtner [sic!]" (S. 84). Das ist ihnen also vorzuwerfen, und ganz besonders in einem von Rassentrennung und Diskriminierung geprägten Südafrika? Ernsthaft?

Immerhin erwähnt Bierling dann doch, dass „die Kommunisten die einzige organisierte weiße Gruppe [bildeten], die die Anliegen der Schwarzen, Inder und Farbigen unterstützte, mit ihnen auf Augenhöhe zusammenarbeitete und ihr volles Wahlrecht forderte" (S. 84). Dies als etwas genuin Positives zu bezeichnen, dazu ringt er sich freilich weder hier noch sonst wo durch. Schwerer wiegt für ihn etwas, das ihm in seiner ideologischen Verblendung als negativ erscheint: die Tatsache, dass sich „schwarze" ANC-Granden Anfang der 1950er Jahre zu einer kritischen sozialrevolutionären Position durchrangen. In seiner Wahrnehmung war das freilich einer kommunistischen Unterwanderung geschuldet: „In den folgenden Jahren baute die SACP ihren Einfluss im ANC systematisch aus" (S. 84). So lautet der Satz, der nahtlos an den vorigen anschließt.

Um seine Bewunderung für den Erfolg des späten Mandela mit seiner Verachtung für den gesellschaftsverändernden Einsatz vereinbaren zu können, den Mandela und Abertausende andere Südafrikaner und Südafrikanerinnen über Jahrzehnte hinweg alltäglich gelebt haben, suggeriert Bierling den Eindruck eines radikalen Bruchs in Mandelas Position. Er erzählt willkürlich eine Geschichte von Gewaltbereitschaft zu Gewaltlosigkeit, die völlig unstimmig ist. (Beides waren für Mandela opportune Strategien der politischen Auseinandersetzung, sofern es – seiner Einschätzung nach – die Situation verlangte; und zwar zeitlebens.) Schlimmer als die faktischen Fehldeutungen, von denen diese Biographie nur so strotzt, ist freilich die ideologische Verblendung, die zu solchen Irrtümern Anlass gibt. In einer Art einleitendem Vorwort, das Bierling tolldreist exotisierend „Madibas Magie" nennt, wird das schon gleich zu Beginn des Buches offenkundig. Dort lobt er die Maßnahme des Apartheid-Staates, Mandela jahrzehntelang wegzusperren, gleichsam wohlwollend wegen ihres (angeblichen) domestizierenden Effekts auf dessen Persönlichkeitsentwicklung: „Er hat sich in den 27 Jahren der Haft neu geformt. Der Mann, den die Regierung 1963 aburteilen ließ, war eine imposante Figur des Widerstands, aber auch heißblütig [sic!] und gewaltbereit. Als Mandela am 11. Februar 1990 das Gefängnis als freier Mann verließ [sic!], [...] war er zu einer besonnenen, abgeklärten Führungspersönlichkeit gereift [...] [mit] moralische[r] Autorität, Willenskraft und Verhandlungsgeschick [...]" (S. 11).

Wer gegen Herrschende opponiert, gar emotional aufgebracht und eventuell sogar handgreiflich gegen Ungerechtigkeiten einschreitet, besitzt demnach keine Reife, keine Führungsqualität, keine moralische Autorität, keine Willenskraft, kein Verhandlungsgeschick?

In vielem faktisch falsch, grundsätzlich unseriös in der Herangehensweise und plakativ in der Darstellung. So lautet meine kürzest mögliche Beurteilung des Buchs.

Plakativ nennt schon der Untertitel drei rhetorische Figuren, um diesen großen Mann der neueren politischen Geschichte Südafrikas zu charakterisieren: „Rebell, Häftling, Präsident." Auf zwei davon greift der Autor auch ganz explizit zurück, um zwei seiner insgesamt 13 Kapitel zu überschreiben. So tritt die Beschreibung der langen Inhaftierung Mandelas von 1963 bis 1990 unter der Überschrift „Häftling Nummer 466/64" (Kapitel 8) in Erscheinung, und seine Präsidentschaft von 1994 bis 1999, die erste in Südafrika, die aus allgemeinen freien Wahlen hervorging, wird einfach „Der Präsident" (Kapitel 12) genannt. Andere plakative Rollenzuschreibungen, durch die Bierling seine Themenbehandlung strukturiert, die im Wesentlichen einfach der Chronologie gehorcht, haben es hingegen nicht in den Untertitel geschafft; etwa „Der Junge vom Land" (Kapitel 1), „Der Freiheitskämpfer" (Kapitel 3), „Kommunist und Terrorist?" (Kapitel 6), „Der Verhandler" (Kapitel 10), „Der Retter" (Kapitel 11), „Elder Statesman" (Kapitel 13). Weitere mehr oder weniger knackige, aber jedenfalls stereotype Zuschreibungen – wie etwa „Der Versöhner" (S. 320), „Unbeugsamer

Menschenfischer" (S. 202), „Bestseller-Autor" (S. 346), „Der Tod des Patriarchen" (S. 368), „Als Schwarzer im Land der Weißen" (S. 23) – sind als Zwischenüberschriften prominent platziert.

Die Darstellung insgesamt folgt einfach linear dem Zeitverlauf. Eine ernsthafte Überlegung, wie seriöse biographische Forschung funktioniert, ist nicht zu erkennen. Was kann und soll eine Biographie leisten? Sie soll Leben und Werk eines Menschen schildern, seine Entwicklung nachzeichnen, Konstanten und Brüche herausarbeiten. Sie kann das im Rückgriff auf dokumentiertes Material, Quellen, auch tun. Allerdings erschöpft sich keine Biographie in der schlichten Beschreibung, sondern sie strickt immer ein Narrativ, eine bestimmte Erzählung, eine gewisse Deutung. Um dies in seriöser Weise überzeugend zu machen, ist es freilich notwendig, Verständnis zu entwickeln – für den Menschen, der biographisch beschrieben wird, vor allem aber auch für die Kontexte, die Lebensumstände und Bedingungen, unter denen jener gelebt hat. Schließlich erfordert biographisches Schreiben, zumindest im 21. Jahrhundert, auch eine gewisse selbstkritische Reflexionsleistung des Biographen selbst. Nichts davon bei Bierling: eine vergebene Chance.

Vielleicht ist das zu viel erwartet? Ich denke nicht, und Bierling schürt die Erwartungshaltung, denn er setzt sein Ziel kaum bescheidener an: „Den Mann aus Fleisch und Blut herauszuarbeiten, zu zeigen, was ihn antrieb, wie sich seine politische Philosophie entwickelte und wie er zur moralischen Instanz Südafrikas, ja der Welt aufstieg, ist das zentrale Anliegen dieses Buchs" (S. 14). Keines dieser Anliegen löst er in befriedigender Weise ein. Mandela in Fleisch und Blut ist auch am Ende der Lektüre nicht in Sicht. Einer überzeugenden Erklärung von Mandelas Motivation, sein Leben dem Kampf um Gleichberechtigung in Südafrika zu widmen, kommt Bierling kein bisschen nahe. Mandelas politische Philosophie bleibt ihm in ganz grundsätzlichem Sinn rätselhaft und verschlossen. Und seine Behandlung von Mandelas Aufstieg zur moralischen Instanz leidet darunter, dass Bierling daran gelegen scheint, an ihr auf Teufel komm raus zu rütteln. Man bemerkt eine gewisse Leidenschaft für das Thema, besonders auffällig auch an dem triefenden Pathos zahlloser Formulierungen, aber keine Sympathie für den Charakter Mandela und kein über die Oberfläche hinausgehendes Interesse an südafrikanischer Geschichte.

Arno Sonderegger

Auf eine seriöse „kritische Biographie" Mandelas bleibt also nach wie vor zu warten. Es soll nichts Schlimmeres passieren. Um sich die Zeit zu vertreiben, bleiben Mandelas autobiographische Schriften, zahlreiche Lebensbeschreibungen von Zeitgenossen, Mitstreitern und Konkurrenten, Sympathisanten und Gegnern, und unzählige seriöse Bücher zur Geschichte und Gegenwart Südafrikas.

Arno Sonderegger
Institut für Afrikawissenschaften, Universität Wien
arno.sonderegger@univie.ac.at

Sabine Hess, Bernd Kasparek, Stefanie Kron, Mathias Rodatz, Maria Schwertl, Simon Sontowski (Hg.): Der lange Sommer der Migration. Grenzregime III. Berlin, Hamburg: Assoziation A 2017, 272 Seiten, 18,50 Euro.

Der Terminus der „Flücht-lings-krise" dominiert seit 2015 den politischen Diskurs. Gemeint ist damit die Migrations- und Fluchtbewegung, die im Sommer 2015 auch Mitteleuropa erreichte. Der Sammelband *Der lange Sommer der Migration. Grenzregime III*, der 2017 erschien, zeigt auf, dass der Begriff der „Flüchtlings-krise" jedoch auch anders interpretiert werden kann: „Bei näherer Betrachtung ist die *Europäische Flüchtlingskrise* die Krise des europäischen Grenzregimes – eine Krise des Schengen-Systems selbst" (S. 38). In den 18 Beiträgen, die der Sammelband umfasst, gelingt es, durch eine Vielzahl an Perspektiven und Theorien ein differenziertes Bild der Migrations- und Fluchtbewegung zu schaffen, die im Jahr 2015 das europäische Grenzregime herausforderte.

Der einleitende Beitrag der HerausgeberInnen analysiert die Inszenierung des Notstandes im Sommer 2015. Damit geht auch die Kritik an der Hegemonie des Humanitarismus einher. So dominierte in öffentlichen Debatten oftmals die „Vulnerabilität" von Flüchtlingen. Das Recht auf Flucht blieb im medialen Diskurs fast unsichtbar. Doch wie die HerausgeberInnen in der Einleitung treffend festhalten: Geflüchtete „kamen als politische Subjekte, die ihr Schicksal gegen alle Widerstände und Widrigkeiten in die Hand genommen haben" (S. 18). Dies wird auch in den darauffolgenden Beiträgen klar skizziert: Sabine Hess und Serhat Karakayali stellen das Grenzregime in den Mittelpunkt ihrer Analyse und diskutieren es unter dem Ansatz der Autonomie der Migration, dabei wird die Handlungsmacht von Migrationsbewegungen unterstrichen. Bereits im Frühling 2015 zeichnete sich ab, dass immer mehr Menschen die griechischen Inseln erreichen würden, doch zu dieser Zeit stand in der EU noch alles im Zeichen der Euro-Krise, argumentiert Bernd Kasparek. Er stellt einen detaillierten Ablauf der Migrationsbewegung dar und verweist auf Parallelen zur Euro-Krise. Hervorgehoben soll an dieser Stelle der Text von Lina Ewert werden, da sich dieser auch mit den politischen Ansprüchen der deutschen NGO *Sea Watch* auseinandersetzt. Durch das Zitieren von zahlreichen Interviewpassagen lassen Sarah Nimführ, Laura Otto und Gabriel Samateh Geflüchtete, die in Malta leben, direkt zu Wort kommen und stellen so deren Erfahrungen in den Mittelpunkt.

Johanna Neuhauser, Sabine Hess und Helen Schwenken beschäftigen sich mit der Ambivalenz, dass die Kategorie *Gender* im öffentlichen Diskurs über Migration und Flucht omnipräsent ist, aber kaum in wissenschaftlichen Ansätzen zu finden ist. Um dies zu ändern, wird auf das Konzept des Geschlechterwissens und auf postkoloniale Theorie verwiesen. Besonders spannend ist der Artikel von Chandra-Milena Danielzik und Daniel Bendix, da sie Willkommensinitiativen in Deutschland gemeinsam mit der *Refugee-Bewegung*, die sich im Jahr 2012 bildete, diskutieren. Sowohl 2012 als auch 2015 fungierte „Refugees welcome" als der zentrale Slogan, wurde aber unterschiedlich von der Gesellschaft rezipiert. So war die *Refugee-Bewegung* 2015 im öffentlichen Diskurs nahezu unsichtbar. Die Auseinandersetzung mit dieser Thematik stellt bislang weitgehend eine Leerstelle dar.

Eine detaillierte Chronologie der Entwicklungen zwischen August und Oktober 2015 sowie Einblicke mehrerer KommentatorInnen finden sich im Beitrag der Initiative „Moving Europe". Hier wäre es eine Überlegung wert gewesen, diesen Text mit dem von Kasparek, der den gleichen Zeitraum behandelt, besser aufeinander abzustimmen, um den spannenden Analysen und Einblicken, die in beiden Beiträgen vorzufinden sind, mehr Raum zu geben. Darüber hinaus hätten auch die Kürzungen der internationalen Hilfsgelder und die damit einhergehenden Folgen in den Flüchtlingslagern im Nahen Osten durchaus ausgiebiger beschrieben werden können, da dieser Aspekt den Zynismus unterstreicht, mit dem einige Staaten operierten.

Trotz des Facettenreichtums, mit dem sich die Beiträge auseinandersetzen, gibt es einige Gemeinsamkeiten: So gilt unter anderem der „Arabische Frühling" als zentraler Referenzpunkt, da einerseits die damit verbundenen politischen Umbrüche bzw. Kriege das europäische Grenzregime destabilisiert haben und andererseits das kollektive Handeln des „Arabischen Frühlings" auch als zentrales

Charakteristikum im *March of Hope* festgemacht wurde.

Die Stärke des Werkes liegt neben seiner Aktualität darin, dass Handlungsoptionen und Widerstandspraxen aufgezeigt werden, ohne diese zu romantisieren. Flüchtlinge und MigrantInnen werden als Subjekte repräsentiert, die selbst über ihr Leben entscheiden wollen und sich dieses Recht nicht von militarisierten Grenzen nehmen lassen. So werden auch die Repressionen, die Gewalterfahrungen und der Tod tausender Menschen thematisiert, jedoch ohne dabei in einen Viktimisierungsdiskurs abzurutschen. Das Buch hinterlässt eine klare Botschaft: Legale Fluchtrouten müssen das Dogma des Grenzschutzes ablösen. Genauso klar ist auch die Sprache, die das Buch nicht nur für ein akademisches Publikum interessant macht.

Bettina Rosenberger

Schwerpunktredakteurinnen und Autorinnen

Juliana Gomes Campos has recently earned her M.A. degree on Global Political Economy at the University of Kassel. Her main research focuses are development and Latin American studies, especially as regards Brazil.

Julia Eder is a Research Associate and PhD candidate in Sociology at the Department of Politics and Development Research, Institute of Sociology, Johannes Kepler University, Linz, Austria. Her research focuses on the political economy of regional integration in Latin America and Eurasia. In particular, she is interested in regional trade and industrial policy, as well as development finance.

Jan Grumiller is a researcher at the Austrian Foundation for Development Research (ÖFSE), an external lecturer at the University of Applied Sciences BFI Vienna, and a doctoral student in Social and Economic Sciences at the Vienna University of Economics and Business (WU). His research focuses on international trade, global value chains and industrial policy.

Claus-Dieter König is Senior Advisor in the Africa Unit of Rosa-Luxemburg-Stiftung. Previously, he was the director of the Foundation's Western Africa regional office in Dakar and deputy director in its Europe Office in Brussels. He works mostly on social movements and economic alternatives.

Roland Kulke is facilitating the "productive transformation" project for *transform! europe*, a political foundation of the Party of the European Left. Besides working for a systemic change of the economic system of the EU, he works on trade policies and on the reform proposals for the EU.

Anita Pelle, PhD in Economics (2010), is working as an Associate Professor and Jean Monnet Chair at the Faculty of Economics and Business Administration of the University of Szeged (Hungary). Her teaching and research cover the economy of the EU, the EU internal market and, most lately, the EU internal divide.

Etienne Schneider is University Assistant at the Department of Political Science of the University of Vienna and editor of the journal Prokla. His work focuses on the political economy of European integration and progressive monetary and industrial policy.

Sarolta Somosi, PhD in Economics (2012), is an Assistant Professor at the Faculty of Economics and Business Administration of the University of Szeged (Hungary). She studies and lectures on the micro policies of the EU which target competition, trade and industry, including energy markets, services and intellectual property.

Arno Sonderegger is Senior Lecturer at the Department of African Studies of the University of Vienna. He is a historian interested in African history, global history and intellectual history. Among his recent publications are a short history of ancient Africa (*Kurze Geschichte des Alten Afrika*, Marix, 2017), an introduction to global history (*Nord-Süd-Ost-West-Beziehungen*, Mandelbaum, 2015) and one volume on *African Thoughts on Colonial and Neo-Colonial Worlds* (Neofelis, 2015).

Rudy Weissenbacher is researcher and lecturer at the Vienna University of Economics and Business. His research focuses on uneven development and core-periphery relations in Europe.

Latest issues

2/14 Financialisation of Food, Land, and Nature / Finanzialisierung von Nahrung, Land und Natur

3/14 Rohstoffpolitik und Entwicklung / Ressource Politics and Development

4/14 Capitalist Peripheries: Perspectives on Precarisation from the Global South and North

1/15 Civil Society, Cooperation and Development / Zivilgesellschaft, Kooperation und Entwicklung

2/15 Gewerkschaftsarbeit in Nord und Süd / Unionism in the Global North and South

3/15 Dependenztheorien reloaded / Dependency Theories reloaded

4/15 Grauzonen der Arbeit / Grey Areas of Labour

1-2/16 Turkey: The Politics of National Conservatism / Türkei: Politik des National-Konservatismus

3/16 The EU Trade Regime and the Global South

4/16 Hunters and Gatherers in the Industrialised World / Jäger und Sammlergesellschaften in der Industrialisierten Welt

1/17 Migrationsmanagement: Praktiken, Intentionen, Interventionen / Migration Management: Practices, Intentions, Interventions

2/17 Social Innovation and the Transformation of Welfare States / Soziale Innovation und die Transformation des Wohlfahrtsstaates

3/17 Socialisms in Development / Sozialismen in Entwicklung

4/17 Middle Class in Latin America / Mittelklasse in Lateinamerika

1/18 Food Sovereignty and Alternative Development in Palestine / Ernährungssouveränität und alternative Entwicklung in Palästina

2/18 Fußball und ungleiche Entwicklung / Football and Unequal Development

Upcoming issues

1/19 Rosa Luxemburg, Imperialismus und der Globale Süden / Rosa Luxemburg, Imperialism and the Global South

2-3/19 Waste and Globalised Inequalities / Müll und globalisierte Ungleichheiten

Informationen für AutorInnen

Das Journal für Entwicklungs-politik (JEP) ist eine der führenden wissenschaftlichen Zeitschriften für Fragen von Entwicklungstheorie und -politik im deutschsprachigen Raum. Alle Beiträge werden anonym begutachtet (double-blind, peer-reviewed). Die Publikation erfolgt in Englisch oder Deutsch. Die Zielsetzung des JEP ist es, ein Forum für eine breite kritische Diskussion und Reflexion für verschiedene Dimensionen gesellschaftlicher Entwicklungen in Süd und Nord zu bieten. Dabei wird auch das Verhältnis zwischen theoretischen Weiterentwicklungen im Bereich von Entwicklungsforschung und konkreten entwicklungspolitischen Prozessen ausgelotet. Gesellschaftlich relevantes Wissen über Entwicklungsprobleme und Entwicklungspolitik wird in einer interdisziplinären Herangehensweise aufbereitet und zugänglich gemacht.

Manuskriptvorschläge können eingesendet werden an:
office@mattersburgerkreis.at
Weitere Hinweise unter:
www.mattersburgerkreis.at/jep

Siehe auch: www.facebook.com/
journalfuerentwicklungspolitik

Information for Contributors

The Austrian Journal of Development Studies is one of the leading journals in its field in the German speaking area. Articles are reviewed anonymously (double-blind, peer-reviewed) and published in German or English. The journal provides a forum for a broad critical debate and reflection on different dimensions of societal transformation and on North-South relations. Specifically, the relationship between cutting edge theoretical advances in the field of development studies and actual development policies is addressed. Politically relevant knowledge about issues of development is provided in an accessible, interdisciplinary way.

Article proposals can be sent to:
office@mattersburgerkreis.at
Further information:
www.mattersburgerkreis.at/jep

See also: www.facebook.com/
journalfuerentwicklungspolitik

GEFÖRDERT DURCH DIE
ÖSTERREICHISCHE
ENTWICKLUNGS
ZUSAMMENARBEIT

Journal für Entwicklungspolitik (JEP)
ISSN 0258-2384, Erscheinungsweise: vierteljährlich
Heft XXXIV, 3/4-2018, ISBN 978-3-902996-18-3
Preis des Einzelhefts: Euro 11,90
Preis des Doppelhefts: 19,80 Euro
Preis des Jahresabonnements: Euro 42,00 (Österreich);
Euro 52,00 (Europa); 62,00 (Welt).
Weitere Informationen: www.mattersburgerkreis.at
Abonnementbezug über die Redaktion:
Journal für Entwicklungspolitik, Sensengasse 3, A-1090 Wien,
office@mattersburgerkreis.at, www.mattersburgerkreis.at/jep
Das Abonnement kann unter Einhaltung einer dreimonatigen
Kündigungsfrist zum Jahresende gekündigt werden.

Offenlegung nach § 25 Mediengesetz
Medieninhaber: Mattersburger Kreis für Entwicklungspolitik an den
österreichischen Universitäten, Sensengasse 3, A-1090 Wien
Grundlegende Richtung des JEP: Wissenschaftliche Analysen und
Diskussionen von entwicklungspolitischen Fragestellungen und Berichte
über die entwicklungspolitische Praxis. Verantwortlich für Inhalt und
Korrekturen sind die AutorInnen bzw. die Redaktion.